the
LEADING EDUCATOR
S E R I E S

A Summing Up

Teaching & Learning in Effective
Schools & PLCs at Work®

ROBERT EAKER

Foreword by Douglas Reeves

Solution Tree | Press *a division of*
Solution Tree

555 North Morton Street
Bloomington, IN 47404
800.733.6786 (toll free) / 812.336.7700
FAX: 812.336.7790

email: info@SolutionTree.com

SolutionTree.com

Printed in the United States of America

Library of Congress Cataloging-in-Publication Data

Names: Eaker, Robert E., author.
Title: A summing up : teaching and learning in effective schools and PLCs at work / Robert Eaker.
Description: Bloomington, IN : Solution Tree Press, 2020. | Includes bibliographical references.
Identifiers: LCCN 2019038848 (print) | LCCN 2019038849 (ebook) | ISBN 9781949539738 (hardcover) | ISBN 9781949539745 (ebook)
Subjects: LCSH: Professional learning communities--United States. | School improvement programs--United States. | Effective teaching--United States. | Eaker, Robert E. | Educators--United States--Biography.
Classification: LCC LB1731 .E129 2020 (print) | LCC LB1731 (ebook) | DDC 370.71/1--dc23
LC record available at https://lccn.loc.gov/2019038848
LC ebook record available at https://lccn.loc.gov/2019038849

Solution Tree
Jeffrey C. Jones, CEO
Edmund M. Ackerman, President

Solution Tree Press
President and Publisher: Douglas M. Rife
Associate Publisher: Sarah Payne-Mills
Art Director: Rian Anderson
Managing Production Editor: Kendra Slayton
Senior Production Editor: Suzanne Kraszewski
Content Development Specialist: Amy Rubenstein
Proofreader: Elisabeth Abrams
Text and Cover Designer: Abigail Bowen
Editorial Assistant: Sarah Ludwig

Acknowledgments

Writing and publishing a book involve much hard work by a significant number of people. I was blessed to have the editing expertise of Lesley Bolton. To say I appreciate her and value her contributions seems woefully inadequate. It has been a pleasure to partner with Lesley on this project. She is the consummate professional.

As always, I enjoyed the support and encouragement of my colleagues and close friends Douglas Rife and Jeff Jones. To them and everyone at Solution Tree Press, I am grateful.

It is impossible for me to describe the many ways Gretchen Knapp helped on this book. She provided initial editing of the manuscript before it was submitted to Solution Tree Press. Equally important, Gretchen was a solid sounding board who provided advice and encouragement along the way. While her professional advice is appreciated, her friendship is treasured.

Writing is a time-consuming and, at times, frustrating undertaking. In this project, and throughout my career, I have enjoyed the support of Star, my wife for over five decades. For her support and encouragement, I offer my heartfelt thanks.

"There is a distinct difference between knowledge and wisdom. Many educational books address facts, information, and skills deemed best practice—the knowledge of our profession. But wisdom requires deep understanding, insightfulness, and good judgment regarding how to best apply what we know. *A Summing Up* is a book of true wisdom. Using his own journey as the backdrop, Bob Eaker provides context to the major educational research movements of the past fifty years and describes how leveraging this knowledge with practitioner experience led to the creation of the PLC at Work process. It is a wonderfully personal story, written with humor and humility. If I could, I would make this book required reading for every educator."

—MIKE MATTOS
Educational Consultant and Author

Table of Contents

About the Author

Robert Eaker, EdD, is professor emeritus at Middle Tennessee State University, where he also served as dean of the College of Education and interim vice president and provost. Dr. Eaker is a former fellow with the National Center for Effective Schools Research and Development. He has written widely on the issues of effective teaching, effective schools, teachers' use of research findings, and high expectations for student achievement.

Dr. Eaker has been a frequent consultant to schools and school districts across North America. He is a regular speaker at national, regional, and state professional meetings.

To learn more about Dr. Eaker's work, visit AllThingsPLC (www.allthingsplc.info).

To book Robert Eaker for professional development, contact pd@ SolutionTree.com.

Gamble, Carouse, and Explore

By Douglas Reeves

D o not play intellectual poker with Bob Eaker. Just when you've been suckered into his good-ol'-boy routine, he is quoting W. Somerset Maugham, Shakespeare, and Voltaire. Maugham, from whom the title of this book is inspired, in one of his most famous short stories, relates the tale of the father who admonishes his son not to gamble, carouse, or explore the wider world. The son, of course, defies all three commands and, confounding the father, wins at the table, finds love, and learns lessons from exploration that his father could never have taught him. So, in the spirit of Maugham, I offer the following foreword to this wonderful book: gamble, carouse, and explore.

Gamble

Take a chance on Bob Eaker's lessons. I'm not asking you to buy in, and I'm not asking you to believe. Every leadership decision, as world champion poker player Annie Duke (2018) has demonstrated, is a combination of strategy and chance. You may not yet believe in his work on Professional Learning Communities at Work® (PLCs), but take a chance. Even though the probabilities are strongly in your favor, Eaker would be the first to admit that you may run into resistance, defiance, and roadblocks. Do it anyway. As Duke (2018) would say, go all in for your students and staff. In this context, gambling is neither a vice nor an addiction but rather the result of the calculated risks that leaders take every day. In our world of education, the risk-to-reward ratio is clear. The risks are criticism and resistance; the rewards are the lives of children. It's not a difficult calculation to make.

Carouse

Fall in love, as Rick and Becky DuFour did with each other, and as Eaker has done, with generations of students, teachers, and leaders. Just as gambling can be entirely rational, falling in love can be entirely irrational, but it is precisely this irrational passion—loving students and colleagues even when they are not very lovable—that Eaker calls us to embrace.

In chapter 8, Eaker addresses the imperative of passionate persistence. All the research and strategies in the world are not a replacement for passionate persistence. Therefore, like Maugham's hero, defy rationality and passionately pursue those values that drive you, and fall in love with the futures that your students and colleagues have, even when your students and colleagues don't necessarily believe in those futures.

Explore

We hear the voice of authority in Maugham's story: stay close, don't stray, don't take risks, don't explore. But Eaker takes us beyond our comfort zones. Along with Rick and Becky DuFour, Eaker asks us to consider how we can improve, from our first years in the profession to the twilight of our careers. My best days as a researcher are when I hear teachers in their thirty-ninth year of work seek, in the context of their PLC, to make their fortieth year even better. I watch new teachers take risks in trying professional practices that were omitted in their undergraduate training. I watch twenty-year veterans defy conventions of tradition to have dramatic impacts on student achievement. I watch leaders who are inclined toward safety and convention explore new ways to engage students, faculty, and staff. Read this book and follow their example.

So, take it from Bob Eaker and W. Somerset Maugham: gamble, carouse, and explore. The journey in the pages ahead will be richly rewarding.

Accidental Friendships

Titles, especially titles for books that are autobiographical in nature, can be tricky. Gore Vidal thought *Palimpsest* was the perfect title for his 1995 memoir. Curious to learn more about the word, I turned to the dictionary: "Something reused or altered but still bearing visible traces of its earlier form" ("Palimpsest," n.d.). Since my professional life has taken any number of distinct—and often unexpected—twists and turns, always retaining elements of previous events, people, and experiences, *palimpsest* provided a strong possibility for my title.

But, alas, W. Somerset Maugham provided another possibility. In 1938, Maugham's *The Summing Up* was published. At sixty-four years of age, after a career that had earned him widespread critical acclaim as a playwright, novelist, and writer of short stories, Maugham (1938) undertook to sum up his reflections about writing, his career, influences on his work, and to some degree, the journey of his life.

After a career in education that has spanned almost half a century, I can relate to Maugham's desire to sum up what one has learned and come to believe. And, like Maugham, I recognize that my beliefs and what I've learned have been shaped by events, experiences, and especially people I've encountered. As I approach the end of my professional journey, it seems natural that I sum up what I have come to believe and know about teaching, effective schools, and school improvement. So, *A Summing Up* it is!

I must admit, however, a feeling of trepidation. There is something inherently narcissistic about a book that is, even to a small degree, autobiographical. Although my overarching intent with this effort is to provide readers with information and insights regarding what I've learned about school improvement, instruction, and student learning throughout my professional journey, I believe context matters. So, I am placing what I've learned within the context of my life during various stages of my professional journey.

And, there is always the risk associated with not providing appropriate recognition to those who have helped along the way. I have never believed in the idea of the *self-made man*. Each of us has received support in one way or another, and my goal is to put what I've learned within the appropriate context of those who helped me, supported me, taught me, and in many cases, became my dearest friends. However, I acknowledge it is impossible to recognize everyone. Any errors of judgment in this regard should not be viewed as a lack of recognition and appreciation.

I have been blessed with a wonderful and fulfilling personal life. That being said, I have chosen to write about my personal life only to the degree that there is a direct connection to what I have learned professionally. I would be remiss, however, if I did not recognize that in a few cases it is impossible for me to separate my personal and professional lives; this is especially true regarding Rick DuFour.

Rick was my professional partner and close friend for nearly four decades. Our friendship and our professional lives became intertwined and inseparable. Readers will quickly discover that a summing up of what I've learned and come to believe is, to a great extent, a summing up that includes Rick. There have been both high and low points in my personal and professional journey. Certainly, the death of Rick in 2017, followed by Becky's passing in 2018, was a staggering loss—not only for me, but also for the countless number of people whose lives they touched. After the losses of Rick and Becky, my journey has continued, but it will never be quite the same. A huge part of me is missing.

A Few Caveats

A few caveats are in order. Since attitudes and beliefs are a result, in part, of experiences, I fully recognize that what follows is based on my own unique history—both personal and professional. Others who have had different experiences may have entirely different views. This is perfectly understandable. While I acknowledge that people have differing views, I also think that one's beliefs (and the resulting practices) must be measured against the standard of what works. When it comes to improving learning for all students, I have tried to filter my ideas through the prism of *Does it work, and is it doable?* In retrospect, I think this pragmatism behind an evidence-based way of thinking and ultimately *doing* explains, to a great extent, the popularity of the Professional Learning Communities at Work® (PLC) approach.

In short, for me, the proof was in the pudding; the value of ideas was found in the impact they would have on school improvement and student learning. Few things influence the attitude and behavior of others as much as evidence of results. Seeing results in actual classrooms and schools certainly had a deep impact on my commitment to action research, especially within a culture reflective of a PLC. While I recognize others have had different experiences and, therefore, see the world of education differently, it comes down to this: everyone has a right to an opinion, but all opinions do not hold an equal promise of effectiveness.

Upon reflection, I realize that, to a great degree, my ideas for improving schools are interconnected. For example, collaboration, a sharp focus on learning, assessment, time and support, passion, commitment, persistence, and a myriad of other best practices must be brought together, maintained, and supported by effective leadership at all levels for long-term, systemic improvement. Each individual aspect of effective schooling is enhanced by its connection to the larger whole. In this sense, we must become students of best practices and understand how each effective practice is connected to and enhanced by other concepts and practices. We can learn much from organizations outside the arena of public education. It is my hope that readers will conclude that my professional career reflects such a record.

Any summing up of what I've learned and come to believe about improving student success is deeply influenced by what I learned from research findings during each stretch of my professional journey. As I moved to new and different research interests, my thinking regarding earlier research was never fully erased. Traces of each stage of my professional journey can be seen in each successive step along the way. (Palimpsest!)

I mention this because I believe there is a tendency, particularly in the social sciences, to dismiss any research findings viewed as dated. More than one editor, I'm sure, has encouraged writers to avoid older research and emphasize more current findings. But I've found that research findings, like life's experiences and personal discoveries, are usually built on earlier foundations. All legitimate research, even that which becomes overwritten later, fuels the drive to move forward and keep searching for new and better answers. I'm sure Stephen Hawking did not dismiss Einstein, nor did Einstein dismiss Newton. I make no apologies for referencing research that might seem dated to some but formed the basis for those things I was learning as I moved forward.

A word is also in order about what this book is not. Although the concepts and practices that I have come to value are research based, this book is not intended to be a synthesis or meta-analysis of research findings regarding effective teaching, effective schools, or organizational development. As a professor for over four decades, I have certainly valued research and have learned a great deal from it. That said, what follows is grounded in my *experiences*—the result of my attempts at using research findings to improve student learning.

Last, I want to recognize up front that I do not claim these ideas as my own. Obviously, my thinking has been influenced greatly by several people, and many are included in this summing up. And as I pointed out earlier, it is impossible to separate my ideas from those of Rick DuFour. During our decades of working and writing together, it was a rare week when we did not communicate by phone, text, or email. (At times, I felt we communicated simply by thinking about the same things, usually in the same way!) We viewed the world of education through the same lens. Many of our ideas about teaching and learning, school improvement, and ultimately the PLC at Work process were serendipitous.

The Professional Learning Communities at Work Movement

The ideas that form the framework for the PLC at Work concept and practices were not the result of a sudden flash of insight. In many ways, the PLC at Work process was an umbrella under which best practices that were found in highly successful organizations, both within and outside the arena of public education, were connected—especially proven strategies that had a positive impact on learning, school and district improvement, organizational culture, and leadership. Rick and I viewed our thinking as more than a synthesis of *what works*. The PLC at Work process was also the result of our personal and professional relationships with others.

The Birth of a Friendship

Each summer, Jerry Bellon—who in the late 1960s served as chair of the Department of Curriculum and Instruction at the University of Tennessee in Knoxville (and my major professor for my doctoral studies)—led a leadership conference for educators from across the United States. Most participants were from the suburban areas of Chicago or Long Island since Jerry was consulting with many school districts in those areas.

In 1979, I was making a presentation at one of Jerry's leadership conferences and in the audience was a young principal from Chicago—Rick DuFour. After my session, Rick introduced himself to me, and we agreed to have dinner together. I have often thought about how different my life would have been had Rick decided he was simply too busy to spend three days in Knoxville that summer. Both of our lives were changed by Rick's decision to attend that conference.

The topic of my presentation that day was linking the clinical supervision model that Jerry Bellon had helped pioneer with the emerging findings from the research on effective teaching being undertaken primarily at Michigan State University and the University of Texas. As improbable as it might seem today, in the late 1970s, research on the topic of specific teacher behaviors that impact student learning and behavior was relatively new. Rick immediately saw the importance of this research and asked me if I would present these early findings to his faculty at West Chicago High School.

I can't recall the exact date I visited West Chicago, but I do remember that it was a cold and rainy Friday afternoon. Rick had offered to take me to dinner in Chicago that evening, but after my presentation to the faculty, Rick told me he needed to speak to a faculty member and it would be a few minutes before we could leave for dinner. As I stood in the hall waiting, I noticed he was talking to this faculty member rather intensely. After a few minutes, Rick joined me.

Since the conversation was rather intense, and the faculty member didn't seem happy about it, out of curiosity, I asked, "What was that about?" His response, I later came to learn, was pure Rick DuFour. He said that he had noticed that the faculty member was sitting in the back of the room during my presentation glancing through a magazine. Rick simply told the faculty member, clearly and directly, that at West Chicago High School this was unacceptable—not the way things were done—and it must not happen again.

I distinctly remember thinking that in my experience, most principals overlooked such behavior. After all, the presentation was well received, and most faculty were very professional in their behavior. In the car driving into Chicago for dinner, I asked Rick why he made a big deal out of one teacher slacking off. "What's important isn't what that one specific teacher was doing," he said, "or what I said to that specific teacher. What's important is what that teacher will say to others."

Obviously, the teacher was not happy that Rick had confronted his behavior, and he would voice his displeasure to others often and loudly. This was just what Rick wanted. He wanted the word to spread: "Hey, Rick is a serious guy, and he pays attention. He is not willing to turn his head and let things go." That theme of "monitoring and paying attention to what we collectively have said we value" would recur in our writing and presentations for almost four decades.

At that point in my career, I was beginning my professorship at Middle Tennessee State University and was heavily engaged in consulting with school districts, primarily through my work with Jerry Bellon and increasingly with Larry Lezotte, a pioneer in the effective schools research movement. As our friendship grew deeper, I also began to partner with Rick to assist schools and districts in their efforts to improve student learning.

Rick moved from West Chicago High School to become the principal at Adlai E. Stevenson High School in Lincolnshire, Illinois. It doesn't do justice to simply say that Rick was an innovator. He led Stevenson from being viewed as an average school at best to the high school that the U.S. Department of Education would later describe as the most celebrated and recognized high school in the United States. And, as Rick's reputation at Stevenson grew and my involvement with Larry Lezotte and effective schools research increased my national profile, Rick and I were increasingly asked to present in various districts or at state or national meetings—especially at summer leadership institutes hosted by the Association for Supervision and Curriculum Development (ASCD) and summer leadership conferences sponsored by the Tennessee Department of Education.

Rick suggested we begin to coauthor articles. The resulting effort led us to being asked to write our first book, *Fulfilling the Promise of Excellence* (DuFour & Eaker, 1987), which we followed up with *Creating the New American School* (DuFour & Eaker, 1992).

Both books gave increased impetus to our work with schools and school districts. Meanwhile, Rick was embedding truly innovative initiatives at Stevenson High School. Additionally, he was becoming heavily involved with educational organizations such as the National Staff Development Council (what is now Learning Forward) and ASCD. I continued my work with districts on implementing findings from the effective schools research. Both Rick and I were asked to be fellows with the National Center for Effective Schools Research and Development, an organization founded by Larry Lezotte. This increased exposure culminated in our decision to write *Professional Learning Communities at Work*, published in 1998—a turning point in our careers.

Another turning point was soon to follow. In 2002, Rick married Becky Burnette. Obviously, marrying Becky changed Rick's personal life significantly, but it also had an important, and positive, impact on our work with the PLC at Work process. Both Rick and I had experience at the high school level, and I was working in higher education. What was missing in our experience base was a strong elementary school perspective. Enter Becky. Becky had served in roles ranging from elementary teacher to central office staff, but when she married Rick, her most recent experience was as principal of Boones Mill Elementary School in Franklin County, Virginia, where she had successfully implemented PLC at Work concepts and practices.

Becky completed the team. In addition to being a highly successful practitioner, she proved to be a solid thinker, presenter, and writer. Following the marriage of Rick and Becky, further refining and promoting the PLC at Work concept became the work of the three of us.

Who *Is* That Guy?

It's safe to say that without Jeff Jones, there would just be a warehouse full of PLC at Work books somewhere in Bloomington, Indiana. Jeff Jones and his partner, D. G. Elmore, purchased National Educational Service (NES) in 1998. The company name was changed to Solution Tree in 2005. While Rick and I developed the basic conceptual framework for embedding PLC at Work concepts and practices in school districts, schools, and teams, Jeff Jones provided the business acumen, marketing skills, and vision that moved the PLC at Work ideas off the page and into schools and districts all over the United States and, eventually, around the globe. Jeff and his wonderful wife, Margaret, took the financial risks involved in purchasing and growing a company to support that work. The PLC at Work movement was a collaborative team effort involving Rick, myself, Becky, and Jeff. Importantly, in addition to our professional teamwork, we developed a very close personal friendship with Jeff and Margaret.

Just as the beginning of my friendship with Rick was serendipitous, so was our association with Jeff. The second book Rick and I wrote was *Creating the New American School* (DuFour & Eaker, 1992). It had been published by NES in Bloomington, Indiana. With the success of the book, coupled with the increasing work that Rick and I were doing with school districts, ASCD, and the Tennessee Department of Education, NES began to plan for a few small events, we labeled *institutes*, during which educators could spend two or three days gaining our insights on how schools could improve student achievement.

The impetus for these institutes was twofold. First, Rick and I had conducted a couple of small, relatively successful workshops for educators in the western suburbs of Chicago. Second, Rick's reputation as a principal was gaining momentum, and my reputation gained increased national exposure as a result of an interview that had appeared in the *Phi Delta Kappan* (Duckett, 1986).

In 1998, NES planned an institute to be held at Mont-Tremblant, a resort area near Montreal. Rick and I planned the agenda, while the associated activities and logistics were handled by NES. When Rick and I arrived at Mont-Tremblant the evening before the institute was to begin, we were casually informed that the company had been sold to a person named Jeff Jones and his business partner but that the people and the day-to-day operations would be unaffected. In a very brief visit, we were introduced to Jeff. And just like that, the handoff was complete.

Rick and I were somewhat taken aback by the change in ownership. In the movie classic *Butch Cassidy and the Sundance Kid* (Foreman & Hill, 1969), as the Pinkerton agents relentlessly chase Butch and Sundance, Butch keeps observing the pursuit and rhetorically asking, "Who *are* those guys?" Watching Jeff at the Mont-Tremblant institute, Rick and I joked that we were just like Butch. We kept asking each other, "Who *is* that guy?" Little did we know, *that guy* would change our lives—and our families' lives—in ways that would be both positive and dramatic.

Shortly after Jeff purchased NES, our book *Professional Learning Communities at Work: Best Practices for Enhancing Student Achievement* (1998) was published. When writing the book, Rick and I wanted to accomplish a number of things that we thought were unique. First, as we represented two different professional worlds—Rick offered a practitioner's perspective, while I brought higher education's insights and research focus—we believed we could create a research-based, effective approach to improving student learning that preK–12 practitioners would find both doable and appealing.

Second, we both felt strongly that our study of best practices should not be limited to those from the field of education. We wanted to highlight best practices from business, medicine, and other professions.

Third, we wanted to present a framework for embedding these practices in schools by capturing the power of the basic principles of the learning community "at work" concept. Rick and I never claimed that we were the first to use the term *professional learning communities* or the first to propose that professional learning communities held promise for improving schools. What we were proud of was that we developed a framework of processes, practices, and procedures that educators could use to reculture schools into highly functional professional learning communities and, as a result, positively impact student achievement. We saw *Professional Learning Communities at Work* as a how-to book for school practitioners.

To say that *Professional Learning Communities at Work* was a success would be an understatement. Due to Jeff's business and marketing innovations, coupled with Professional Learning Communities at Work Institutes, the book quickly gained momentum and proved very successful, not only for us, but also for those who used the book to help guide their school improvement efforts. Jeff was very innovative in his vision for growing Solution Tree, initially through marketing the PLC at Work process. His brilliance was connecting book sales to PLC at Work Institutes and ultimately connecting both to high-quality professional development services. This vision of publishing books and offering institutes and professional development—

much like a three-legged stool—proved to be highly successful, and as a result, our books and attendance at our institutes and professional development activities grew quickly, with each leg of the stool enhancing the others.

The concepts and practices of the PLC at Work process have been endorsed by virtually every major educational organization in the United States and have been supported by researchers and practitioners alike. Districts and schools that have successfully embedded the PLC at Work concepts and practices can be found in every state and province in North America—and increasingly, around the world.

I often meet people who believe my thinking and ideas about systemic initiatives to improve student learning began with the publication of *Professional Learning Communities at Work* (DuFour & Eaker, 1998). In actuality, the PLC at Work process was the culmination of many years of collaboration with a number of people who had a significant impact, not only on my thinking, but also, in fact, on my life. And although I have continued to refine my thinking since 1998 (and hopefully, I will continue to do so), my serious thinking around enhancing student achievement began in the early 1970s, when I was a doctoral student at the University of Tennessee in Knoxville and was influenced enormously by Jerry Bellon.

So, with an appreciative nod to W. Somerset Maugham, what follows is my attempt, after almost half a century as a professional educator, to sort out my thoughts on how to create the kinds of schools and classrooms for *all* kids that we would want for our own children.

CHAPTER 1

Clinical Supervision
Improving Classroom Instruction

Like many things in my life, my first opportunity to study best practices for improving student learning—my work with Jerry Bellon on clinical supervision—was accidental. In my mind, the journey began at Brainerd High School in Chattanooga, Tennessee, in 1968, with my first teaching position. But perhaps it began even earlier, when I was an undergraduate.

I have generally paid attention to suggestions and advice from others, especially people I know well and admire. However, in college, there was one piece of advice I chose not to accept. I chose to major in history and become a teacher, despite many friends pointing out that teaching positions in history were few and far between, and if I didn't become a teacher, what employment could I count on with a degree in history?

Regardless of the odds, I stuck with it. I enjoyed my history classes, and without exception, I enjoyed my history professors at the University of Chattanooga. In the 1960s, the University of Chattanooga was still a small private liberal arts university, only later becoming part of the University of Tennessee system. I thrived in such a place. The classes were small, I got to know my professors, and they likewise knew me. I decided to stick with history, believing that somehow I would be able to get a teaching position following graduation.

A huge break came when I was assigned to Brainerd High School for my student teaching experience. In the late 1960s, Brainerd was considered by many to be the top public high school in the Chattanooga public school system, both academically and athletically. The school had only been open a few years (my wife, Star, was in the first graduating class) and was located in an upper-middle-class section of the city.

I can't remember anything remarkable about the experience, except that it gave the principal and others the opportunity to know me, both personally and as a teacher. However, the prospects of attaining a teaching position there were very bleak. The history staff had been at the school since it had opened, and since none were near retirement, no openings were likely in the foreseeable future.

And then, a stroke of luck! One of the history teachers at Brainerd accepted a position at a nearby community college, and I was offered his position. At the time, I didn't realize there was a storm brewing at Brainerd and in the larger Chattanooga community—a storm that would set my life on a new, and profoundly different, path.

Although over a decade had passed since the *Brown v. Board of Education of Topeka* (1954) decision, by and large Chattanooga's public schools remained segregated. Of Brainerd's approximately twelve hundred students, just over a hundred were African American. Through the lens of the white population of the school—both students and adults—race relations seemed to be very positive, especially since some of the star athletes were black students.

As the number of African American students increased, however, so did their confidence and willingness to air their grievances. In retrospect, it's astonishing that most white students and adults were *surprised* when black students expressed displeasure regarding the school's nickname (the Rebels), fight song ("Dixie"), and logo (the Confederate flag).

In 1969, conflict erupted when word spread that the principal had met with a group of black students and was considering changing the offending symbols. Brainerd's white students walked out of the school and gathered on the front lawn and in the parking lot. After some time, the principal met with them and assured them that no real consideration was being given to changing the name, the fight song, or the flag. Word of this news also spread, and as the white students walked back into their classes, the black students walked out!

Over the next few days, tensions intensified and ultimately stretched beyond the school. People with no connection to the school rode through predominately black neighborhoods of Chattanooga flying Confederate flags from their cars. Shots were fired into the air. Groups such as the John Birch Society joined in the fray by contending students had every right to not only support the school symbols but to proudly display them on their clothing, even though doing so was obviously provocative. The situation worsened to the point that some small but serious riots broke out, and the school was closed as district leaders struggled to find a solution.

At the time of these events, I was serving as dean of students and trying to de-escalate the conflict. Obviously, if the symbols remained, the black students were going to continue to protest, and the potential for more serious rioting was real—along with the likelihood that the rioting could spread throughout the city. As we struggled to find a solution, someone at the district office suggested the Educational Opportunity Planning Center at the University of Tennessee at Knoxville as a possible resource.

As school districts all over Tennessee were grappling with how to successfully desegregate, the University of Tennessee had received a federal grant to create the Educational Opportunity Planning Center to assist districts as they struggled with both practical and cultural issues associated with school desegregation. Dr. Fred Venditti served as director of the center and agreed to offer the center's assistance with the problems in Chattanooga. Ultimately, the Confederate symbols and fight song were changed, and although the climate remained tense, eventually things returned to order.

I have been blessed by the people who have helped and encouraged me along my life's journey, and certainly Fred Venditti was one of those people. Fred changed my life trajectory without really realizing the full effect of what he was doing. We got to know each other during his days of meeting with faculty and student groups at Brainerd, and eventually, Fred asked if I had ever considered pursuing a doctoral degree.

With Fred's encouragement, as well as a rather sizable bank loan, I applied for and was accepted into the doctoral program at the University of Tennessee at Knoxville. Fred's efforts to ease racial tensions at Brainerd High School had little impact on the school's culture, but his encouragement and support had a huge impact on me, and I have been forever grateful. Although Fred and I were friends until his death, I did not ask him to chair my doctoral committee. Instead, I turned to Jerry Bellon, the new chair of the Department of Curriculum and Instruction. Little did I realize the positive impact this decision would have on my life, both professionally and personally.

Jerry Bellon and Clinical Supervision

To say that I was unprepared for doctoral study is an understatement. I was confident academically, but I really did not have a clue about the processes and procedures for advanced graduate study at a major university. When Star and I arrived in Knoxville in March for the beginning of the spring quarter of classes, I assumed I should enroll in classes and get underway, which is exactly what I did.

I registered for three or four doctoral-level courses that first quarter. I simply selected courses I thought would be interesting and helpful. Since my background was history, I enrolled in a doctoral history course taught by a visiting professor from Yale University. Given my recent experiences with race relations at Brainerd High School, I was interested in his course in African American history. Only five or six students were enrolled, and in the first class meeting, I was taken aback when the professor assigned *six* books to read and noted that in each class meeting, we would discuss one of those books. And this was only one class in which I was enrolled! But I quickly adjusted and was able to hold my own in the class discussions and writing assignments.

My most immediate problem was that although I had been accepted into the university's graduate school, I had not been accepted into a particular program of study. When my friends and fellow students would ask, "What program are you in?" I would respond, "I'm in the doctoral program." To which they would say, "No, I mean what program of study are you in—administration, curriculum and instruction, or what?" I began to realize I had a big decision to make.

It was logical that I enroll in the administration and supervision program, since Fred Venditti was a prominent faculty member in the department and had been so encouraging to me. Plus, I was on leave from the Chattanooga public school system, where I had most recently served as dean of students. Returning to Chattanooga as a principal after I completed my degree would be a practical course of action.

On the other hand, deep down, I recognized I did not find the nuts and bolts of administration interesting, at least intellectually. This is odd considering that I later served as an administrator for most of my career in higher education. But I never applied for or actively pursued any of the administrative positions I subsequently held, and quite honestly, the administrative duties of my positions were never of deep interest to me. I did, however, value the fact that I was in a position of leadership, and with leadership opportunities came opportunities to make a positive difference.

The curriculum and instruction program was broader and more flexible than the program in administration, so my friends encouraged me to make an appointment to meet with the department chair, Jerry Bellon. Most of us, when we reflect on our life, can point to a few moments that radically shifted its trajectory. Such was my meeting with Jerry. Literally, my life and the lives of everyone in my family were changed forever.

Jerry explained that, yes, I would need to apply for admittance to the curriculum and instruction doctoral program. I would also need a faculty doctoral committee to guide my study, and asking someone to chair my committee was an extremely important decision. When he asked whom I thought I would like to chair my doctoral committee, I had no idea how to respond. I had taken a philosophy class from a professor who seemed to be encouraging, open-minded, and flexible, so I mentioned him as a possibility. Jerry responded by asking me to take a few days to think about it.

Throughout the years when Jerry and I would get together and reminisce about those early days together, we would laugh about how long it took me to figure out what Jerry was trying his best to convey: perhaps Jerry himself would be an excellent person to chair my doctoral studies! Jerry had to keep asking, "So, Bob, have you given any more thought about the chair of your committee?" And invariably, after I would mention a name, Jerry would tell me to give it some thought and then come back and see him. It was perhaps our fourth meeting during which the light bulb finally clicked on and I said, "I was wondering if you would be willing to chair my doctoral committee." Not only did Jerry agree to chair my committee, but we also began to talk about a graduate assistantship. I have often thought about what my life experiences would have been had Jerry simply agreed to another chairperson for my studies.

To say that Jerry had presence doesn't do him justice. He was a strong person, both intellectually and physically. When Jerry was in a room, he became the center of the conversation. People gravitated to the power of his personality. Balancing this commanding personality was a good heart. Jerry was adamantly opposed to discrimination of any kind. He was demanding and fair. He had high expectations but was always willing to help. His professional career was on an upward flight, and he was willing to take me—and others—along with him.

Jerry had first become interested in improving classroom instruction while he was a doctoral student at Berkeley and later in his work as a faculty member at Stanislaus State, in California. With his friend and colleague Dick Jones, he began to sharpen his thinking around a concept and practices that at the time were referred to as *clinical supervision*. Importantly, Jerry also had developed a reputation as an effective consultant to schools and districts that were interested in improving classroom instruction and, ultimately, student learning through the clinical supervision process.

While working on my degree, I focused on the clinical supervision process in addition to the typical course of study, and Jerry began to include me in his consulting work, primarily in the western suburbs of Chicago and in districts on Long Island. Throughout my years in Knoxville, and later at Middle Tennessee State University, I continued to do consulting work with Jerry. Additionally, Jerry, Dick Jones, Jim Huffman, and I authored *Classroom Supervision and Instructional Improvement* (Bellon, Eaker, Huffman, & Jones, 1976). Almost immediately, I began to understand the added benefit of connecting consulting and publishing. Consulting was the perfect vehicle for connecting research and practice. While my publishing efforts were important, especially in the world of higher education, the practical upshot was increasingly being asked to speak at conferences or consult with schools and districts. I learned that publishing and consulting were inextricably linked. More importantly, these formative years gave me confidence and insights into working with schools and districts of all sizes and laid the groundwork for my own consulting work that was to follow.

A Brief History of Classroom Supervision

To fully understand the emergence of a clinical approach to supervision in the 1960s, I find it helpful to place it in a historical context. The supervision of classroom instruction in U.S. public schools has continually evolved and continues to do so with an emphasis on student testing, teacher evaluation, and enhanced accountability. In 1976, in *Classroom Supervision and Instructional Improvement*, we wrote, "A look at the historical development of supervision indicates that supervision has sometimes been detrimental, sometimes helpful, sometimes useless, but usually maligned" (Bellon et al., 1976, p. 3). This observation still rings true.

Supervision of schools and classrooms in colonial America is often described as the period of administrative inspection, which was predominant until roughly 1900. During the early years of schooling in America, there was little concern for improving teachers. Supervisory practices were heavily top-down, and the remedy for poor instruction or classroom management was simply to replace the teacher—a cure currently regaining popularity.

During the first part of the 20th century, influenced by the work of Frederick Taylor and his promotion of scientific management as a means for improving organizational effectiveness and efficiency, supervision practices shifted to focus on research and measurement. The role of the supervisor during this period was to discover the best instructional and classroom management methods and procedures and then ensure that teachers utilized these approaches, often by making unannounced classroom observations.

Clearly, this kind of supervision was not a cooperative endeavor. That began to change in the 1930s, when human relations became emphasized. The human relations approach suggested that supervisors and teachers work together to help teachers realize their potential for improving instruction. The new *democratic supervision* diminished the authority of supervisors and their perceived threat to teachers. This wane was further influenced by the rapid expansion of schools after World War II, which overwhelmed administrators with administrative and maintenance issues and consequently left less time for instructional improvement.

The increased emphasis on management issues and proclivity to democratic thought led to a virtual absence of serious efforts to actively improve the classroom instruction of individual teachers. This hands-off approach has been referred to as a period of laissez-faire supervision (Bellon et al., 1976).

During the 1950s, new strategies such as microteaching, interaction analysis, and the use of performance objectives and goal setting were introduced and showed much promise as ways to help individual teachers improve their classroom performance. These initiatives set the stage for the Harvard-Newton Project at Harvard University, led by Morris Cogan (1973).

The Emergence of a Clinical Approach to Improving Classroom Instruction

The instructional improvement framework that Cogan and his associates developed is referred to as a *clinical approach* because of its emphasis on direct, objective, trained observation of classroom behaviors. In a clinical supervision approach, the supervisor (the observer) eschews personal bias and does not deal in generalities;

rather, the observer focuses on specific behaviors of both students and teachers that occur during the lesson. The foundation of the clinical supervision process (which was refined by Jerry Bellon) is grounded in the following four basic assumptions that drive the entire process.

Assumption One

Teaching is a set of identifiable patterns of behavior. This assumption is based on the belief that together supervisors and teachers can identify specific, observable, recurring actions and techniques that form the core of a given teacher's classroom instruction.

Assumption Two

When selected patterns of teaching behavior are changed, improvement of instruction can be achieved. Teaching is a set of complex, interconnected, and recurring verbal and physical actions. The underlying assumption is that improvement is more likely to occur when specific patterns of teaching are isolated for observation and study.

Assumption Three

The supervisor-teacher relationship must be built on mutual trust if change is to take place. Teaching is highly personal, and because it is so personal, meaningful change is more likely to take place in a climate of support and mutual trust. Building mutual support is the result of behavioral interactions, over time, between the supervisor and the teacher, rather than the supervisor merely verbalizing the need for trust. Trust is the result of people behaving in ways that are trustworthy. Primarily, this involves a consistency between what supervisors and teachers say and what they do.

Assumption Four

The improvement of instruction is the primary goal of supervision. The clinical supervision process is designed for the purpose of assisting teachers in the improvement of their instructional practices, not for the purpose of evaluating teachers. Any use of the clinical approach for evaluation is clearly secondary to the primary goal of improving classroom instruction.

The Clinical Supervision Process

The clinical supervision process described in *Classroom Supervision and Instructional Improvement* (Bellon et al., 1976) is built around four distinct but interconnected phases (figure 1.1, page 24). The process is also prescriptive in that within each phase are specific interactive steps that must be completed by the supervisor (observer) and the teacher.

Phase 1: Pre-Observation Conference

It is important for both the supervisor (or anyone who is conducting the observation) and the teacher to understand the context of the lesson that is to be observed and the role of the supervisor in the process. It is also important to recognize that this conference is an interactive dialogue between the supervisor and the teacher rather than a one-way conversation that is dominated by the supervisor. The role of the supervisor is to guide the conversation, ensuring that each of the following steps is performed.

1. **Discuss the class setting:** Teaching is contextual. Rarely is a lesson taught in isolation. This general introductory step provides an opportunity for the teacher to share with the supervisor how this lesson fits into a larger unit, including what has previously occurred and what is expected to follow. The teacher can also share any unique aspects of the lesson, the class, or specific students. Last, the supervisor and the teacher agree on the date and time that the observation will take place.

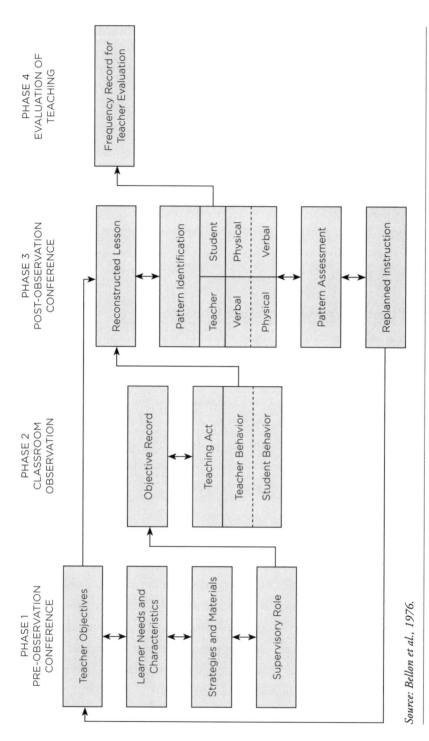

Source: Bellon et al., 1976.

FIGURE 1.1: Schematic representation of the supervisory process.

2. **Clarify the objectives:** What are the students expected to learn as a result of the lesson? During this conversation, the supervisor may need to help the teacher sharpen the objectives by making sure they are ultimately stated in learner outcomes—either content or process objectives.

3. **Discuss learner characteristics and evaluation:** This discussion extends the earlier conversation about the context of the lesson by focusing specifically on the readiness of the learners, as well as how the teacher will evaluate whether the students have attained the lesson objectives. In short, this discussion sharpens both the supervisor's and the teacher's understanding of the teacher's pre- and post-assessment processes.

4. **Identify strategies and materials to be used:** In this step, the teacher shares with the supervisor the teaching strategies that he or she will use during the lesson, in essence describing what will occur throughout the lesson, as well as any materials or technology that will be used.

5. **Establish the supervisory role:** Once the supervisor has a clear understanding of both the teacher's objectives and what will be occurring during the lesson, the supervisor and the teacher should agree on a focus of the observation that will be the most helpful to the teacher.

During my years of consulting, writing, and presenting on the clinical supervision process, one of the most frequently asked questions has been, "Are you getting an accurate view of a teacher's classroom if the teacher knows ahead of time he or she is going to be observed? Wouldn't it be more helpful for the observation to be unannounced?" I always thought this question revealed a certain underlying philosophy and assumption about the purpose of supervision, which I would challenge by asking, "Do you want to observe teachers at their very best or to *catch* them at their worst?"

If a formal observation is unannounced, the teacher has a ready-made excuse if things do not go well. The teacher can point out it was "just one of those days," or say, "This is not the way my classes typically go." On the other hand, if the teacher knows ahead of time he or she will be observed, there is little reason not to expect the teacher's best performance. I must also note that very few administrators think it would be a good idea for school board members to drop in unannounced for the purpose of conducting a formal observation of their own work!

Certainly, principals and assistant principals need to be aware of what is occurring throughout the school and particularly in classrooms. But there is a difference between conducting a formal observation and simply dropping in on a classroom for a few minutes, or talking with students about their experiences, or meeting with a grade-level or content team. The Bellon approach to the clinical observation process emphasizes that trust is established by agreeing on a time for the observation and creating the conditions for seeing teachers at their best.

Phase 2: Classroom Observation

During the classroom observation phase, the supervisor observes and records the behavior of the teacher and students. The supervisor does not attempt to make general observational notes but rather focuses on the specific aspect of the lesson that was designated as being the most important during the pre-observation conference. Importantly, the supervisor only records what is occurring during the lessons, not his or her feelings or opinions about the observation. The description should be as objective as possible.

The supervisor may choose to focus on what the teacher or the students are saying or on what they are doing. In many observations, the supervisor will choose to focus on a combination of both verbal and physical behaviors as activities within the lesson change.

The supervisor's notes might take the form of a script of what the teacher says or what students are saying. For example, if the teacher's objective is for the students to gain a clear understanding of a particular concept, the supervisor might choose to record, as verbatim as possible, what the teacher says as he or she explains the concept. Alternatively, the supervisor and teacher might have agreed to record students' questions after the concept is explained.

In some cases, the supervisor might record the physical movements of the teacher. Such diagrams can be particularly insightful in laboratory classes or physical education classes. Perhaps the focus might be diagramming where students are during an activity.

Regardless of the focus of the observation, the supervisor must observe two parameters. One, he or she must become skilled at recording classroom behaviors, and two, value judgments must not be part of the record.

Phase 3: Post-Observation Conference

The post-observation conference should be conducted as soon as possible after the lesson. During the classroom observation phase, the primary skill required of the supervisor is accurate recording of what the teachers or students are saying and doing, or a combination of both. In the post-observation conference, the primary skill required of the supervisor is interpersonal. An element of trust is essential if the post-observation conference and, by extension, the clinical process are to be productive. This trust must have been developed over time, before the clinical process even began. It cannot be built on the spot during the post-observation conference.

In this conference, the supervisor and the teacher sit side by side and examine the data the supervisor recorded (typically on a long legal pad). With the data in front of them, the supervisor and the teacher proceed through five distinct steps.

1. **Reconstruct what took place:** The supervisor reviews the data with the teacher regarding what took place during the lesson. The teacher might ask questions, or the supervisor might ask for the teacher's view of what the data indicate. The important point is that the supervisor and teacher agree that the data portray an accurate representation of what occurred during the lesson.

2. **Identify patterns of behavior from the recorded data:** Patterns are defined as recurring behavior. A pattern may be verbal or physical. A pattern may be a teacher pattern or a student pattern. Often a pattern is a combination of behaviors. The point is, in this part of the post-observation conference, the supervisor is leading the teacher in the identification of actions that recurred during the lesson.

    Ideally, the teacher will identify the most obvious patterns first. However, the supervisor may also point out a pattern that the teacher has failed to identify. This is a joint dialogue in which two professionals are doing their best to identify recurring patterns of behavior during the lesson.

3. **Restate the content and process objectives for the lesson from the pre-observation conference:** At this point, the supervisor quickly restates the objectives the teacher had for the lesson. The supervisor is setting the stage for a discussion of each pattern that occurred in relation to the teacher's objectives, rather than to any preconceived notion the supervisor has about good teaching.

4. **Compare the patterns that have been identified with the stated objectives:** Together, the supervisor and the teacher assess the effects of each identified pattern on the teacher's objectives for the lesson. The patterns either supported the attainment of or were detrimental to the lesson objectives. In many cases, it will be determined that

some had no effect. It is important to emphasize that this discussion is a *joint* discussion. Ideally, the teacher will readily state his or her view regarding pattern effectiveness, but often the supervisor needs to take a more active role, pointing out effects that perhaps the teacher has not seen. Likely, there will be a good deal of anxiety during the first observations, but after being participants in the clinical process a few times, teachers become much more comfortable and trusting, active partners—providing, of course, the supervisor performs the role well.

5. **Use the analysis for future teaching:** Once the supervisor and the teacher have agreed on patterns that supported the attainment of the teacher's objectives, the continued use of those patterns should be recommended and supported. There should also be agreement regarding detrimental patterns that need to be changed or modified.

    For example, the supervisor might ask, "If you taught this or a similar lesson again, what would you do differently?" Such questions hopefully will cause the teacher to reflect not only on teaching behavior but also on how it might be improved. And, of course, the supervisor might offer suggestions on how to improve patterns.

At its core, the post-observation conference creates a mirror in which the teacher, along with the supervisor, reflects on the effectiveness of each pattern of teacher behavior in light of the stated objectives for the lesson and serves the purpose of enhancing purposeful reflection regarding teaching effectiveness, not only with individual teachers, but over time also with the entire teaching staff.

Phase 4: Evaluation of Teaching

In the early 1970s, we discouraged linking teacher evaluation and the clinical supervision process. Occasionally, a district administrator would ask, "Why not use the notes from the clinical classroom observation as a major aspect of the evaluation of teachers?" Our response was that we believed it was very difficult to develop and maintain a high level of trust between the supervisor and teachers if evaluation became part of the process.

The latter part of the 1970s witnessed an increased focus on accountability and evaluation across the United States. Increasingly, districts were including classroom observations as part of their teacher evaluation programs. Districts consulting with Jerry Bellon and his associates (including me) asked how they could connect what they were doing within the clinical supervision process with their emerging teacher evaluation programs. So we began to assist them and offered the following suggestions:

a. The observational data should only be used in the part of the evaluation process that deals with classroom instruction.

b. The evaluation program should be based on the assumption that the major purpose of evaluation is to gather information for decision making that will improve the instructional program.

c. All aspects of the evaluation program should be philosophically and procedurally in harmony with the clinical supervision approach.

d. Agreement should be reached about which important behaviors will be evaluated.

e. Evaluation forms should be congruent with gathering objective data that can be used for decision making. Rating sheets that are heavily laden with value statements that require subjective judgments should be avoided.

f. And, given the fact that each school district is different, each district should engage in an inclusive process to develop its own unique evaluation program. (Bellon, Eaker, Huffman, & Jones, 1976, pp. 24–25)

I find it amazing that the clinical supervision process that I experienced in the late 1960s is so prominent in the 21st century. While not referred to as *clinical supervision*, classroom observation has become a feature of virtually every state evaluation system. Palimpsest indeed!

A Summing Up

Clearly, the decade of the 1970s was a seminal period in my life. In retrospect, this was the time that I seriously and purposefully began to delve into issues related to both instructional improvement and, toward the end of the decade, school improvement.

The consulting work with Jerry Bellon gave me the confidence to work in schools and school districts of all shapes and sizes. I increased my understanding not only of instructional improvement but also of the importance of appreciating each school and school district's unique history and culture. I also acquired valuable experience handling the political issues that often accompany any attempts at change.

I was fortunate to work in all types of schools. Most were upper-middle-class suburban schools, but because I worked in so many different schools in a wide variety of districts, I was able to gain insights into rural schools, inner-city schools, wealthy schools, and poor schools, as well as schools of all sizes.

This period was also important in that I made new and enduring friendships, both personal and professional. My relationship with Jerry evolved from being his graduate assistant to being close friends with both him and his family. Also during this period, my friendship with Rick DuFour grew and deepened. We realized we viewed the world through the same lens, including things beyond educational issues. We found humor in many of the same things. Not all who knew Rick had the opportunity to witness his sharp sense of humor.

Boy, did they miss out! He was one of the wittiest people I ever met. Simply put, for four decades, we had great fun together.

Working in schools also gave me the opportunity to make new friends, especially in the districts of suburban Chicago and Long Island, such as Hinsdale, Illinois, and West Islip, New York. I often traveled with Jim Huffman, who also was a graduate assistant of Jerry's and after receiving his doctorate joined me on the faculty at Middle Tennessee State University. In the evenings, we would have dinner with friends, such as Roger Miller from Hinsdale and, of course, Rick.

My experiences in these schools sharpened my belief in the critically important role leadership plays in regard to district, school, team, and classroom effectiveness, particularly the quality of superintendent and principal leadership. I realized quickly that the defining difference between success or lack thereof was leadership. Programs, regardless of how well they may be conceived or supported by research, will have limited impact in districts and schools in the absence of strong leadership. It is ironic that teacher empowerment, ownership, and improvement depend on strong top-down leadership.

I also gained a greater appreciation of the role that attitudes play in instructional improvement. In many ways, attitudes are the lubrication that makes things work—or not. In *Kid by Kid, Skill by Skill* (Eaker & Keating, 2015), Janel Keating and I write of the difference between *have-to* educators and *get-to* educators. I was amazed at the differences between schools and within schools regarding this basic attitude. Some educators seemed to have an attitude of "I have to come to work and do these things I am told to do," while others expressed excitement or gratitude that "I get to work with my colleagues and these kids." What a difference!

A get-to teacher attitude is exemplified by Eleanor Roosevelt. After her husband, Franklin Roosevelt, was elected governor of New York in the election of 1928, Mrs. Roosevelt refused to give up the job that meant the most to her. She was teaching American history and 19th century literature three days a week at the Todhunter School for girls in Manhattan. She remarked, "I teach because I love it. I cannot give it up" (Ward & Burns, 2014, pp. 268–269).

Another example: For years one of my dearest friends was Richard Marius. Although Richard passed away in 1999, I often think of him and his impact on me—and countless others. For almost two decades, Richard was director of expository writing at Harvard University. Beyond directing expository writing, Richard frequently taught a course in the Harvard Graduate School of Arts and Sciences on William Faulkner's novels, from *Soldiers' Pay* to *Go Down, Moses*. Although the university catalog course description noted enrollment was limited to fifteen students, in the fall of 1996 his final grade sheet listed grades for seventy-one students (Anderson, 2006)!

Richard did not feel he *had to* teach those additional students. Instead, he felt grateful that he *got to* share his knowledge of and enthusiasm for Faulkner's life and novels with students. Later in my career, as a university dean, I witnessed get-to attitudes like Richard's time and again. Unfortunately, I also occasionally encountered faculty members who would not allow any additional students in their courses beyond the published class size limits, regardless of the circumstances.

What a difference attitude makes! What would lead us to believe that students will have a better attitude than their teachers or that teachers' attitudes will be more positive and enthusiastic than the attitude of their principal? Doesn't the attitude of the superintendent have an effect on an entire school district—especially on principals, teachers, and support staff? The answer: absolutely!

During this period of utilizing the clinical supervision process as a vehicle for improving instruction, both Jim Huffman and I (and, I am sure, others) began to realize the process had some severe limitations. While the process offered educators helpful skills at observing and recording classroom interactions, along with a framework for partnering with teachers to reflect on their instructional effectiveness, the process did not place a heavy emphasis on providing teachers specific research-based approaches for improving their classroom effectiveness.

We saw that at the end of post-observation conferences, teachers would often agree that some changes in their classroom instruction would enhance their effectiveness and asked for recommendations on what to change, but the supervisors had only limited knowledge of research-based effective instructional practices. Interestingly, in many cases, the teachers were much more knowledgeable regarding effective teaching strategies than those conducting the observation!

Fortunately, the latter part of the 1970s witnessed an increased interest within both the U.S. Department of Education and the research community in pursuing research around teaching effectiveness. And fortunately for me, like so many times in my life, I serendipitously met a person who would make a significant impact on my professional career and greatly enhance my knowledge of and thinking about instructional improvement—a meeting I'll describe in the next chapter. But it's safe to say that without my prior decades of experience with classroom observation through the clinical supervision process and the friendship and mentorship of Jerry Bellon, this new research wouldn't have had nearly the impact on me that it ultimately did.

CHAPTER 2

The Consumer-Validation Approach

Research Into Practice

T he clinical supervision framework continued to be the focus
of my thinking about instructional improvement well into
the mid-1970s. In the fall of 1972, I joined the faculty at Middle
Tennessee State University. I was sure I would stay at the university
for four or five years and then move to a larger university. Instead, I
remained for the next forty-one years!

There were many reasons. Some were personal. We were settled
in the Murfreesboro community, and our extended family was in
nearby Chattanooga. Other reasons were professional. I eventually
worked for five university presidents, all of whom treated me wonderfully. From the time I joined the faculty until I became dean of
the College of Education, I was mentored by Ralph White, chair of
the Department of Educational Leadership. More than a mentor,
Ralph became a great friend. And importantly, each dean, vice president, and president not only allowed me to continue my consulting
work with K–12 schools but also encouraged me to do so. Although
in subsequent years I had opportunities to move to the University
of Georgia and the University of Virginia, both of which I seriously

considered, in the end, I realized I could not find another university culture as supportive as Middle Tennessee State.

In the early 1970s—along with Peabody College, Tennessee State University, and the Metropolitan Nashville Public Schools—Middle Tennessee State joined a consortium, the Teacher Education Alliance for Metro, to supervise and develop preservice teachers and provide in-service opportunities for educators. When I joined the university faculty, my initial assignment was with the consortium. During my second year on the faculty, I was joined by my good friend and colleague Jim Huffman, who had also received his doctorate from the University of Tennessee. Working daily in Nashville's schools gave us the opportunity to expand our public school experiences, particularly in inner-city schools, even though we were full-time university faculty. Although the consortium was our primary responsibility, we were also assigned to teach graduate classes.

The combination of working in schools within a large metropolitan district, consulting in suburban districts in Chicago and Long Island, and teaching graduate classes composed primarily of teachers from surrounding suburban and rural districts in Tennessee provided a perfect laboratory for our interest in research-based instructional improvement.

As a university faculty member, my interest in the research on effective teaching practices became more focused. I learned of efforts by the U.S. Department of Education and the educational research community, particularly at Michigan State University and the University of Texas, to improve student achievement through research to identify specific teaching behaviors that directly affected student learning and behavior—what was at the time referred to as the *teacher effects research*. One of the researchers who had an early impact on our thinking was Jacob S. Kounin (1970).

The Kounin Research on Classroom Management

The work of Kounin (1970) was groundbreaking in two ways: one, it impacted the way both researchers and practitioners viewed classroom management, and two, it fueled the emerging interest among researchers in objectively observing classroom instruction and its effect on student learning and behavior.

Kounin's (1970) interest in classroom management began quite accidentally. During one of his classes, he reprimanded a student for reading a newspaper during the lesson. He noticed that although he had reprimanded only one student, his reprimand had an effect on other students in the class. He later asked, "Why were students who weren't targets of the reprimand affected by it? Do differences in the qualities of the reprimand produce different effects, if any, on non-target students?" (Kounin, 1970, p. iii).

Kounin's curiosity eventually led to years of research on the subject of classroom discipline—specifically, the effects of how teachers handle student misbehavior. He sought to discover if some discipline techniques are more effective than others when it comes to affecting the behavior of an entire class. He also wanted to learn if and how the discipline techniques of teachers who are perceived as good disciplinarians differ from the techniques of those who are perceived as weak disciplinarians (Eaker & Keating, 2015).

After five years of study, Kounin did not find many, if any, differences in the effects of various disciplinary techniques on the larger classroom environment. He found that the manner in which teachers handled misbehavior made no difference in how audience students reacted. He was unable to predict any ripple effect from the quality of a disciplinary event. Further, he found that a teacher's actions after a student misbehaves (desist techniques) "are not significant determinants of managerial success in classrooms" (Kounin, 1970, p. 71).

Kounin was not deterred. He sought to know why some teachers are generally viewed as better disciplinarians than others. What differentiates good disciplinarians from weak disciplinarians? To answer this question, he began another research project. This second study differed in that Kounin and his colleagues collected data from videotapes. The use of videotapes allowed the researchers to gather data about the larger issues related to how teachers manage their classrooms, rather than only data focusing on the more specific issue of how teachers respond to misbehavior (Eaker & Keating, 2015). Kounin and his researchers were able to analytically review teacher and student behavior in real classrooms without relying on classroom observations in real time.

The findings in this second study were significant. Kounin and his colleagues found that how teachers managed their lessons prior to student misbehavior had a far more powerful effect on student behavior than teachers' disciplinary actions after student misbehavior occurred. In other words, what teachers were doing *prior* to misbehavior to manage the whole classroom was more significant than how they dealt with individual incidents.

Kounin (1970) was able to group various classroom management behaviors into four categories.

1. **Withitness and overlapping:** Kounin (1970) defines *teacher withitness* as "a teacher's communicating to the children by her actual behavior (rather than by simple verbal announcing: 'I know what's going on') that she knows what the children are doing, or has the proverbial 'eyes in the back of her head'" (p. 82). Associated with withitness is overlap: "what the teacher does when she has two matters to deal with at the same time. Does she somehow attend to both issues simultaneously, or does she remain or become immersed in one issue only, to the neglect of the other?" (p. 85).

2. **Smoothness and momentum:** Kounin and his colleagues found that effectively managing instructional and noninstructional transitions and movement reduced student misbehavior:

> A teacher in a self-contained classroom, then, must initiate, sustain, and terminate many activities. Some of this involves having children move physically from one point of the room to another, as when a group must move from their own desks to the reading circle. At other times it involves some psychological movement, or some change in props, as when children change from doing arithmetic problems at their desks to studying spelling words at the same desks. (Kounin, 1970, p. 92)

There are any number of teacher behaviors that affect smoothness and momentum in classrooms. One such behavior identified by Kounin and his team is *stimulus-boundedness*—an event in which the teacher:

> Behaves as though she has no will of her own and reacts to some unplanned and irrelevant stimulus as an iron filing reacts to some magnet: she gets magnetized and lured into reacting to some minutia that pulls her out of the main activity stream. (Kounin, 1970, p. 98)

Another such behavior they identify is *dangle*. This occurs when "a teacher started, or was in, some activity and then left it 'hanging in mid-air' by going off to some other activity. Following such a 'fade away' she would then resume the activity" (Kounin, 1970, p. 100). Kounin also found that smoothness and momentum were affected by *flip-flops* during transitions, when a teacher stops one activity, starts another, then returns to the original activity. Momentum is also affected by *slowdowns*, and slowdowns are, in turn, affected by such behaviors as *over-dwelling* and *fragmentation*. Kounin (1970) defines *fragmentation* as "a slowdown produced by a teacher's breaking down an activity into subparts when the activity could have been performed as a single unit" (p. 105).

In short, Kounin found that teachers who exhibit behaviors that contribute to smoothness and momentum have fewer student behavior problems and receive the added benefit of keeping students more involved and focused on their work (Eaker & Keating, 2015).

3. **Group alerting and accountability; valence and challenge arousal:** Teachers who have fewer student behavior problems can keep the class focused on the lesson using a skill Kounin refers to as *group alerting*, which is the degree to which teachers are able to involve nonreciting students in the recitation task, maintain their attention, and keep them on their toes or alerted. Kounin also cited an additional dimension of maintaining group focus, *formatting*, which is what other students are required to do when a person or a small group is being called on to perform or recite (Eaker & Keating, 2015).

    Kounin found that misbehavior is decreased when students are motivated to engage in lessons and feel appropriately challenged by classroom activities. He grouped these findings into the category of *valence and challenge arousal*.

4. **Seatwork, variety, and challenge:** Closely associated with motivating and challenging students are behaviors related to variety. Teachers who plan for variability in lessons have fewer classroom management problems than teachers who have a limited repertoire of instructional approaches and tend to rely on the same approaches time and again (Eaker & Keating, 2015).

The research of Kounin was seminal for me and, I assume, many others. First, it shifted my professional focus from the clinical supervision process to research-based instructional effectiveness. I did not abandon the idea that observing teachers is important; rather, I found Kounin's findings provided much-needed support for teachers—especially when linked with classroom observation. I began to see that observers could be armed with a toolbox of proven research strategies they could share with teachers to enhance the likelihood of instructional improvement.

Second, Kounin's work differed from much of the existing research base in that it was practical, focusing on specific teacher behaviors that practitioners could easily grasp and understand. The findings simply made sense in the real world of schools. Rather than focusing on areas of schooling over which teachers had little or no control—for example, the impact of poverty or the lack of parental support—Kounin's findings focused on specific things teachers could do or avoid doing to improve their classroom management skills and, thus, improve student behavior.

The work of Kounin was part of a rapidly growing body of research exploring new and exciting prospects for improving what happens in classrooms. My interest in Kounin's research led me to increasingly focus on the correlation between what teachers do and say in classrooms and student achievement. This led me and Jim Huffman to a new area of interest—again rather accidentally—that would have a significant impact on my professional career.

The Consumer-Validated Research Model

As findings from a growing body of research became available, mainly through journals, newsletters, and meetings, Jim and I began sharing findings from the teacher effects research with teachers. We had a significant number of teachers in our graduate courses and in-service programs who were interested in improving their instructional effectiveness, and they saw research findings as a viable resource.

Initially, our work with teachers involved simply sharing a specific research finding and engaging in discussions that included question-and-answer sessions and teachers sharing their personal experiences. These meetings were somewhat helpful. They created an awareness about the research on teaching and enhanced teacher interest in and appreciation for research findings as a helpful tool. The nonthreatening discussions created a climate in which teachers felt comfortable reflecting on and sharing ideas and issues related to the effectiveness—or lack thereof—of teacher behaviors in certain classroom situations.

But our early approach did not result in teachers trying, to any great extent, to implement any of the research findings in their classrooms (Eaker & Huffman, 1980). Simply informing teachers about research findings was not making an impact on their instructional practices. We began to question the larger process of how practitioners acquire and use research findings.

The Limitations of Traditional Dissemination Processes

Even though most teachers genuinely want to improve their instructional effectiveness and value research findings, the impact of such findings on classroom behavior has traditionally been weak. Most dissemination approaches have relied on the expository mode (both verbal and print) to distribute research findings to teachers. Such approaches are only marginally effective, at best.

Although we learn through experience and the use of multiple senses, teachers are often expected to change personal and complex teaching behaviors by simply reading about research findings or listening to someone present the findings. Moreover, the research in question has usually been conducted by college professors. While professors might be best suited to conduct research studies, teachers often perceive many, if not most, college professors as having an unrealistic understanding of real-world preK–12 classrooms, and their findings, as a result, lack credibility with teachers. Further, teachers find many research conclusions to be vague or even contradictory. As a result, they often have difficulty thinking of specific things they can do in their classrooms to benefit from those conclusions (Eaker & Huffman, 1980).

Jim and I sought to develop a new process for disseminating research findings, one in which teachers would actively engage with the findings on effective instructional practices in their classrooms. We felt that higher education's findings should be validated by those teachers who are intended to use them. Just as *Consumer Reports* researchers test product claims of effectiveness, teachers would test instructional practices, following the consumer-validation model.

A New Model for Testing and Implementing Research Findings

Using our previous work with teachers in the Murfreesboro, Tennessee, school system, Jim and I decided to create a dissemination model that would go beyond informing and actually affect teachers' classroom behavior. Our primary source of research studies was the Institute for Research on Teaching at Michigan State University. At that time, the institute was heavily involved in researching such areas as teacher decision making; reading diagnosis and remediation; classroom management strategies; instruction in language arts, reading, and mathematics; teacher education; teacher planning; effects of external pressures on teachers' decisions; sociocultural factors; and teachers' perceptions of student affect. Some of the most highly respected researchers in the United States conducted these studies and many others, such as Lee Shulman, Jere Brophy, Christopher Clark, Andrew Porter, and Larry Lezotte, to name a few.

Additionally, we utilized the research from others outside the institute, namely Thomas Good, Barak Rosenshine, and Jacob Kounin.

As we conceptualized this new dissemination model, our goals began to emerge (Eaker & Huffman, 1980).

> Increase awareness among the participant teachers of current research findings in the area of teacher behavior and student achievement.

> Improve individual teaching skills by having teachers apply research findings in their individual classrooms.

> Help teachers become more analytical and reflective about their own teaching behavior.

> Help teachers critically evaluate research findings in terms of their applicability to the classroom.

We planned our framework and activities based on certain assumptions. First, we assumed that the quality of interpersonal relations between us and the teachers, as well as within the participant group, would be a key factor in the success of the project. We knew that if our goal was to encourage experimentation, creativity, imagination, and a willingness to try new things, the process would need to be as nonthreatening as possible.

Second, teachers would need to feel secure and confident in their knowledge and understanding of the research. Simply put, we recognized that unless teachers developed a clear and accurate understanding of the findings, implementing them would be problematic and the odds of changing teacher behavior slim.

Third, we recognized that to be effective, the dissemination plan would have to focus on teacher behavior in K–12 classrooms. We would have to shift the focus from the *university* classroom, where teachers were *informed* of research findings, to *K–12* classrooms, where teachers could *apply, use, and test* the practicality of specific research findings—an approach that in later years came to be known as action research.

And, finally, we assumed we would need a tool for collecting data from teachers' experiences as they tried new instructional behaviors:

> If teachers were to reflect on the effects of their teaching, and if they were to share information with others, then some sort of format needed to be developed in which teachers' ideas, activities, insights, criticisms, attitudes, and feelings could be recorded. (Eaker & Huffman, 1980, p. 5)

The plan that eventually emerged contained four types of activities, or steps.

1. Seminars
2. Implementation
3. Classroom visitations
4. Sharing sessions

Seminars

Seminars provided deep, rich discussion around specific research findings related to instructional effectiveness. To avoid information overload, we decided to limit our seminars to four research areas.

1. Planning and organization of classroom activities
2. Student planning and time on task
3. Discipline and classroom management
4. Affective teaching skills

Research findings in each of these four areas were synthesized by myself and Jim and made as clear and concise as possible. Gathering, synthesizing, translating, and discussing research findings so that they could be more easily understood by teachers became a central aspect of the consumer-validation approach (Eaker & Huffman, 1980).

Implementation

Once teachers felt confident they understood the specifics and implications of a set of research findings, they implemented the findings in their day-to-day classroom instruction and recorded their observations and outcomes on a simple form:

- Section One contained a brief description of the specific research findings that the teacher was integrating into classroom instruction.

- Section Two was a blank page with the heading "Description of Classroom Behaviors Engaged in While Implementing the Above Research Findings." Teachers were asked to list and briefly describe the things they did in their classrooms to implement specific research findings.

- Section Three was another blank page with the heading "Analyze What You Think and Feel About What Happened When You Tried Each of the Behaviors Listed in Section Two." The purpose of this section was to prompt teachers to reflect on the results or impact of their implementation. We wanted the teachers to analyze what occurred and evaluate the classroom efficacy of specific research findings. Recording their perceptions also enabled teachers to be better equipped to share their experiences with the other participant teachers. (Eaker & Huffman, 1980, p. 7)

After each seminar, teachers worked to integrate the research findings into their regular classroom routines and keep the record form up to date.

Classroom Visitations

We recognized that teachers would have questions during implementation. Some would need simple reassurance, while others would need more technical assistance. To a great extent, success of the consumer-validation project hinged on our classroom visitations to support teachers.

My years of focus on the clinical supervision process with its emphasis on objective classroom observation provided me with a wealth of experience in visiting teachers' classrooms, and those earlier experiences proved invaluable to me as I now visited classrooms for an entirely different purpose.

The classroom visits that Jim and I made in the consumer-validation project were unlike those that were part of the clinical supervision process. These visitations were not so much observational as they were collegial and assistance oriented. Often, a great deal of time was spent with a teacher in an individual school. On other occasions, one of us met with a small group of teachers in the same school. There was no set way for conducting these visits. The goal was simply to assist teachers during the implementation phase.

Sharing Sessions

After teachers spent two or three weeks (depending on the complexity of the research focus) implementing research findings in their classrooms, they met in post-implementation seminars to share and discuss what had occurred during the implementation phase. The purpose of these seminars was threefold.

First and most obvious, the sessions were geared to engage teachers in sharing how they approached implementing each research finding. Sharing ideas, activities, and materials significantly increased the number and variety of instructional ideas that each teacher learned beyond those tried in his or her individual classroom. For example, as a group, the teachers tried thirty-four distinct ways of improving classroom organization and planning for instruction (Eaker & Huffman, 1980).

The second purpose of these seminars was to share conclusions about the instructional impact of specific research findings. Teachers reported that some ideas had a very positive impact on the effectiveness of their instructional practice, while others had a marginal impact. Some activities and approaches did not work well at all. Teachers learned to evaluate research findings, not after studying those findings, but rather after *using* those findings in their own classrooms. In this regard, teachers were becoming wise consumers of research findings.

The third purpose of the post-implementation seminars was to improve teachers' instructional effectiveness through high-quality interactions with other teachers who had experimented with the same set of research findings. In short, the seminars provided a setting in which teachers engaged in rich dialogue with their professional colleagues. One teacher remarked that teachers rarely get to engage in extensive discussions with other teachers about teaching in an organized setting (Eaker & Huffman, 1980). It was interesting to learn that teachers perceived the experiences and perceptions of other teachers who had implemented research findings to be more credible than those of university professors.

We made significant discoveries about teacher perspectives as a result of the consumer-validation experiments (Eaker & Huffman, 1980). First, we learned that teachers valued research findings that focused on classroom instruction, and they believed research findings could have a positive impact on improved teaching. However, teachers often viewed findings to be contradictory, and they did not perceive principals, faculty meetings, supervisors, in-service meetings, or professional meetings as resources providing them with useful research findings that focused on effective classroom instructional practices.

Likewise, they did not believe undergraduate teacher preparation programs provided effective, specific information regarding classroom-related research. (However, they had a more positive view of graduate programs in this regard.) Teachers received most of their information regarding research related to effective teaching practices from professional journals, but there, too, they felt this approach to research dissemination should be expanded (Eaker & Huffman, 1980).

We also learned how to more effectively disseminate educational research findings. For example, we learned there must be a person who has the specific responsibility for studying relevant research, interpreting those findings to small groups of teachers who teach the same or similar content, demonstrating how specific findings can be effectively implemented in classrooms, then monitoring and analyzing with teachers in a collaborative setting the effects of their efforts to improve their instructional practice.

This is a complex responsibility requiring special skills. First, people in these roles must genuinely be interested in and know about research efforts that focus on instructional effectiveness. They do not need to possess the sophisticated skills required to *generate* research findings, but they must have the skills to accurately *interpret* such research. In addition, they must be familiar with and appreciate the challenging world of the classroom teacher. Researchers often lack recent preK–12 teaching experience, and this leads to a general lack of credibility with classroom teachers. Finally, effective interpersonal and communication skills are a must. A person who works with teachers to enhance their instructional effectiveness through the implementation of proven research findings must be sensitive and empathetic and possess the skills that can lead to a climate of trust (Eaker & Huffman, 1980).

Our consumer-validation experiments reinforced our belief about the necessity of trust-based collaboration with teachers. The term *consumer-validated research* implies that the *consumers* of research findings—classroom teachers—play an important role in *validating* both the degree to which such findings are workable and relevant to the day-to-day world of classroom teachers and how research findings can be effectively implemented, modified, and improved on. This undertaking is collaborative in nature and, if successfully implemented, can result in a body of research findings that are *teacher validated* and thus more likely to be useful to other teachers.

Jim and I thoroughly enjoyed our work with classroom teachers as we sought to find ways to effectively implement research findings in classrooms, but perhaps the most professionally significant outcome, like most of the major stages in my professional life, occurred rather serendipitously. Another accidental friendship developed— this time with Judith Lanier, the dean of the College of Education at Michigan State University and co-director, along with Lee Shulman, of the Institute for Research on Teaching. Judy's friendship was a professional life changer for me.

The Institute for Research on Teaching: Michigan State University

From the mid-1970s through the 1980s, the College of Education at Michigan State University, led by Judy Lanier, was widely considered by many to be the top educational research center in the United States—and justly so. The college was home to the Institute for Research on Teaching, which was funded by a $3.6 million grant from the U.S. Department of Education, in addition to funds from various other sources. Specifically, the focus of the institute was to investigate a broad spectrum of teacher behaviors and their effects on student learning, student behavior, and student motivation.

As mentioned earlier, the institute was home to many of the most highly respected researchers, representing a wide variety of backgrounds and areas of interest and expertise. Additionally, public school teachers worked in the institute as half-time collaborators in research initiatives. Judy Lanier and Lee Shulman were co-directors of the institute, with Larry Lezotte and Andrew Porter serving as associate directors. Larry had additional responsibilities for the areas of communication and dissemination. Although the institute published research reports, notes from conference proceedings, and occasional papers, it was their quarterly newsletter that was the vehicle for my association with the institute generally, and Judy and Larry specifically.

I don't recall ever requesting the newsletters, but I do recall a newsletter showing up in my mail one day. As I was glancing through it, I became particularly interested in a short column written by Judy. I was impressed by her comments about the important role teachers played in the work of the institute. I wrote a letter to her, thinking, perhaps, she might be interested in knowing of the work that Jim and I were doing to enhance teachers' instructional effectiveness through helping teachers use research findings in their classrooms. I had no expectation of a response, much less her high degree of interest.

Shortly after receiving my letter, Judy left a message for me to call her. We chatted a bit, and she expressed genuine interest and enthusiasm for our work. Fairly soon afterward, she invited Jim and me to visit the institute in Lansing and share our work at one of the regular faculty convocations. She explained the purpose of these meetings was for faculty to share and discuss their work and their thinking with each other, and occasionally, researchers other than the institute faculty were invited to speak.

Of course, we were excited and accepted the invitation. I clearly recall a great degree of anxiety, too. After all, we were simply two faculty members from a comprehensive mid-level university who had a background in using, rather than producing, original research results. In retrospect, I believe this was what fascinated Judy the most. She was genuinely interested in the question, How can we at the institute make a positive difference in the improvement of classroom instruction beyond merely engaging in and writing about research on teaching effectiveness?

Our initial visit to Michigan State could not have gone better. Judy, Larry, Jere Brophy, and the entire faculty were welcoming and hospitable. In addition to our presentation to the group, Judy had arranged for many one-on-one conversations with faculty. Although they were very busy with their teaching and their research, they were welcoming and engaging, on both a professional level and a personal level. (We learned early on in our conversation with Jere Brophy that he was a country music fan!)

Judy also hosted an informal gathering at her home that evening where we could mix and mingle with the faculty and her friends. It was truly delightful, and I like to think that it was at this gathering that we really began our friendship with Judy and with Larry. Larry drove us back to the airport, and as we chatted, I remember thinking, *This is one of the nicest people I have ever met.* Little did I know that Larry and I would be working much more closely together in the future as the research on effective schools began to gain national prominence.

I don't recall how many times we visited the institute, but each time, I felt we became closer friends with Judy. I remember thinking that there was the possibility of a position offer in the works and wondered how I would respond. On a personal level, my wife, Star, and I wanted very much to remain within driving distance of our family in Chattanooga, and I was concerned about the high-pressure culture of a large, research-oriented university. No such offer ever materialized, although I believe Judy did give the possibility some thought.

A Summing Up

My experience with the Institute for Research on Teaching and Judy Lanier had a positive impact on my career (and personal life) in a number of ways. First, I gained a much deeper knowledge of and interest in research-based approaches for improving classroom effectiveness. In retrospect, I think this played a significant part in the emphasis Rick DuFour and I placed on gaining shared knowledge about best practices and on collaborative teams engaging in action research in the Professional Learning Communities at Work process.

Rick and I both saw the potential for connecting the findings from the effective teaching research to the clinical supervision observation process. In his inimitable, witty way, Rick frequently pointed out the problem of the *Now what?* question in post-observation conferences.

Rick remarked that observations of teachers, even if done well and accurately recorded, are of little value if the person conducting the interview has little to offer when a teacher asks, "I see that I need to improve my instruction in certain areas. What do you suggest I do?" Rick, with what Becky DuFour and I came to refer to as his *dripping sarcasm*, would observe that at this point most principals and supervisors are left to say, "Well, actually, I don't have a clue about how you can improve your teaching or classroom management practices. You see, my skills are in observing and recording, not in the knowledge of effective teaching practices. Sorry."

The research findings on effective teaching didn't just help teachers; they also armed observers with a knowledge base that enhanced the effectiveness of the clinical supervision process. Jerry Bellon quickly saw the value in this emerging field of research and began including examples of the research findings in his consulting work with districts. In fact, within a few years, Jerry coauthored one of the first books that synthesized many of the research findings into a handbook for improving classroom instruction (Bellon, Bellon, & Blank, 1992).

Second, I gained confidence in working with schools and school districts and in speaking to groups about effective, research-based teaching practices. This knowledge and confidence enabled me to work with many more districts across the United States. Interestingly, this also changed my relationship with Jerry Bellon. He had viewed me, appropriately, as an associate who helped him work with districts that were interested in improving teaching through the clinical supervision process. As a result of my association with the Institute for Research on Teaching and my friendships with Judy Lanier and Larry Lezotte, as well as my individual work with districts regarding the teacher effects research, he came to view me as a person with my own area of expertise and, to some extent, a growing national reputation.

Third, my professional reputation was given a huge boost by an interview conducted by Willard Duckett, who was the assistant director of the Phi Delta Kappa Center on Evaluation, Development, and Research, that appeared in the *Phi Delta Kappan* in 1986. Duckett (1986) began the article by noting that the center and the *Kappan* were undertaking an initiative to introduce readers to individuals "who make exemplary contributions to research or who make effective, practical applications of research in the administration of public schools" (p. 16). Although I never asked, I always felt the interview was the result of some intervention by Judy Lanier. For this alone, but for much more, I have always been grateful for Judy's friendship and support during this period of my professional journey.

The article certainly enhanced my national exposure. I think the point that received the most attention was the idea of "legitimizing" research, which Jim Huffman and I had picked up from Herbert Lionberger:

> **Duckett:** By *legitimizing*, you obviously mean something more than passive acceptance.
>
> **Eaker:** Exactly, it's the process of becoming convinced, as opposed to being informed. Being informed doesn't motivate one to do much. Legitimizing an idea is a process of dispelling fears or inhibitions and coming around to a favorable disposition leading to acceptance. When an idea has been legitimized, one is willing to act on it.
>
> **Duckett:** Give me an example of how a consumer might legitimize, or go through experiential validation, with regard to research data.
>
> **Eaker:** Manufacturers often do extensive testing of their products in both the development and the production stages; it is generally to their advantage, in a competitive market, to at least advertise supporting data. General Motors, for example, will have elaborate data on the performance capabilities of Car X. Those data might reveal that Car X can be expected to get between 16 to 31 miles per gallon of fuel (quite an indeterminate range, incidentally).

Regardless of how thoroughly Car X was tested, you and I, as consumers, are probably skeptical about how closely "laboratory" conditions at GM match our own local driving conditions. Without questioning the validity of the GM tests, you and I will probably prefer to legitimize or validate such data at the experimental level. So, we ask our neighbors or co-workers about their experiences with Car X. We seek to validate the data in terms of *our* normal use of a car in everyday driving. To what extent will our driving habits approximate those of the professional drivers at the GM test ranges? How many variables in our environment approximate those at GM? In short, can we expect to average closer to 31 miles per gallon than to 16? If not, why not?

Thus, in seeking to validate the research data from a consumer's point of view, we do not repeat the manufacturer's tests, nor do we mount a formal challenge to the methodology. We simply set out to validate by determining the appropriateness of the data for use in our own specific situations.

Duckett: Does the analogy hold for teachers?

Eaker: Yes, we [Jim Huffman and I] think that teachers react to educational research reports in much the same way. Teachers can easily be informed about the research coming from Stanford, the University of Texas, or Michigan State University. But they want to know whether their own classrooms are similar enough to those of the experimental groups to lead them to expect similar results. Their questions go something like this: "Okay, these classroom variables worked well for the research group, but will they work in *my* classroom?" Our answer is simply, "Let's check them out. Let's check the applicability of that research for your situation, your instructional context." That is what I mean by experiential validation of research. (Duckett, 1986, p. 14)

In addition to the publication of the *Kappan* interview, in 1986, I accepted the position of dean of the College of Education at Middle Tennessee State University. The university had a large teacher education program (the largest in Tennessee) that educated approximately one-fourth of all the new teachers in the state. My interactions with the people at Michigan State, and especially my observations of Judy Lanier in her role as dean, helped me think of ways the College of Education at Middle Tennessee State could partner with school districts to not only prepare more effective teachers but to also use research findings to improve the instructional effectiveness of classroom teachers.

Last, these experiences enabled me to meet and become friends with people who had a huge impact on me professionally and personally. I developed a close professional relationship and a personal friendship with Lynn Canady at the University of Virginia during this time. I knew of Lynn from my teaching days in Chattanooga. While I was at Brainerd High School, Lynn was the principal at Dalewood Jr. High School in the same suburban area. Under his leadership, Dalewood developed a growing reputation for innovation, particularly in the area of flexible scheduling. Lynn became a faculty member at the University of Virginia and was widely regarded for his work in developing block scheduling, grading, and assisting school districts in school improvement initiatives.

I don't recall exactly when Lynn contacted me—perhaps it was a result of the *Kappan* interview—but regardless, he invited me to present to a group of public school administrators and teachers at the University of Virginia. Lynn had created a consortium between Virginia school districts and the university through which the university would assist districts in school improvement efforts, especially by arranging for a variety of presenters on school and instructional improvement topics.

Called the School Improvement Program (or SIP), the basic idea was that it would be more cost effective for each participating district to pay a rather small membership fee and have access to a number of presenters throughout the year than each district bearing the costs of bringing speakers to their individual districts. It was through his efforts, such as the SIP initiative, as well as his willingness to assist districts himself, that Lynn became highly respected in Virginia. And, through this work—and his writing—Lynn developed a highly regarded national reputation.

After my first visit to the University of Virginia, Lynn invited me to work with him and numerous districts in Virginia, particularly in the valley that ran from Bristol, Tennessee, to Roanoke, Virginia. Through my work with Lynn, I consulted in Winchester, Virginia, on occasion. Interestingly, my work in Winchester led me to become acquainted with a former superintendent of the district who had retired and become an executive with one of the largest concrete manufacturing companies in Virginia, the Shockey Precast Group.

We enjoyed each other's company very much, and he decided the Shockey Precast Group could benefit from the concepts that were the focus of my work in Winchester—building an organizational culture through focused, collaboratively developed mission, vision, values, and goals. I had dinner with the owner of the company and the top executives, which led to my consulting with the company on a number of occasions and eventually being asked to present at the annual meeting of the Virginia Concrete Association.

I mention this not only because it was a great experience and I met some wonderful people but also because it was the first time I realized that the work Rick and I were doing, and the ideas we were talking and writing about, were applicable to organizations in general. Through the years, Rick and I were asked to speak to quite a few corporate executives and business groups.

The larger point is this: these experiences, which broadened my thinking and enhanced my confidence, would not have happened if Lynn Canady had not invited me to work with him at the University of Virginia. More important, Lynn and I would not have met, become friends, and remained so for the next forty years or so. I am much indebted to and thankful for Lynn Canady.

As I've noted, through my association with the Institute for Research on Teaching, I became friends with Larry Lezotte. While most of the time I spent at the institute was with Judy Lanier or researchers such as Jere Brophy, Larry usually sat in on meetings, and he was also nice enough to drive Jim Huffman and me to and from the airport. Little did I know that Larry and I would become friends and spend considerable time together in the next phase of my professional journey—more about that in the next chapter.

It's interesting to think that as a result of Judy Lanier writing a column in the institute's newsletter, which I accidentally read and then responded to with a short note, Larry Lezotte and I would eventually work together in the area of effective schools research. I would not have met Larry if Judy Lanier had not reached out to me and included me in her circle of friends who were heavily engaged in the research on effective teaching and in her work as a national leader in higher education. Again, accidental friendships!

CHAPTER 3

The Teacher Effects Research

Practices for Improving Instruction and Student Learning

The more interested I became in helping teachers use research findings to improve their classroom effectiveness, the more interested I became in the research on effective teaching (the so-called *teacher effects research*) and how specific teacher behaviors affected student learning. In retrospect, I suppose this interest was a natural progression of my career and my learning. I had moved from a deep interest in clinical supervision and classroom observation as a way to improve teacher effectiveness to helping teachers improve their effectiveness through the use of research findings to sharpening my focus on the actual research on the effect teacher behavior can have on student success.

Although the most fundamental shift that occurs when a traditional school transitions into a PLC is a shift from a focus on *teaching* to a focus on *learning*, this shift does not diminish the importance of teaching. The difference is one of purpose. In more traditional schools, when we ask, "What is the primary purpose of schools?" it's not unusual to hear, "Schools are a place where kids go to be taught." In a PLC, teaching is viewed as a means to an end: "Schools are a place where kids go to learn." The goal is to ensure that students are learning, and the most critical *in-school* tools available to educators are effective teaching practices (Eaker & Keating, 2015).

This traditional misplaced focus on teaching has unfortunately led to misuse of the findings from the effective teaching research. Increasingly, teachers are being subjected to classroom observations and teacher evaluation schemes based on the false assumption that the research demonstrates there is one set of effective teaching behaviors that virtually all teachers should include in their lessons. Time and again, researchers have warned against their findings being used as *effective teaching checklists*, yet the use of such observational checklists continues to expand.

Leaders of PLCs understand that successful teaching—that is, teaching that results in students learning—is highly contextual, affected by the subject and topic being taught, student characteristics, the relationship of a specific lesson to previous and future lessons, and so on. There is simply no one-size-fits-all method of effective teaching. Robert Marzano (2007) succinctly writes, "It is certainly true that research provides us with guidance as to the nature of effective teaching, and yet I strongly believe there is not (nor will there ever be) a formula for effective teaching" (p. 4). He also points out that we have known this for decades, as researchers have long characterized effective teaching as part art and part science (Eaker & Keating, 2015; Marzano, 2007).

Of course, effective teaching is also dependent on a teacher's knowledge of and enthusiasm for the subject and content. Methodology will take a teacher only so far; content knowledge is such an obvious prerequisite for teaching success it often goes overlooked. It is entirely possible for a teacher to receive a very high rating on an observation checklist of teaching methodology and at the same time teach content that is inappropriate or simply incorrect.

Thus, effective teaching is not only contextual but also an interplay among three elements: (1) the science of teaching (instructional skills), (2) artfulness in delivery, and (3) content knowledge (figure 3.1). Effective teachers are competent in all three areas.

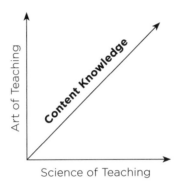

Source: Eaker & Keating, 2015.

FIGURE 3.1: *A three-dimensional model of effective teaching.*

The Power of High-Performing Teams

The importance of collaborative teams is well documented. An individual teacher's instructional effectiveness is enhanced by being a member of a high-performing team that focuses on the right issues—that is, the personal learning of each student, skill by skill, name by name.

Few issues related to student learning are as misunderstood and misinterpreted as collaboration. Most people consider collaboration a good thing, and many studies, particularly studies on effective schooling practices, point to the desirability of a collaborative culture. But what is collaboration, and what does effective collaboration look like in schools? Equally important, what does *not* qualify as collaboration?

We (DuFour, DuFour, & Eaker, 2008) define a *teacher team* as a group of teachers who teach roughly the same content and who work interdependently to achieve common goals, for which they hold each other mutually accountable. This interdependency is grounded in members of the team sharing with each other and learning together—all for the common goal of improving the learning levels of every student.

In many ways, the culture (and structure) of most traditional schools is a recipe for failure. Teachers are expected to successfully teach all students *more standards* at a *higher level* than ever before, within a *reduced time frame* (due to statewide testing in April in most states) and with *less (and declining) support* than ever before. Simply put, it is impossible for most teachers to feel—or be—successful in such an environment.

In the White River School District in Buckley, Washington, superintendent Janel Keating and the board hold two meetings per month. One is devoted to the more traditional (and formal) business meeting, and the other is referred to as a learning meeting. The learning board meeting is an informal session in which the board learns about a particular aspect of the district's efforts to improve student learning. For example, the session might be devoted to principals showing how they are leading the efforts in their schools to improve student writing or to students explaining how they use learning targets to guide their learning. These meetings are highly interactive. Board members genuinely seek to gain a greater insight and understanding about the district's touted focus on learning.

One meeting I attended focused on how teacher teams are organized in each school, their purpose, how they work, and why they are important. Significantly, the people interacting with board members were teachers, not administrators. The teachers gave us their firsthand accounts of the important role teacher teams played in instructional effectiveness. One teacher near retirement said that in thinking back on her career in White River, she thought of most of that time as "the wonder years." I thought she was referring to the television show of the same name, but that wasn't it. She explained that until the school organized into meaningful collaborative teams, she didn't have any idea what her fellow teachers were doing. She'd be walking down the hall and hear highly engaged activity occurring in a classroom, and she would wonder, "What are they doing?" If another teacher got great results, she would wonder how he or she did that. If she heard of an activity or piece of material that a teacher found effective, she would wonder how he or she used it. In essence, until she worked as a contributing member of a high-performing team, she had no opportunities to interact professionally with her peers and was left to wonder how they taught and what worked for them.

I've come to believe that the impact of virtually every research finding related to effective instructional practices can be enhanced when teachers are organized and collaboratively engaged in planning, sharing, learning, analyzing the impact of their instructional efforts, monitoring the learning of each student, and setting meaningful improvement goals.

Many of the findings concerning effective teaching practices are very specific. On the other hand, some are broader. For example, effective teachers organize their classrooms and lessons in such a way that instructional effectiveness is enhanced. Classroom organization skills play an important role in classroom management, and student learning is affected by the degree to which the overall classroom environment is organized and focused for the task at hand—student learning. And again, the effectiveness of a teacher's organizational skills is enhanced by being a member of a high-performing team.

Organizing classrooms and lessons for learning can best be accomplished through *collaborative* unit planning. Effective unit planning begins with teams developing a deep, rich understanding of what the standard means, along with a clear understanding of what the standard, if met, would look like in student work. Additionally, teams discuss each standard's relative importance to and relationship with other standards. This leads to the obvious question of how much time, roughly, should be devoted to the teaching of each standard. In other words, teams develop a flexible pacing guide for the entire academic year.

The final format of the team's unit plans is not nearly as important as the process to get there: the *quality* of the collaboration, inquiry, and sharing and the *focus* on the right issues. Team discussions should center on four critical questions associated with student learning: (1) What is essential that every student learn in this unit? (2) How will we know if they have learned it? (3) How will we respond to students who struggle with particular skills or concepts? and (4) How will we respond to students who exhibit proficiency? (DuFour et al., 2008).

It's through this process of collaboratively planning units of learning that teachers share instructional strategies, materials, and experiences. In short, by planning together, teachers learn together, and as a result, their teaching practices are more deliberate and instructional effectiveness is enhanced.

One particular aspect of collaborative unit planning that is often overlooked has to do with collaborative reflection and record keeping. After a unit has been taught and teachers have collaboratively reviewed the results of their collaborative formative assessments, they should collaboratively reflect on the effectiveness of their instructional practices: what seemed to work well, what could have gone better, whether enough time was allotted to specific activities, and so forth. The essential question is this: when we teach this unit in the future, how could it be improved? By recording team decisions, a list of suggested improvements will be readily available when it comes time to teach the unit again.

A Teacher's Toolbox of Instructional Techniques

As in all professions, in education, our understanding of best practices is constantly changing in response to new information. As professionals, teachers should continually hone their skills. Like skilled woodworkers, teachers should not only increase the number of tools in their repertoire, they should also improve the skill with which they use their tools. The word *professional* also implies the ability to exercise judgment, and indeed, teachers must learn which tools to use in a wide-ranging set of circumstances they are likely to encounter (Eaker & Keating, 2015).

There is no definitive number of effective instructional tools a teacher should have in the toolbox. Since the late 1970s, researchers have gained considerable insight into instructional practices that are likely to have a positive effect on student learning—again, depending on certain variables, many of which are beyond a teacher's control. Findings from the major research studies on effective teaching practices have been synthesized through meta-analysis into a few excellent resources. Two of the more prominent are Robert Marzano's (2017) *The New Art and Science of Teaching* and *Visible Learning* by John Hattie (2009). And although it is somewhat dated, I still find Jerry Bellon, Elner Bellon, and Mary Ann Blank's (1992) *Teaching From a Research Knowledge Base* to be helpful.

There is no one list of teacher behaviors that all teachers should employ. That's not to say the research findings on effective teaching practices are not important. What follows is a *sampling* of what I've come to believe are findings from the teacher effects research that are the most significant.

Two important points should be made about the following research findings. One, simply *knowing* that an instructional practice can be effective isn't enough. Teachers must develop the skill for *employing* research findings in their lessons. This leads to the second point: developing skills for effectively implementing multiple new research-based practices in classrooms is best accomplished in teacher teams composed of teachers who teach the same or similar content. The positive impact of new practices is enhanced by teacher teams sharing, planning, analyzing student learning data, and reflecting on the effectiveness of their instructional practices.

Differentiating Instruction

Most everyone agrees that students (and adults) learn at different rates and in different ways. This fact has huge implications for instructional effectiveness and for how teacher teams plan units of learning. Differentiating instruction must be a topic of team discussion, with the goal of expanding each teacher's instructional toolbox—not with a checklist of strategies that must be included in each unit, but with knowledge and skills each teacher can draw on as needed in his or her classroom.

At the most basic level, planning for differentiated instruction involves recognizing and understanding variances in student learning profiles and, based on these profiles, planning to monitor learning and adjust instructional strategies accordingly. Carol Ann Tomlinson and Susan Demirsky Allan (2000) define differentiated instruction as:

> A teacher's reacting responsively to a learner's needs. A teacher who is differentiating understands a student's needs to express humor, or work with a group, or have additional teaching on a particular skill, or delve more deeply into a particular topic, or have guided help with a reading passage—and the teacher responds actively and positively to that need. Differentiation is simply attending to the learning needs of a particular student or small group of students rather than the more typical pattern of teaching the class as though all individuals were basically alike. (p. 4)

Teachers can gain shared knowledge on differentiation of instruction through book studies, workshops, and so on. However, perhaps the best approach is to be a member of a high-performing team in which teachers share effective instructional practices and materials— and, of course, to improve instructional practice through feedback, analysis, and reflection.

Ensuring Clarity of Instruction

Evidence shows that student learning is positively affected when lessons are taught in a clear and cogent manner. This clarity is, of course, enhanced when teachers' lessons are also well planned and organized.

Researchers have used various terminology when discussing the issue of clarity. For example, Bellon et al. (1992) group teacher behaviors that impact clarity into three categories.

1. **Substantive:** Factors related to content to be learned
2. **Semantic:** Factors related to the way teachers use language
3. **Strategic:** Deliberate use of strategies to improve learning

Educators and researchers Jon Saphier, Mary Ann Haley-Speca, and Robert Gower (2008) organize teacher behaviors affecting clarity into five categories.

1. Framing the learning
2. Presenting information
3. Creating mental engagements
4. Getting inside students' heads (cognitive empathy)
5. Consolidating and anchoring the learning

Regardless of the terms used, the findings are clear; effective teaching is impacted to the degree that teachers employ instructional techniques designed to clearly communicate both process and content information to students (Eaker & Keating, 2015).

Communicating Specific Learning Objectives in a Task-Oriented Culture

Clarity of instruction is affected to the degree that teachers plan and teach to specific, clearly communicated learning objectives. Whether they are referred to as *objectives, learning targets,* or specific *learning outcomes,* the point is this: effective teachers are experts at aligning their classroom instruction to specific learning objectives. Not only do effective teachers teach to specific learning objectives, they also communicate those objectives to the students in multiple ways and encourage questions to ensure students understand exactly what they're going to learn.

The degree to which teachers are able to clearly communicate specific learning objectives goes a long way in developing a task-oriented classroom culture. A task-oriented culture—one in which students learn quickly that doing their work, behaving appropriately, and learning are important—is the result of any number of small teacher behaviors. It is difficult to expect students to be organized and do their work correctly and on time if the teacher is not organized, task oriented, and teaching to specific learning outcomes.

Developing lessons around specific learning outcomes allows teachers to better communicate the essential points of those lessons and better enables teachers to focus student attention on the essential aspects of the lesson, thus increasing time on task. Effective teachers employ a variety of techniques to make essential points stand out. They do this before the lesson, during the lesson, and in summarizing and revisiting the lesson. Some of the most frequently used techniques are (Eaker & Keating, 2015):

> › Clear communication of learning targets that are emphasized throughout the instructional process

> › Student self-assessment of progress (Students learn to self-assess their progress toward specific learning targets by

frequently assessing their own work on a continuum in relation to the target.)

> Peer check-in (Students engage in student talk to provide feedback to each other regarding how they are progressing toward the learning target.)

> High-quality exemplars of student work that reflect the targets

A quick reminder is in order. There is no one place for teachers to go to learn all the effective ways to make essential points stand out and to improve time on task. Again, the best way to improve one's skill set is to be engaged with a teacher team in gaining and sharing knowledge.

Planning for Student Products and Performances

I've found that one of the most frequently overlooked aspects of collaborative unit planning is planning for student products and performances. Ultimately, students must *do* something to demonstrate their learning. What will learning look like in terms of student work if the standard or target is met? Collaboratively answering this question is one way to clarify the essential things students must learn and make essential points stand out. Additionally, if teachers can clearly articulate and communicate the expectations for student products and performances, they can accurately align student exemplars of high-quality work with the standard. Plus, there is the important benefit of student motivation. When students are engaged in meaningful activities that result in specific products or performances, they become more involved and interested in what they are doing and the quality of their work is enhanced.

Another aspect of collaboratively planning for student products and performances is planning against a set of predetermined standards—rubrics that reflect various levels of quality. Importantly, these rubrics should be clearly articulated to, and discussed with, students—and at the elementary level, with parents, too. Judging the quality of student work should involve both *internal* and *external* reviews. Internal review includes both teachers and students, while external review involves an external audience in front of which student work is exhibited or students perform. Again, student engagement and motivation are enhanced when students know their work will become public. (Think of school plays, music or dance performances, mathematics competitions, and invention conventions. Public performance is one reason athletics are so motivating for some students.)

Planning for Variability of Instruction

As teachers plan units of instruction—hopefully with their collaborative team—they should pay attention to planning for variability of their instructional methodology. In many ways, the research on variability of instruction was the foundational research on differentiation; differentiation of instruction is simply more specific and based on knowledge of individual student needs and characteristics. If we know students learn in different ways and at different rates, making differentiation a necessity, then planning for a variety of instructional approaches within units simply make sense. The quality of the variation that is included in teacher plans, coupled with ensuring smooth transitions between activities, can have a positive effect on student learning.

How much variety is appropriate? There is no right answer. Teachers can have too many activities or too few. Simply put, the answer is a judgment call. This is but one reason that collaborative teams discuss the effectiveness of their instructional practices after analyzing the results of their formative assessment data and as they plan for future instruction.

Relating to the Students' Frame of Reference

As teachers plan units of instruction and organize their lessons around student learning, it is helpful to consider the students' frame of reference. In other words, ask, "If I was a student in this class during this lesson, how could I best learn this material?" Many teachers consistently use adult examples to frame a concept when student examples would be much more effective. When I was a high school teacher in Chattanooga, I taught economics. When I taught the unit on inflation, I described the concept of a general rise in prices by giving examples of buying and selling a home. In retrospect, I could have been more effective by using examples of products that students routinely purchase. (Students think they will buy a home when they are really old—like thirty!)

While teachers should reflect on the examples they use in their instructional framework, they should also think of analogies and other aspects of students' lives that are important to them. Much of the improvement in instructional effectiveness that comes from relating to students' frame of reference can be gained by simply becoming aware of one's instructional practices and becoming more deliberate when planning for instruction.

Planning for Purposeful Student Practice

Student practice is such an obvious instructional strategy that it is often overlooked. Most everyone agrees that through practice we get better at most everything we undertake. But because the very idea of practice is so obvious, it is often not part of the collaborative unit-planning process. As I pointed out previously, research findings on effective teaching are interrelated and interdependent. Nowhere is this fact more apparent than in planning for *appropriate practice*.

For practice to be effective, it must be appropriate. This raises the obvious question, How can a team determine just what practice is appropriate in each unit or lesson? This is where research findings become interrelated. When a team engages in collaboratively planning a unit of learning, they must clarify what is essential that every student learn from the unit. But to harness the full power of that process of clarifying essential standards, they must also answer, What would these learning outcomes look like *in student work* if they were met? Addressing this question with specificity and fidelity allows teachers to follow through more effectively throughout the unit. Knowing what an essential outcome looks like in student work informs the design of formative assessments, which, in turn, helps teachers determine the most appropriate practice leading up to those assessments.

Of course, effective teams deal with a number of additional issues regarding student practice, such as how much practice is appropriate, what materials can assist students in their practice (for example, excellent examples of previous work by other students), and where students can receive immediate assistance if they hit a snag in their practice efforts. The bottom line is this: student learning can be significantly enhanced when teacher teams collaboratively address the issue of student practice as an integral piece of their unit-planning process. Student practice that is aligned and purposeful is a powerful tool to help students not just improve but improve on the right things by reinforcing the most essential learning within each standard.

Providing Detailed and Descriptive Feedback to Students

Importantly, to be effective, student practice must be coupled with meaningful feedback. Unfortunately, many teachers give students feedback without much thought. Researchers have described several different kinds of feedback, such as *product feedback* (informing students whether their work is correct or incorrect) and *process feedback* (informing students where they have made mistakes and how to correct them). It is generally more effective for teachers to utilize both product and process feedback, rather than only product feedback.

In other words, feedback should be purposeful and support further learning, not merely indicate whether learning has occurred. To this end, feedback also needs to be timely (to enable students to incorporate it into further efforts), and it should be specific.

After I graduated from high school, I attended Mississippi State University on a band scholarship. As I reflect on my experience playing in a large university band, I can see analogies to the feedback process that I did not fully appreciate at the time. For example, when we would rehearse a piece of music, it was not uncommon for Dr. West, the conductor, to stop the playing and say something to the effect of, "Bob, that should be a B flat in bar nineteen." Or he might give feedback to the group, such as, "Hold it just a second; we seem to be rushing through this section. Pay closer attention to me." The point is, Dr. West didn't wait until after the performance (the summative assessment) to provide feedback. Feedback was simply a normal part of the learning process, and it was specific, focused, and timely. There are countless examples of coaches, drama teachers, music teachers, career and technical education teachers, and many others who do not wait until after the season, or the summative assessment, to provide students with feedback.

Additionally, feedback should encourage learning. There is a tendency, I think, to assume that all feedback is good, at least to the extent that it's giving students information about their work. Yet, feedback that is inappropriate, or given in a way that is inappropriate, can be hurtful—not just to the learning process, but also to a student's sense of self and attitude. A sarcastic comment from a teacher can be very hurtful, as can making fun of a student in front of the class. Feedback should be positive and geared toward improvement: "Stick with it." "You can do this." "You're getting better." "Try this next time."

Hattie (2009) writes that the key takeaway regarding feedback is the feedback teachers receive from their students.

> When teachers seek, or at least are open to, feedback from students as to what students know, what they understand, where they make errors, when they have misconceptions, when they are engaged—then teaching and learning can be synchronized and powerful. (p. 173)

In keeping with the theme of summing up, I've found that effective teams (those that make a significant positive impact on student learning) engage in deep, rich collaborative discussions about connecting learning targets to student practice, feedback, and encouragement in thoughtful, purposeful ways.

Using Formative Assessments

Since roughly the mid-1990s, the use of formative assessments to improve student learning has become increasingly popular. There was limited research regarding the impact of various types of assessment (product versus process assessments, for example) during the early days of the teacher effects research. It has been only fairly recently that educators have begun to use formative assessments on any widespread and consistent basis, despite the powerful impact formative assessment can have on student learning—and yet I suspect they are still not used nearly to the extent we might think.

It's surprising that it took so long to understand the power of formative assessments. Think about it: in our daily lives, we know the importance of assessing how we're doing along the way (either through self-assessment or assessment by someone else) rather than waiting until we are finished, in virtually every task we undertake. For example, when we engage in a task as simple as hanging a picture, we almost always ask someone else to tell us whether it's level, high enough, and so forth before nailing the hanger into the wall.

Ironically, now that we've come to understand the power of assessing *for* learning during the teaching-learning process, the federal government, state legislatures, and state departments of education have dramatically increased the emphasis on summative assessments—assessment *of* learning. (I generally turn to the work of Rick Stiggins [2005] to differentiate between assessment *of* learning and assessment *for* learning and to Dylan Wiliam [2011, 2018] regarding the power of formative assessments to impact student achievement.)

I think of formative assessment as actions that are taken *during* the teaching and learning process to move the learner toward success. Summative assessments, on the other hand, are actions taken after instruction has occurred to determine if the learner was successful. Formative assessments can, and should, be used in multiple ways and in a wide variety of circumstances.

Obviously, teachers, and teams of teachers, should plan for formative assessments that will occur during their instructional processes. Importantly, unit plans should be developed that include students, both individually and in groups, assessing their own learning progress and setting improvement goals. At the district level, formative assessment strategies should be created to assist staff who are pursuing professional development and personal learning goals. In short, the power of formative assessments should not be limited to teachers monitoring the progress of their students.

Further, when it comes to improving student learning, districts should work to develop a culture of formative assessment that extends beyond the classroom. For example, there are many ways that district leaders can check on the learning progress of students during the year rather than waiting until the results of summative assessments are available. The same is true of individual schools. Teacher teams, along with a schoolwide leadership team, should use formative assessment results throughout the year to improve student learning.

Individual teachers should use a variety of classroom formative assessment strategies, from quick checks for understanding to exit passes to various methods of questioning to students evaluating their own learning progress during the learning unit. The point is, formative assessments take many forms, and it is the collective power of a formative assessment culture that can drive goal attainment and continuous improvement—of both students and adults.

The power of formative assessments to improve student learning can best be achieved when teacher teams collaboratively develop *common* formative assessments as the cornerstone to their efforts to improve student learning. In our earlier work, Rick and I did not fully grasp just how the power of formative assessments could be enhanced by having teams of teachers collaboratively develop common assessments. It was only when we began working with schools to clarify the work of teacher teams and when we began to summarize our thinking about what collaborative teams should do in *Professional Learning Communities at Work* (DuFour & Eaker, 1998) that we truly began to understand and clarify the importance of teams developing—and more importantly, using—common formative assessments.

Why should teams develop common formative assessments? In *Revisiting Professional Learning Communities at Work* (DuFour et al., 2008), Rick, Becky, and I elaborated on our rationale as to why teams should use *commonly developed* formative assessments.

› **Team-developed common formative assessments are effective tools for monitoring and improving student learning:** Research has shown that team-developed common formative assessments are one of the most powerful strategies available to educators for improving student achievement.

> **Team-developed common formative assessments are essential to systematic interventions when students experience difficulty in their learning:** When teams collaboratively analyze the results of their common formative assessments, they are able to monitor the learning of each student—skill by skill. This enables teams and individual teachers to more effectively focus extra time and support strategies.

> **Team-developed common assessments are more efficient:** Rather than each teacher developing his or her own individual formative assessments, it is simply more efficient for the team to develop *one* set of assessments.

> **Team-developed common assessments promote equity:** Common assessments enhance the likelihood that students will experience the same curriculum, learn the same essential knowledge and skills, take assessments of the same rigor, and have their work judged according to the same criteria.

> **Team-developed common formative assessments can inform and improve the practice of both individual teachers and teams of teachers:** When teams of teachers who teach the same content create and use common formative assessments, they receive ongoing feedback regarding the progress their students are making toward a standard that the team has previously agreed on. (And importantly, the teams have agreed on what the standard, if met, would look like in student work.) Since the team developed the common formative assessment, they have agreed that the assessment represents a valid way to assess what students should learn, *in comparison to other students attempting to achieve the same standard.* This process transforms student learning data into useful information.

The process of teacher teams collaboratively analyzing student learning data also enables teachers to reflect on and improve their own teaching, as well as the instructional effectiveness of the team as a whole. Because of the commonality of the formative assessments, the results become one of the most powerful motivators for teachers to reflect on their own instructional practices.

> When teachers are presented with clear evidence their students are not becoming proficient in skills they agreed were essential, as measured on an assessment they helped create, and that similar students taught by their colleagues have demonstrated proficiency on the same assessment, they are open to exploring new practices. (DuFour et al., 2008, p. 214)

› **Team-developed common formative assessments can build the capacity of the team to achieve at higher levels:** The very process of collaboratively developing, using, and analyzing the results from common formative assessments enhances team effectiveness. The interaction and the deep, rich dialogue involved in collaboratively developing common formative assessments not only elevate the assessment skills of the team, they also sharpen and clarify the questions of what is essential for all students to learn and what that learning should look like in student work.

Making Questioning More Purposeful

When it comes to actual instructional behaviors, it would be difficult to overestimate the important role questioning plays in the teaching process. Think about these findings: Kathleen Cotton (1988) reports that teacher questioning is only surpassed by teacher talk when it comes to frequency of specific instructional strategies. Michael Long and Charlene Sato (1983) report that teachers spend between 35 and 50 percent of their classroom time asking questions. Kathleen Mohr (1998) reports that teachers ask as many as one hundred questions per hour, and Amy C. Brualdi (1998) reports that teachers ask between three hundred and four hundred questions per day. Simply because questioning is such an inevitable part of teaching, it can become rote or unexamined. The key to capturing the effectiveness of questioning as an instructional tool is making questioning more purposeful (Eaker & Keating, 2015).

Purposeful questioning involves, in part, thinking about the types of questions to ask and knowing how each type affects student responses. The most common question types are often categorized as (1) *convergent*, which demand one specific correct answer (thus tending to limit classroom interaction); (2) *divergent*, which are open-ended and enhance classroom discussion; and (3) *choral*, which require the entire class to respond and thus help the teacher refocus students' attention.

Purposeful questioning also addresses the level of the questions being asked. While a number of classifications exist, I've found the most frequently utilized is based on the *Taxonomy of Educational Objectives* (Bloom, 1956). Regardless of which taxonomy is used, the important action takeaway for teachers is to tie the level of their questions to the lesson's learning objectives. In this way, questions become purposeful by eliciting specific responses from the students.

Teachers should also be deliberate in how they respond to students' answers to questions, using wait time, hints, clues, or restatement as needed to enhance learning. Teacher response behaviors vary among teachers and even in how individual teachers respond to different students. In retrospect, I think questioning is so pervasive that many, if not most, teachers simply ask questions and respond to student answers automatically, without much thought. What the research findings tell us is that questioning is such a huge aspect of teaching, it must be a thoughtful and purposeful aspect of teaching.

Increasing Time on Task

There is a difference between the amount of time that is *allocated* for teaching and learning and the amount of time students are actually *engaged* in the learning process. For example, David C. Berliner (1986) reports that students are engaged only about 40 percent of the time. In addition, the amount of high-quality, academic engaged time often varies significantly from teacher to teacher, even within the same school, grade level, and course.

Equally important, there is a huge difference between students simply being engaged in learning something and being engaged in learning high-quality content that links directly to the essential learning outcomes of the unit. Enhancing the amount of high-quality academic time on task begins with teacher teams collaboratively planning lessons that are meaningful, engaging, and tied directly to the standards, using fully the amount of time that is allotted to teaching and learning each day (Eaker & Keating, 2015).

I've found, however, that much that is related to academic engaged time is also beyond teachers' control. For example, academic engaged time is impacted if the school schedule requires students to move from class to class or from one activity to another too frequently, or if instruction is frequently interrupted by intrusions, such as announcements. In short, academic engaged time can be enhanced when the principal works directly with teacher teams to ensure that the overall school operation reflects a task-oriented culture that keeps a sharp focus on teaching and learning. *I am not saying that schools should never do anything but purely academic work.* What I am saying is that administrators and teachers must work collaboratively to ensure that the allocated time for teaching and learning is used thoughtfully, purposefully, and wisely.

As I mentioned earlier, these examples of the teacher effects research are just that—examples. There are many more areas of research to explore, and while teachers shouldn't be expected to master all

With Rick DuFour, Bob Eaker's best friend and professional colleague for almost four decades (2013)

Rick DuFour, Bob Eaker, and Jeff Jones, our dear friend and an indispensable advocate and promoter of Professional Learning Communities at Work (2008)

research, they can become passionate *students of teaching*. Schools, teams, and individual teachers should work to create a culture in which research is valued. There are any number of ways teachers can learn best practices, but research findings on effective teaching behaviors are invaluable.

Teacher Behaviors That Communicate High Expectations for Student Learning

Pioneering mathematician and cryptanalyst Alan Turing, who led the effort in World War II to break the German Enigma code, developed what is viewed by many as the forerunner of the modern computer. In the movie *The Imitation Game* (Grossman, Ostrowsky, Schwarzman, & Tyldum, 2014), based on his life, Turing is credited with saying, "Sometimes it is the people no one imagines anything of who do the things no one can imagine."

History may show this to be true. But what would it mean, for most of us, to be a person of whom no one imagines anything? And what would be the impact of becoming a person someone believes in? As I learned more about the research on teacher behaviors and student achievement, I became particularly interested in how teachers' expectations affect student learning and behavior.

Since the publication of Robert Rosenthal and Lenore Jacobson's (1968) *Pygmalion in the Classroom*, few aspects of teaching have been as widely researched—and as widely misunderstood. One key finding is that teachers' behavior is driven by their beliefs, values, attitudes, and assumptions. For example, some teachers believe that student achievement is basically a result of students' innate *ability* and that ability is *unequally distributed* among the student population, and most importantly, because ability is innate, it is *unalterable*. Simply put, for some teachers, this explains why some students learn and some don't.

During the time when I was focusing on the role teacher expectations play on student learning and behavior, much attention was being paid nationally to the issue of racial equity—or lack thereof—in schools. The insights I gained into the expectations research and how different students are treated differently *during* instruction—in literally dozens of small ways—contributed to my realization that while equity is a huge issue at the district and school levels, *instructional equity in classrooms* is often overlooked.

In *Kid by Kid, Skill by Skill* (Eaker & Keating, 2015), Janel Keating and I include one of my favorite examples of how expectations can affect behavior and attitudes. In act 5 of George Bernard Shaw's *Pygmalion* (1916/2003), Eliza Doolittle explains to Colonel Pickering how he differed from Professor Henry Higgins. While Rosenthal and Jacobson's (1968) *Pygmalion in the Classroom* is often cited as a classic example of the role expectations can play as a self-fulfilling prophecy, my favorite example remains Shaw's (1916/2003) *Pygmalion*, partly because of how much I enjoyed the subsequent movie production, *My Fair Lady* (Warner & Cukor, 1964). This particular piece of dialogue from *Pygmalion* captures the power of expectations:

> **Liza:** But do you know what began my real education?
>
> **Pickering:** What?
>
> **Liza:** Your calling me Miss Doolittle that day when I first came to Winpole Street. That was the beginning of self-respect for me. And there were a hundred little things you never noticed, because they came naturally to you. Things about standing up and taking off your hat and opening doors—
>
> **Pickering:** Oh, that was nothing.
>
> **Liza:** Yes. Things that showed you thought and felt about me as if I were something better than a scullery-maid; though of course I know you would have been the same to a scullery-maid if she had been let into the drawing room. You never took off your boots in the dining room when I was there.

Pickering: You mustn't mind that. Higgins takes off his boots all over the place.

Liza: I know. I am not blaming him. It is his way, isn't it? But it made such a difference to me that you didn't do it. You see, really and truly, apart from the things anyone can pick up (the dressing and the proper way of speaking, and so on), the difference between a lady and a flower girl is not how she behaves, but how she is treated. I shall always be a flower girl to Professor Higgins, because he always treats me as a flower girl, and always will; but I know I can be a lady to you, because you always treat me as a lady, and always will. (Shaw, 1916/2003, pp. 94–95)

This piece of dialogue has much to teach us. Many of my graduate students missed the point when we discussed the passage. It wasn't simply that Colonel Pickering had different expectations for Liza than did Henry Higgins. What affected Liza was Colonel Pickering's *behavior*. Similarly, findings from the research on teaching are clear on this point: teachers behave differently toward different students, hence communicating differing expectations.

Thomas L. Good and Jere E. Brophy (1980) define *teacher expectations* as inferences teachers make about the future academic performance of students—the assumptions teachers hold about whether certain students are capable of learning or doing specific things. Harris M. Cooper and Thomas L. Good (1983) differentiate between two types of expectations: the sustaining expectation effect and the self-fulfilling prophecy.

The *sustaining expectation effect* reinforces and maintains existing behaviors and thus plays an important role in preventing change. On the other hand, the *self-fulfilling prophecy* occurs when the expectations of a teacher actually cause students to behave differently. The self-fulfilling prophecy effect is dramatic and rare, while the sustaining expectation effect is subtle and pervasive.

In *Kid by Kid, Skill by Skill* (Eaker & Keating, 2015), Janel and I choose a conversation between Malcom X and his high school English teacher as recorded by Alex Haley (1965) in *The Autobiography of Malcom X* to demonstrate the sustaining expectation effect.

> He told me, "Malcom, you ought to be thinking about a career. Have you been giving it thought?"
>
> The truth is I hadn't. I never figured out why I told him, "Well, yes, sir, I've been thinking I'd like to be a lawyer." Lansing certainly had no Negro lawyers—or doctors either—in those days, to hold up an image I might have aspired to. All I really knew for certain was that a lawyer didn't wash dishes, as I was doing.
>
> Mr. Ostrowski looked surprised, I remember, and leaned back in his chair and clasped his hands behind his head. He kind of half smiled and said, "Malcom, one of life's first needs is for us to be realistic. Don't misunderstand me now. We all here like you, you know that. But you've got to be realistic about being a nigger. A lawyer—that's no realistic goal for a nigger. You need to think about something you can be. You're good with your hands—making things. Everybody admires your carpentry shop work. Why don't you plan on carpentry? People like you as a person—you'd get all kinds of work." (p. 43)

How does the expectation effect play out in the everyday world of classrooms? Good and Brophy (1980) identified twelve of the most common ways teachers treat high-expectation and low-expectation students differently. While there is no single authoritative list, I still consider this work by Good and Brophy (1980) to be the standard:

1. Seating low-expectation students far from the teacher or seating them in a group

2. Paying less attention to low-expectation students in academic situations (smiling less often or maintaining less eye contact)

3. Calling on low-expectation students less often to answer questions or make public demonstrations

4. Waiting less time for low-expectation students to answer questions

5. Not staying with low-expectation students in failure situations (for example, providing fewer clues, asking fewer follow-up questions)

6. Criticizing low-expectation students more frequently than high-expectation learners for incorrect responses

7. Praising low-expectation students less frequently than high-expectation learners after successful public responses

8. Praising low-expectation students more frequently than high-expectation learners for marginal or inadequate public responses

9. Praising low-expectation students with less accurate and less detailed feedback than high-expectation students

10. Failing to provide low-expectation students with feedback about their responses as often as high-expectation students

11. Demanding less work and effort from low-expectation students than from high-expectation students

12. Interrupting low-expectation students' performances more frequently than high-expectation students

Research like this, I've found, enables teachers to reflect deeply on their own instructional behavior, and when used in groups, it can spark important discussions related to any number of complex issues regarding teacher—and school—expectations of students.

Enhancing student success by merely expecting students to do well is far too simplistic. Many more complex factors are related to the expectations effect. For example, teachers' high expectations must be genuine to impact student learning. Perhaps unsurprisingly, teachers' expectations of students are affected, to a large degree, by their expectations of and belief in themselves—what is referred to as *self-efficacy*. The expectation effect is much more likely to impact student success if teachers truly believe not only in the students' potential but also in their own—that they have the knowledge, skills, and persistence to ensure their students learn.

For example, Henry Higgins is often offered as an example of a person who had high expectations for his student (Liza Doolittle) and, because of this, was successful. In fact, Henry Higgins's success is a result of his expectations of himself—his self-efficacy. When Colonel Pickering offers a wager as to whether Professor Higgins can teach Liza to speak well enough that she can pass as a duchess, Henry accepts the challenge, proclaiming, "In six months—in three if she has a good ear and quick tongue—I'll take her anywhere and pass her off as anything" (Shaw, 1916/2003, p. 29). In short, teachers with high (and realistic) self-efficacy believe they can *positively impact the learning level* of *all* of their students (Eaker & Keating, 2015).

Two final thoughts on self-efficacy. First, teachers' individual self-efficacy can be positively impacted by membership in a high-performing collaborative team. Teachers who work in teams not only learn from each other but can also call on the resources of their teammates for assistance. They plan ways to provide additional time and support to students who experience difficulty. So, while an individual teacher might feel a sense of hopelessness from time to time, those who are members of a collaborative team realize that while *I* alone might not be able to help every student succeed, together *we* can do it! Team efficacy builds self-efficacy.

Second, developing a sense of self-efficacy is also critical for students. Teachers *and* students must believe in students' ability to learn. This is unlikely to happen by chance; it will require proactive behaviors. There is a huge difference in *valuing* student self-efficacy and *planning specific ways to nurture* student self-efficacy. Building student self-efficacy should be a goal of every teacher and teacher team.

A Summing Up

At the heart of any profession lies a clear core purpose and a knowledge base of current best practice. For educators, our fundamental, overarching purpose is student learning. Our knowledge base is composed of subject-area content, developmental psychology (including child growth and development, and how students and adults learn), leadership and organizational development theory, and research surrounding instructional practice—the so-called teacher effects research.

Although teaching as a practice dates back to society's earliest days, the idea of teaching as a *profession* is very young, especially in comparison to other professions. The research foundation on instructional effectiveness is even more recent. Prior to the mid-1970s, most of the research on teaching focused on characteristics of excellent teachers and on child growth and development, including learning theory.

However, in the mid-1970s, researchers made a significant, focused effort to learn the effects of specific teacher behaviors on student learning and behavior. In retrospect, I realize how fortunate I was to be in the early stages of my career when these new initiatives began. I was even more fortunate to have a background in clinical supervision that extended to an interest in how teachers learned of and used research findings and to have the sheer luck of reading the Institute for Research on Teaching newsletter and becoming friends with Judy Lanier.

In summing up this period in my professional career, two words of caution are in order. First, our profession suffers from the misuse of findings from the teacher effects research. Virtually every major research from this period cautions against the one-strategy-fits-all mindset. There is no one right way to teach and no checklist of teaching behaviors that every teacher should follow; anyone who suggests otherwise is simply misusing the research. Teaching is a contextual endeavor requiring educated professional judgment in varied situations.

Second, being an effective teacher also requires touching the emotions; instructional strategies, as important as they are, will only take us so far. The teachers who made an impact on our own lives possessed affective skills beyond mastery of content knowledge or effective teaching research. They had the ability to inspire us. They were masters of motivation. As students, we believed they cared for us. They made us feel special.

Palimpsest again. As my interest in the teacher effects research grew, I never completely erased what I had learned from my experiences with the consumer-validation approach of helping teachers test research findings in the classroom or from my years of experience with the clinical supervision approach to objective, nonjudgmental classroom observations. Together, these experiences laid a solid foundation for my later focus on research findings related to specific teaching behaviors and their effect on student learning and behavior.

As with every stage of my adult life, I had no idea where the next stop on my professional journey would take me. I focused on the present without much thought to what would come next. I did not have the slightest idea that getting to know Larry Lezotte during those trips to Michigan State and my interest in teacher expectations and student achievement would prove to be the catalyst for a major new direction in my life.

CHAPTER 4

The Role of Teacher Interpersonal Behavior

Impacting Student Success

The more I delved into teacher effects research, the more I realized both from my own experiences and from my years of classroom observations that teaching strategies, as important as they are, do not paint the complete picture of a highly effective teacher. Clearly, a master teacher is much more than a competent instructional technician.

I think of a master teacher as one who has a significant impact on students beyond ensuring they learn specific learning targets—although mastering learning targets is certainly important. Master teachers, in my view, have a significant, positive impact on students' lives beyond the classroom. The issue is identifying and measuring teacher behaviors in the area of interpersonal relations, or the affective areas of teaching. I've found that researchers tend to measure things that can be measured. But the fact that some areas of teaching and learning are difficult, if not impossible, to measure does not make them any less important.

Consider this example: I think there is universal agreement that it is important for parents to love their children. If someone asked me if I love my children, I would obviously say, "Of course I do! Very much!" But if he then asked, "Well, how much do you love your children?" I would say, "Very, very much!" And if he pushed me by asking, "But how much do you love your children? Give me a number," I would respond, "That's impossible! You cannot measure how much I love my children."

The point is this: the fact that loving one's children cannot be measured does not lessen its importance. While affective aspects of relationships cannot be measured, it *is* possible to look for indicators that positive interpersonal behaviors exist. If the person grilling me on how much I love my children instead asked, "In what ways do you demonstrate your love for your children?" well, that question I could answer.

As with the teacher effects research, there is no comprehensive list of significant interpersonal skills that all teachers should possess. On the other hand, there are some examples that readily come to mind. And, of course, the positive effects of teachers' interpersonal skills can be enhanced when they become the focus of deep, rich learning and are shared within a teacher team. The following are a few affective tools that I have found to positively impact students.

The Secret: Making Students Feel Special

I've come to believe that, at the heart of it, the secret to student motivation is making students feel special—in a genuine and sincere way. One of my favorite authors through the years has been Pat Conroy. I enjoyed each of his books from the first book of his I read, *The Great Santini* (Conroy, 1987), to his last book, *A Lowcountry Heart* (Conroy, 2016). Perhaps my favorite was the autobiographical *My Reading Life* (Conroy, 2010).

There were few people in Conroy's life he respected more than his high school English teacher, Gene Norris. Through the years, as I have spoken and written about the importance of making students feel special, I have usually included a piece from *My Reading Life* in which Conroy (2010) recalls an encounter with a young lady at Gene Norris's funeral. He asks:

> "But why are you here? Did you know Mr. Norris? You're too young to have been a student of his."
>
> "My first year at Robert Smalls," she said, "I was such a mess. In trouble. Boys. Drugs. That sort of thing. They sent me to see Mr. Norris."
>
> "He was good, wasn't he?"
>
> "Mr. Norris told me to come to his office every day at lunch. We could talk and get to know each other. I went there for the next two years. Two years. Yet he didn't even know me."
>
> "You got the best of Gene," I said.
>
> "He saved my life. He literally saved my life."
>
> "Come on in," I said, putting my arm around her. "I'll introduce you to a couple of hundred people who'll tell you the same thing."
>
> "Mr. Norris acted like I was the most important girl in the world," she said.
>
> "You were. That was Gene's secret. All of us were." (pp. 70–71)

Reflect on that interaction for a moment. Think of your own life, especially when you were young. Can the importance of making a student (or an adult, for that matter) feel special be overemphasized? Pat Conroy was right. Want to motivate others? Here's "the secret": make them feel special—and mean it!

A few years ago, I attended an exhibit of Norman Rockwell's covers for the *Saturday Evening Post*. Later, as I was reading Deborah Solomon's (2013) *American Mirror: The Life and Art of Norman Rockwell*, I came across a passage that reinforced my notion that the key to impacting students' lives is to make them feel special. Norman Rockwell was a skinny kid and unathletic. Comparing himself with other boys, particularly his brother, he believed he was unappealing. It was his eighth-grade teacher, Miss Julia M. Smith, who recognized and appreciated his talent for drawing (Solomon, 2013). Solomon (2013) writes of the importance of Miss Smith making him feel special:

> Miss Smith fussed over his drawings. She made him feel that he was artistic and hence special and not required to live by the rules, that being artistic somehow made up for his failure to excel at baseball. He would keep in touch with her for the rest of her life, and she is one of the few people from his childhood for whom he admitted to feeling a special fondness. Later, he would marry three times and each time he married a schoolteacher. (p. 35)

The impact of making someone feel special is validated, for me at least, by my own experiences. Occasionally, I've tried hard to recall the very first thing I can remember as a child. Two or three recollections come to mind, and in each one of them, I am in front of my parents. My friend Janel Keating frequently tells me, "Kids don't get to pick their parents." This is certainly true, and when it came to parents, I hit the lottery. They always seemed so proud of me and encouraged me throughout my life, even into my adulthood. I cannot recall a single time in my life that I did not experience encouragement, care, and support from my parents. In short, I was blessed to have parents who made me feel special.

But the power of positive, caring relationships was not limited to interactions with my parents. I was born during World War II; my father was in Europe in the army. My mother's sisters were a close-knit group, and each seemed to view me as her own child and, together with my mother, took responsibility for raising me.

When my father returned from the war, he built a small house two houses up from his mother and father's house. Since both of my parents worked, I went to my grandparents' house each day. In addition to my grandparents, my father's brother and sisters were nearby. Not only was I blessed by having parents who made me feel special, but that feeling was multiplied by relatives on both my mother's and my father's sides of the family.

My good fortune extended to my schooling. I had wonderful teachers. I say this mostly because of *how they made me feel*. I don't know if it was due to conscious thought or was simply the kind of people they were, but I had teachers who made me feel special—not only in the elementary school years, but in my high school years as well.

A singular experience has remained with me. It occurred in my junior year of high school. I attended a relatively small high school in a small town in north Georgia, very near Chattanooga. The school was not strong academically, but what it lacked in academics, it made up for (as far as could be made up) in interpersonal relationships. Not only was I made to feel special, but so was most everyone.

My junior English class was taught by Mr. Pearson. Students respected Mr. Pearson, not only because he was nice, but also because he seemed to be more intellectual than the other teachers (to the degree we high school students understood that). One day, he told me to come up to his desk when the period was over. He said I should extend my reading interests beyond what was assigned in class and gave me a copy of Maugham's (1916) *The Moon and Sixpence*. He told me to read it and that we would talk about it later.

I did read it. I remember meeting with Mr. Pearson afterward, and I remember distinctly that he explained what Maugham (1916) meant by the title *The Moon and Sixpence*. The point is this: I don't remember what he said about the title, but I've never forgotten how special I felt because Mr. Pearson, the most respected teacher in our high school, had taken an interest in me. Reading became a major theme in my life.

While I was in high school, my aunt's husband ran the bakery at Mississippi State University. Each morning, he would have coffee and donuts with a small group of employees and faculty, one of whom was Dr. West, the director of bands. Since I played in the high school band, my uncle arranged for me to visit the university and audition for a possible scholarship, which I was fortunate enough to receive. (I've always thought the scholarship was a result more of the morning coffee breaks that included my uncle and Dr. West than my talent at playing the trumpet.) The band scholarship, coupled with a job working in the bakery each morning, made it possible for me to attend college, so in 1960, I headed off to Mississippi State University for a taste of college life.

Although I earned very good grades at college, I did not want to return when I was home for Christmas break during my sophomore year. Instead, I made a decision of major importance; I signed up for a three-year hitch in the United States Marine Corps. There again, my luck of being made to feel special held, and oddly enough, I experienced an incident eerily similar to the one with Mr. Pearson and *The Moon and Sixpence* (Maugham, 1916).

After boot camp training at Paris Island, South Carolina, and infantry training at Camp Geiger, North Carolina, I eventually was stationed in Holy Loch, Scotland, as part of a small contingent of approximately twenty marines assigned to guard the Polaris submarine missiles and the ships that were anchored in the Firth of Clyde. (Interestingly, my father had landed in the town of Greenock on the bank of the river Clyde some twenty years earlier as part of the troop buildup for the invasion of Europe.)

I had not been in Scotland long when I was ordered to report to my commanding officer, Captain Sweitzer, who told me I was to report to Rear Admiral David Bell's office for possible assignment as his aide (in Marine Corps jargon, an enlisted person who serves in this capacity is called an *orderly*). Admiral Bell was a highly decorated World War II veteran, having won the Navy Cross and two Silver Stars for heroism as commander of the submarine USS *Pargo*. In 1945, he was commander in chief of the Pacific fleet. In Scotland, he was responsible for the entire United States nuclear Polaris submarine fleet operating from a base near the small town of Dunoon.

After a brief interview with Admiral Bell, I was told henceforth I would be assigned to him for whatever duties he required. Each day, I dressed in my formal dress blue uniform and met the sailors responsible for taking a small boat (called the *Admiral's Gig*) ashore to bring the admiral to the ship and return him to shore each evening. In between, I waited just outside his door near his desk for whatever he asked me to do. There were long stretches in which I simply stood guard at his door.

Recognizing this, one morning Admiral Bell called me in to see him. He said I shouldn't be wasting my time just waiting until I was needed; instead, I should be reading. He ordered that a small lectern be constructed by the carpenter shop so that I could put a book on it and read while standing outside his door. (Obviously, no marine was going to read while sitting at a desk! I could read while standing.)

I don't remember the title of the first book he gave me, only that it was by Ernest Hemingway. Interestingly, he didn't only provide books; he also grilled me on them! My role included driving the admiral when he traveled to cities such as Glasgow or Edinburgh. As we were traveling, he would quiz me on whatever I'd just read. He was very well read himself, and he emphasized that reading a book involves more than being entertained. Books, he said—especially good books—should cause one to think.

The time I was assigned to Admiral Bell had a profound influence on me, not simply because my interest in reading was enhanced. More importantly, here was a man of enormous influence and responsibility who saw in me something more than a marine who was to stand outside his door, do whatever he asked, and serve as his driver. I felt he saw some undefined potential in me and took me under his wing, all the while making me feel special. We stayed in touch through occasional letters after I was discharged from the

Marines and he retired from the navy in 1970. I think he was proud to learn that I had received my doctorate and was a professor at Middle Tennessee State University. I believe that he felt, rightly, that he played a significant part in my interest in teaching and learning—and reading and writing.

My experience as a student in higher education was unique, I think, in that I thoroughly enjoyed it, and my luck of being treated as though I was special continued. Many professors were exceptionally kind and encouraging to me, but one stands out: Bill Butterfield. I think of Bill Butterfield's impact on my life as the *Butterfield Effect*.

After completing my service in the Marines, I returned home to Chattanooga. With the help of the GI Bill, I decided to complete my college degree by enrolling at the University of Chattanooga, which at that time was still a small liberal arts college but one with a very good reputation. (It is now the University of Tennessee at Chattanooga and part of the statewide University of Tennessee system.)

I was a history major during my time at Mississippi State University and continued my studies in history at the University of Chattanooga. Because my goal was to become a high school history teacher, I took classes that would lead to a teaching certification, and after receiving my undergraduate degree and securing a teaching position at Brainerd High School, I began work on my master's degree.

It was during my graduate studies that I developed a friendship with Bill, whom I had first met as an undergraduate. Bill had received his doctorate from The Ohio State University and was very progressive in his thinking, especially regarding issues such as poverty, race, human rights, and so on. He had been successful in leading the efforts to start an Upward Bound program at the University of Chattanooga for inner-city students, and he asked if I would like to serve in the summers as assistant director of the program. Not only was this a great experience for me—and a way to make extra money in the summers—but it also provided the opportunity to get to know Bill better, as well as other members of the university faculty.

Very few of my fellow high school students pursued studies in higher education. So I was somewhat proud of myself for graduating college—the first person in my family tree to do so. But I also thought the master's degree would be my final degree; I never thought of anything beyond that.

I clearly remember the incident during which I realized that how Bill viewed me and my future was much more positive than how I viewed myself. My wife, Star, and I were just awaking one Saturday morning when we noticed Bill's little red Volkswagen Beetle convertible parked on the street in front of our house. As we moved into the kitchen, I saw Bill sitting on our back porch step. I couldn't imagine what this was about. I went out and sat down, and we began to talk.

Bill told me he had spent much of the night trying to decide which university I should attend for my doctoral degree. I was surprised to say the least. I told him I hadn't thought I would even go to college, much less work on a doctorate. He said he had been talking with friends at Ohio State, and he thought I could receive an assistantship if I chose to go there. He thought I had a future teaching in higher education or in other leadership roles, he explained, but unless I received a doctorate, that future would be limited.

After Bill left, Star and I talked. Although we talked about the possibility of moving to Columbus for further graduate study (in those days, virtually all major universities had a one-year residency requirement for a doctorate), much of our conversation was around what a caring, encouraging, and thoughtful person Bill Butterfield was and how his view of me was transforming my view of myself and my professional future.

Earlier I shared how ultimately Dr. Fred Venditti played a pivotal role in our moving to Knoxville as I pursued my doctorate at the

University of Tennessee, but I would never have made the decision to work on a terminal degree if Bill Butterfield hadn't planted the seed of that idea.

My entire professional life has been impacted by people who believed in me—and I never wanted to disappoint a single one of them. At the University of Tennessee, Jerry Bellon practically made Star and me members of his family. He made me feel special, both personally and professionally. At Michigan State, Judy Lanier had a huge impact on my professional career. I remember a faculty member at Michigan State telling me that the dean—Judy Lanier—thought I was special. (It seemed he couldn't quite figure out why!) Later, when I accepted a position at Middle Tennessee State University in Murfreesboro, Tennessee, my department chair, Ralph White, took me under his wing. During my forty-one-year career at Middle Tennessee, I worked for five presidents, and I became especially close to the last four. Along the way, I went up through the ranks from a new assistant professor, to an associate professor, and then to a full professor and later served for twelve years as dean of the College of Education and toward the end of my career as the interim vice president and provost. I can say that I had full support and encouragement from each department chair, dean, provost, and president during my career in higher education.

I fully realize that I am sounding Pollyannaish about my life and the people who made me feel special. Of course, my life journey has included my share of experiences that were unremarkable and people who were downright rude. But, in retrospect, I learned from those people, too. When my daughter Robin prepared for her first day as a teacher, she asked if I had any advice. I told her to think of the very best teachers she had, try to remember the things they did, and choose to emulate them. Equally important, I told her, was to remember the very worst teachers and commit to never engaging in their behaviors.

Bad examples have proven to be beneficial to me, and I think I learned some valuable lessons from them. Still, I must admit that I have been blessed by the fact that the people who were caring, encouraging, and made me feel special outnumbered those who did not. When it comes to motivating students—and adults—at the very core, I think Pat Conroy (2010) got it right when writing about his teacher Gene Norris. Gene Norris dramatically impacted his students' lives because he made them feel special; that was the secret. My experience has been that people are primarily motivated by how *they think others think they are.*

There is a strong research base regarding student motivation beyond my personal experiences. Researchers and writers such as Jere Brophy, Robert J. Marzano, and John Hattie, along with many others, have made important contributions to the knowledge base. The fact that the effects of teachers' affective skills are much harder to statistically measure does not diminish their importance.

In this regard, I highly value the work of Carl R. Rogers (1961). As I first began to seriously think about and study teaching behaviors and their effect on student learning and behavior, the work of psychologist Carl Rogers (1961) was—and still is—held in high esteem. In *Kid by Kid, Skill by Skill* (2015), Janel Keating and I include one of my favorite insights of Dr. Rogers. It can be found in his classic work, *On Becoming a Person: A Therapist's View of Psychotherapy* (Rogers, 1961). For me, it pretty much sums up my thinking about the importance of valuing each student and making him or her feel special. For me, it rings as a universal truth:

> Change appears to come about through experience in a relationship. . . . If I can provide a certain type of relationship, the other person will discover within himself the capacity to use that relationship for growth, and change and personal development will occur. . . .
>
> By acceptance I mean a warm regard for him as a person of unconditional worth—of value no matter what his

condition, his behavior or his feelings. It means respect and liking for him as a separate person, a willingness for him to possess his own feelings in his own way. It means an acceptance of and regard for his attitudes of the moment, no matter how negative or positive, no matter how much they may contradict other attitudes he has held in the past. This acceptance of each fluctuating aspect of this other person makes it for him a relationship of warmth and safety, and the safety of being liked and prized as a person seems a highly important element in a helping relationship. (Rogers, 1961, pp. 333–334)

Interpersonal Interactions and Student Success

As with instructional strategies, there is no authoritative, all-encompassing checklist of affective skills that all teachers should possess. Beyond that, there is also not an agreed-on vocabulary for describing important interpersonal behaviors. On the other hand, effective teaching is a combination of effective instructional strategies and meaningful and effective interpersonal interactions with students—along with a deep, rich knowledge of the subject matter. Students discern rather quickly whether their teacher likes them, cares for them, and is interested in them.

When it comes to thinking of interpersonal behaviors between teachers and students, I like to start with a broad brush: how do we create a classroom culture that supports student success and personal growth? There is no particular order in the following examples, but it is important to note that these examples are interconnected and impact each other. (Again, these examples are not intended to be all-inclusive but are examples of my thinking about some of the more obvious and important affective behaviors.)

Effort-Based Classroom Cultures

Since the beginning of the 21st century we have seen increased emphasis on the value of teachers (and administrators and, importantly, parents) viewing students with an effort-based rather than ability-based mindset. In their studies on the psychology of success, Carol S. Dweck (2008) and her colleagues emphasize that while adults often view students' potential for success as *fixed*—determined by innate ability—their research has shown that when it comes to success, ability is not as important as effort. Angela Duckworth (2016) makes much the same point in *Grit: The Power of Passion and Perseverance*.

Much can be said for creating classroom cultures in which high standards for learning are clear and fixed, time is flexible, and encouragement, feedback, and support are the norm. Creating classroom cultures in which teachers make plans for and celebrate effort enhances the probability of success for all students, rather than a select few. Creating such cultures first requires a shift in the mindset of teachers from an ability-based mindset to an effort-based mindset, with the ultimate goal being to develop an effort-based mindset in their students.

Time and Support

It's impossible to create an effort-based classroom culture in schools and classrooms absent a systematic plan to provide additional time and support for students who experience difficulty with their learning. Virtually all students will need additional time and support on some skill or concept. It has always puzzled me why educators readily accept the fact that students learn at different rates, yet routinely create school schedules and cultures based on all students learning within the same time frame—and label those who don't demonstrate proficiency within the fixed time frame as failures. To add to the irony, adults are quick to point out when they themselves need more time to complete a task or gain deeper understanding!

Recognizing the importance of providing time and support for students isn't enough. District leaders must work to ensure that each school collaboratively develops systematic plans for implementation—plans that are recorded in writing and widely communicated.

The assistance must be, at a minimum (DuFour & Eaker, 1998; Eaker & Keating, 2012):

> › Systematic, occurring within the school day, regardless of the teacher to whom a student is assigned

> › Flexible (Students are not labeled; they move in and out of time and support as needed.)

> › Directive rather than invitational

> › Timely (The system does not wait too long to provide students with additional time and support.)

> › Supplementary (The assistance does not replace core instruction.)

> › Continually monitored for effectiveness and adjusted as needed

A Task-Oriented Classroom Culture

An emphasis on creating classrooms with a caring, encouraging, and helping culture does not imply simply making students feel good. Positive classroom culture cannot come at the expense of high expectations for student learning and appropriate student behavior. Effective teachers rely on their interpersonal skills to ensure that their classrooms reflect a task-oriented culture in which the recurring message is, "This is what we are going to learn. This is why it's important. This is what is expected of you. We can do this." (Jon Saphier, Mary Ann Haley-Speca, and Robert Gower [2008] would encourage us to add, "I won't give up on you!")

Listening

One of the most important, and effective, ways to connect with students is to simply listen—but at a deep level. Often this means listening to what students *aren't* saying and establishing a trusting relationship in which students become more open and willing to share.

Years ago, someone gave me an old reel-to-reel audiotape that someone had made of Carl Rogers's last lecture at, I believe, the University of Wisconsin. I treasure that tape, and for years, I used it in my graduate classes. In it, Rogers shares an example of listening at all levels, especially listening deeply to things not said but perhaps inferred. He tells of counseling a young boy who kept saying that he had no goals—no goals whatsoever. Rogers recalls thinking that perhaps the boy was simply stating a fact; on the other hand, perhaps he was signaling that he had given up. After a period of time, as Rogers showed that he was listening deeply, the boy shared that he had recently considered taking his life.

Obviously, not all situations will be this dramatic. But even ordinary situations can be significant to the student. I remember when I was a teacher at Brainerd High School a student kept hanging around my desk after the period had ended. As we talked, she eventually shared with me that she was pregnant and terrified at what her parents would think. I recall vividly how she cried and cried. She was desperate to talk with someone who would listen in a nonjudgmental way. In many ways, her situation represented a universal truth. All of us, students and adults alike, need people who will listen to us and allow us to share our deepest feelings and thoughts, and do so in an encouraging, caring, empathetic, nonjudgmental way.

A Warm and Caring Classroom Culture

I've found that one of the most powerful ways effective teachers motivate students is simply by communicating in multiple and meaningful ways that they care for their students and their success (and that they care and are passionate about the content they teach and the school as a whole). In doing so, they purposefully create warm and caring classroom cultures. In *Kid by Kid, Skill by Skill* (Eaker & Keating, 2015), Janel Keating and I highlight just a few ways that teachers model a warm and caring demeanor:

Smiling, asking how students are doing, or inquiring about a student's personal life such as his or her family, pet, or car can draw students in and make them feel that you are interested in them. Expressing concern for students' academic, social, and family life can contribute to this sense of warmth. . . . And, when behaviors such as these are demonstrated frequently, consistently, and genuinely, they will go a long way in creating a warm and caring classroom environment. (p. 135)

It has always amazed me that many teachers attempt to motivate those students who are unresponsive and do not do their work at a high level of quality or do not do it at all by threatening to give them a low grade. There is no evidence that the threat of a low grade is an effective way to motivate low-achieving students. On the other hand, the fear of a low grade can be highly motivational for some high-achieving students—at least in the short term. As a professor, I have had conversations with students who shared with me that although they made all As in high school, looking back they wish that early on they had made a B or two, so they could have enjoyed their high school years. Some simply said the pressure to constantly achieve at such a high level made them miserable.

There is no recipe for how to communicate caring, but it must be genuine. Any experienced teacher will point out that students cannot be fooled. They know how their teachers feel about them. Students feel teachers care for them when the teacher takes an interest in them, listens to them, is empathetic to their problems, and lets them know how proud he or she is of their accomplishments.

One particular incident made a huge impression on me when I was serving in the role of dean of students at Brainerd High School. As I mentioned earlier, Brainerd, like many high schools, was struggling with numerous challenges during those early days of desegregation. Two African American students taught me a lesson that I will not forget. They were in my office for some perceived misbehavior, and one student said, "Mr. Eaker, there are some teachers at this school who don't even care enough about black students to correct us when we misbehave!"

I had never thought of this before—that insisting that students learn and behave in ways that are good for them is an important way to communicate, "I care about you and your success, not only as a student, but as a person."

Empathy

Empathy is often misunderstood. Having empathy does not mean *feeling sorry for* certain students. I think of empathy as a vicarious emotional experience: attempting to understand students and their behavior by imagining yourself in their situation. The power of being empathetic lies in action, not feeling; empathy motivates educators to go to extraordinary lengths to help students move forward, often overcoming overwhelming odds. Teachers must go beyond simply empathizing with a student and try to *do* something to help. *Act*, even if your attempts prove fruitless; the very fact that you tried communicates volumes.

As in most cases, demonstrating a sense of empathy and understanding is enhanced by the work of teacher teams. There is only so much an individual teacher can know and do. One teacher may only know so much about a student, but others on the team may possess different helpful information. Even a teacher who is empathetic and knowledgeable may have a sense of helplessness or run out of ideas about what to do. A team of teachers is more likely to think of effective approaches to a difficult situation than an individual teacher who might feel alone and succumb to despair.

Sensitivity and Respect

It's easy to respect students who behave well and are successful in their schoolwork. However, *all* students deserve respect from their teachers. This simply means there are some things—some norms—that teachers should adhere to, one of which is being sensitive to students and their feelings. Students are sensitive about practically everything—their looks, their clothes, and especially what their peers think of them, just to name a few.

Students can be devastated when a teacher makes fun of them in front of the class or says something without realizing its emotional effect. In many ways, being sensitive and respectful involves simply being aware and thinking before saying something that may prove hurtful. Teachers who demonstrate respectfulness can remember what it was like when they were students or think of the way they would want their own child to be treated. The bottom line is this: teachers should always be courteous and respectful to students, *even those who do not reciprocate*. What leads us to believe that students will be more respectful than the adults with whom they interact?

Enthusiasm

I hear this refrain all too often: "Today's students are so apathetic!" It would be more accurate to say, "In *my* classroom, *my* students are apathetic."

Students behave differently for different teachers and in different situations. Any teacher who says his or her students are apathetic or lacking enthusiasm should first look in the mirror! Rarely will students be more enthusiastic than their teacher. The key to understanding student enthusiasm is to understand the power of modeling. Here's a general rule: teachers who are enthusiastic tend to have enthusiastic classroom cultures. Most of us can remember teachers who seemed lethargic and started a unit with an introduction that was less than enthusiastic, such as, "Well, I've always dreaded teaching this unit. Frankly, I think it's boring, and I think you'll find it boring, too. But we have to study it, so let's dig in and get through it."

Pacing also affects enthusiasm. Plodding through content, stalling in one place, repeating points over and over—these simply kill student enthusiasm. It becomes difficult for students to stay awake, much less be excited.

A Summing Up

Throughout my career, I have presented to and spoken with groups of educators countless times. My writing and speaking most often deal with the research on teaching or effective schools or PLCs—what they are like, how they work. But I almost always stop to remind the group that, as educators, we have the opportunity to be a hero to some child every day. While teaching methodology is important, it will only take us so far. Relationships matter—a lot!

I frequently engage educators in the following activity. First, I ask them to think of the best teacher they ever had. After a minute of reflection, I next ask them to think of three adjectives that describe the teacher they chose. I then ask the group to share the adjectives that describe the best teacher they identified. Not surprisingly, almost without exception, they describe the teacher's affect, using words and phrases such as *caring, enthusiastic, a sense of humor, encouraging, a good listener*, and so on. Teaching and learning are a complex interplay between human beings, and in human interactions, emotions matter. Teaching strategies matter. Knowing one's content matters. Additionally, positively affecting students' emotions matters—a lot—and should not be merely left to chance.

CHAPTER 5

The School Effects Research

As my friend and colleague Jim Huffman and I visited the Institute for Research on Teaching at Michigan State, we began spending an increasing amount of time with Larry Lezotte. Although Larry was busy in his role as department chairperson and associate director of the institute, he often would drive us from and back to the airport. I only mention this to emphasize the fact that Larry was very nice and accepting of us, and to this day, he continues to be one of the nicest, most professional people I know. And although we seldom see each other, I consider Larry a good friend and truly admire his contributions to our profession—and to my career.

My primary interest in the work of the institute centered on teacher behaviors and their effect on student learning. Increasingly, my interest had become more focused on the topic of teacher expectations and their effect on student learning and behavior—specifically, how teacher expectations are reflected in teacher behavior. I, of course, had heard of the effective schools research, especially the work that had been done by Ron Edmonds. I had read Edmonds's (1979) highly influential article in *Educational Leadership* and was much impressed. I knew that Edmonds was at Harvard when much of his research was being conducted, so it was interesting to learn from Larry that Edmonds would be joining the faculty at Michigan State. (I was not surprised since I knew the dean, Judy Lanier, well enough to know that she was constantly working to add highly regarded educators to the faculty. Judy never underestimated the importance of highly capable faculty.)

I did not realize it at the time, but that conversation with Larry was the first step in a new direction in my professional life. Although I didn't abandon my interest in the teacher effects research (palimpsest, again!), I began to delve deeper into the emerging research on effective schools.

The Coleman Report

Any deep understanding of the effective schools movement must, I think, be viewed within the context of the 1966 Coleman Report and its impact on the thinking about how to improve America's schools (Dickinson, 2016). In retrospect, it is hard to fathom that the effective schools movement had its beginnings in a report that essentially made the case that what schools do—or don't do—makes very little difference in student achievement (Dickinson, 2016). Simply put, the report sent the clear, and depressing, message that the primary factors impacting student achievement were beyond the purview of schools, residing primarily in the family socioeconomic structure and culture (Dickinson, 2016).

The impetus of the 1966 Coleman Report was the Civil Rights Act of 1964. The act contained a rather obscure directive that the U.S. commissioner of education conduct a survey for the president and Congress concerning the lack of educational opportunities for individuals due to race, color, religion, or national origin in public educational institutions—and the report was to be completed within the short time frame of two years!

James Coleman, a sociologist at Johns Hopkins University, was selected to head the team to develop and conduct the nationwide survey, analyze the results, and write the final report (Coleman et al., 1966). In a little over a year, the team administered one of the largest social science surveys ever conducted, involving six hundred thousand students and sixty thousand teachers in four thousand school districts (Dickinson, 2016).

The survey included topics that had never been the focus of widespread, in-depth research. The study went far beyond the primary issues of the degree to which educational segregation existed and the accompanying disparity of resource allocation. The questions focused on such issues as how well students of all races and economic backgrounds were learning and, importantly, what factors influenced their learning.

Most educators and politicians assumed the results of the report would simply validate what most thought to be the norm—that segregation by race existed in most schools, particularly in the South, and that resources for the education of white students were far superior to those allocated for the education of black students, thus accounting for the disparity in student achievement.

When it was released, the 737-page report painted a far more complex picture of public education than was expected. While the report validated the fact that segregation did exist, it also found that physical amenities and funding were not the most important factors in students' educational success. Instead, a student's family background and a diverse socioeconomic mix in the classroom proved to be the primary factors in student achievement. The 1966 Coleman Report provided data to support what became known as the achievement gap between students of different racial and social backgrounds (Dickinson, 2016). In other words, it suggested that *the determinants of student success in school lay outside of school and classroom boundaries—and there wasn't much schools or teachers could do to impact learning!* More specifically, Coleman et al. (1966) found that schools account for only about 10 percent of the variance in student achievement, with the remaining 90 percent accounted for by student socioeconomic background characteristics (Marzano, 2003).

The report sparked additional interest in the role family background plays in student achievement. One of the most important later works was a reanalysis of the Coleman data by Christopher Jencks (1972). Titled *Inequality: A Reassessment of the Effect of Family and Schooling in America*, Jencks's (1972) analysis found the following (Marzano, 1972).

> ❯ Schools do little to lessen the gap between rich students and poor students.

> ❯ Schools do little to lessen the gap between more and less able students.

> ❯ Student achievement is primarily a function of one factor—the background of the student.

> ❯ Little evidence exists that education reform can improve a school's influence on student achievement.

While the 1966 Coleman Report played an important role in drawing attention to the disparity between the academic achievement of black and white students (as well as wealthy and poor students), perhaps the greatest effect of the report was the impact the findings had on the collective psyche of public school educators and policymakers. After all, if family background is the *primary* factor affecting student academic performance and schools themselves make very little difference, why should school leaders develop initiatives aimed at improving the academic achievement of students? Imagine the practical and psychological impact on educators of learning that the largest, most extensive research study of American public education ever conducted concluded that what schools do makes very little difference to student learning!

Effective Schools: The Early Research

Although the statistical methodology and the validity of the 1966 Coleman Report were not widely criticized, the idea that it makes little difference which school a student attends simply did not make sense to many—if not most—people. After all, to parents, which school their child attended was an issue of major importance. Both educators and the general public knew some schools were better than others. In short, this idea flew in the face of common knowledge, as well as common sense.

Are some schools more effective than others? And, if so, how? What *in-school* factors, if any, contribute to school effectiveness? In the early 1970s, researchers began to ask these questions. Of course, such research efforts had to begin with how one defines an *effective school*. Generally, definitions of school effectiveness contained a few common themes. One, an effective school should reflect minimal mastery of educational achievement for poor children that is on par with children of the middle class (Edmonds, 1979). Two, an effective school is characterized by high overall achievement, with no significant gaps in that achievement across major subgroups (Lezotte & Snyder, 2011). In short, an effective school was one that effectively educated *all* students.

The Weber Study: New York City (1971)

For me, a few of the early studies stood out. One of the first that caught my attention was a study by author and researcher George Weber (1971) of four instructionally effective inner-city schools in New York City that were performing above average in reading on standardized tests. Weber (1971) identified several factors that contributed to student success in the four schools. One factor was strong leadership, particularly the tone set by the principal. The schools reflected a culture of high expectations. Weber (1971) emphasized that although high expectations were necessary, in and of themselves, high expectations alone were not sufficient for school success. The learning atmosphere within the schools was orderly, quiet, and pleasant. Further, these four schools emphasized the acquisition of reading skills and the evaluation of pupil progress on a frequent and timely basis. These schools had additional reading personnel, phonics instruction, and individualized instruction (Edmonds & Frederiksen, 1978; Steller, 1988).

New York State Department of Education Study (1974)

While some of the effective schools studies were descriptive in nature, other researchers relied on a comparison approach—comparing what occurs in schools that have roughly the same demographic profile but attain much different student achievement results. By studying schools that were outliers, researchers were able to identify factors (correlates) in high-achieving schools that differed from their lower-achieving counterparts.

One such study was conducted in 1974 by the State of New York's Office of Education Performance Review. Researchers identified two inner-city public schools in New York City, both serving students that were predominantly poor. One school was high achieving, while the other was low achieving. When researchers studied both schools, they identified the following differences:

- The differences in student achievement in these two schools seemed to be attributed to factors over which the school had control.
- The administrative behavior, policies, and practices in the schools seemed to have a significant impact on student achievement.
- The higher-achieving school was led by an administrative team that reflected a good balance between management skills and instructional skills.
- In the more effective school the administrative team had a plan for raising reading achievement and had implemented the plan throughout the school.

- Reading instruction did not differ between the two schools since teachers in both schools had problems in teaching reading and assessing reading skills of students.

- In the less effective school, many of the staff attributed students' lack of reading success to factors beyond the school's control. Additionally, many of the professional staff were pessimistic about the school's ability to have a positive impact. This view resulted in a culture of low expectations. In the higher-achieving school, teachers expressed more confidence in their ability to positively affect the performance of their students.

- Children were apathetic, disruptive, or absent when exposed to unstimulating learning experiences. (Edmonds & Frederiksen, 1978, pp. 16–17)

The California Study (1976)

Another, much larger study in which researchers utilized the outlier approach was conducted in California (Madden, Lawson, & Sweet, 1976). In this study, the researchers studied twenty-one "matched pairs" of elementary schools (forty-two total schools). Again, the demographics were constant for both groups of schools. The schools only differed in student performance on standardized achievement tests, with twenty-one schools rated as low achieving and twenty-one schools high achieving. The purpose of the study was to determine the school characteristics that seemed responsible for the differences in student achievement levels. Edmonds and Frederiksen (1978) summarize the major findings:

- Teachers in the higher-achieving schools reported that the principals provided them with a significantly greater amount of support.

- Teachers in the higher-achieving schools were more task-oriented and exhibited more evidence of applying appropriate principles of learning.

- Classrooms in the higher-achieving schools reflected more evidence of student monitoring processes, student effort, happier children, and an atmosphere conducive to learning.

- Teachers in higher-achieving schools reported that they spent relatively more time on social studies, less time on mathematics and physical education/health, and about the same amount of time on reading/language development and science. Teachers in higher-achieving schools reported a larger number of adult volunteers in mathematics classes, fewer paid aides in reading, and they were more apt to use teacher aides for nonteaching tasks, such as classroom paperwork, watching children on the playground, and maintaining classroom discipline.

- Teachers in higher-achieving schools reported higher levels of access to "outside the classroom" materials.

- Teachers in the higher-achieving schools believed their faculty as a whole had less influence on educational decisions.

- Teachers in higher-achieving schools rated the district administration higher on support services than did teachers in the lower-achieving schools.

- The higher-achieving schools divided classrooms into fewer groups for purposes of instruction.

- Teachers in the higher-achieving schools reported being more satisfied with various aspects of their work. (pp. 17–18)

The Brookover and Lezotte Study (1979)

One of the more influential effective schools studies was published by Wilbur Brookover and Larry Lezotte in 1979. Much like the California study, the Brookover and Lezotte (1979) study, *Changes in School Characteristics Coincident With Changes in Student Achievement*, compares differences between schools with lower achievement that were declining and schools with higher student achievement that were improving. They chose to study eight schools: six that were improving and two that were declining (Brookover & Lezotte, 1979). Arthur W. Steller (1988), in *Effective Schools Research: Practice and Promise*, summarizes the major findings from the Brookover and Lezotte (1979) study:

- In the improving schools there was more emphasis placed on reading and mathematics.
- The staff and principals of the improving schools demonstrated a belief that all students could master basic learning objectives.
- The staff of the improving schools believed that most of their students would finish high school.
- The staff of improving schools believed they could make a significant difference in student learning, regardless of the students' home background.
- Principals in the improving schools tended to accept responsibility for accountability for student learning measures on criterion-referenced assessments.
- The staff of the improving schools were less satisfied with student achievement, while the staff in the declining schools tended to be more complacent.
- Parent-initiated contact was more prevalent in the improving schools. (p. 10)

In his article on effective schools for the urban poor, Edmonds (1979) included more description on these points from the original Brookover and Lezotte (1979) research.

1. Improving schools accept and emphasize the importance of basic reading and mathematics goals and objectives while declining schools give much less emphasis to such goals and do not specify them as fundamental.

2. The improving schools believe that all students can master the basic objectives, and teachers perceive that the principal shares this belief. They tend to report higher and increasing levels of student ability, while the declining school teachers project the belief that students' ability levels are low and they cannot master these objectives.

3. Staff members of the improving schools hold higher and increasing expectations with regard to student accomplishments. Staff members of the declining schools are much less likely to believe that their students will complete high school or college.

4. Teachers and principals of the improving schools are much more likely to assume responsibility for teaching basic reading and mathematics skills and are much more committed to doing so. The declining schools feel there is not much that teachers can do to influence student achievement, displacing the responsibility for learning on parents or students.

5. Teachers in the declining schools believe there is little they can do to influence basic skill learning, so they spend less time in direct reading instruction than teachers in the improving schools. Improving school staffs devote a much greater amount of time toward achieving reading and mathematics objectives.

6. In the improving schools, the principal is more likely to be an instructional leader, more assertive in his or her leadership role, more of a disciplinarian, and perhaps most of all, assumes responsibility for the evaluation of basic objective achievement. The principals in declining schools appear to be permissive and to emphasize informal and collegial relationships with teachers.

7. Improving staffs show a higher acceptance of the concept of accountability and are further along in the development of an accountability model. Declining schools make little use of state assessment devices and reject their relevance as a reflection of instruction.

8. Generally, teachers in the improving schools are less satisfied than those in the declining schools. The higher levels of satisfaction and morale in the declining schools seem to reflect a pattern of complacency and satisfaction. The improving school staff members appear more likely to experience some tension and dissatisfaction.

9. It seems that there is less overall parent involvement in the improving schools; however, the improving staffs indicated that their schools have higher levels of "parent initiated" involvement. This suggests that we need to look more closely at the nature of the parent involvement. Perhaps parent-initiated contact represents an effective instrument of educational change. (Brookover & Lezotte, 1978, pp. 66-68)

The Fifteen-Thousand-Hour Study (1979)

In the late 1970s, Michael Rutter, Barbara Maughan, Peter Mortimore, Janet Ouston, and Alan Smith (1979) conducted research to answer basic questions such as (1) do a student's experiences in school have any effect on academic attainment and behavior, (2) does it matter which school a student attends, and (3) what are the features of schools that contribute to differences in student academic achievement and behavior? More specifically, the researchers (Rutter et al., 1979) studied four student outcomes—achievement, attendance, behavior, and delinquency—for five years in twelve London secondary schools. Although all participant schools had similar demographics and other input variables, the outcomes among the schools were substantially different (Eaker & Dillard, 2017; Steller, 1988).

Outcomes that were attributable to the schools varied significantly. The more effective schools were characterized by: (1) an emphasis on academics, (2) skills of teachers, (3) teachers' instructional behaviors, (4) rewards and punishments, (5) student climate, (6) student responsibility and participation, and (7) staff responsibility and participation (Steller, 1988).

In a critique of the study (Eaker & Dillard, 2017), the findings were articulated as follows:

- A school's atmosphere is influenced positively by the degree to which it functions as a coherent whole, with agreed-upon ways of doing things that are consistent throughout the school and have the general support of all staff.

- Outcomes were better in schools where teachers expect students to achieve at relatively high levels.

- Outcomes were better in schools that provide pleasant working conditions for students.

- Outcomes were better in schools where immediate, direct praise and approval are the prevalent means of classroom feedback.

- Outcomes were better in schools where teachers present themselves as positive role models demonstrating punctuality, concern for the physical well-being of the school building, concern for the emotional well-being of the pupils, and restraint in the use of physical punishment.

- Children's behavior was better in schools where teachers were readily available to be consulted by students about problems and where many children consult with teachers.

- Outcomes were better in schools where a high proportion of children hold some kind of position of responsibility in the school. (p. 41)

Ron Edmonds and the Effective Schools Movement

Perhaps no single person influenced the widespread interest in the effective schools research more than Ron Edmonds. Edmonds's advocacy of the research, especially as a way to improve schooling practices for children of the urban poor, shifted the effective schools research from the work of a few researchers to what became a nationwide educational movement.

In 1978, Edmonds and John Frederiksen published *Search for Effective Schools: The Identification and Analysis of City Schools That Are Instructionally Effective for Poor Children*. Subsequently, Edmonds joined with Lezotte and Gary Ratner in the Search for Effective Schools project, which was a multiyear, multiphased examination and analysis of effective and ineffective schools in Michigan. Edmonds and his colleagues also engaged in a reanalysis of the 1966 Coleman Report data, in which they found numerous schools that were instructionally effective for poor children.

In an influential article that appeared in *Educational Leadership*, Edmonds outlines the characteristics of schools that were effective for the urban poor as (Edmonds, 1979; Steller, 1988):

> ‣ Having strong administrative leadership without which the disparate elements of good schooling cannot be brought together or maintained

> Having a climate of expectations in which no children are permitted to fall below minimum but efficacious levels of achievement

> Having an atmosphere that is orderly without being rigid, quiet without being oppressive, and generally conducive to the instructional business at hand

> Making it clear that pupil acquisition of the basic school skills takes precedence over all other school activities

> Focusing school energy and resources on the fundamental objectives

> Frequently monitoring pupil progress toward instructional objectives

Prior to his untimely death in 1983 at the age of forty-eight, Edmonds had become a national spokesperson in the United States and an advocate for improved schooling practices for children of poverty. He was certainly the most prominent of the effective schools researchers. He frequently pointed out that the issue was not a lack of knowledge but, rather, a lack of will. I've always felt his passion was best reflected in the closing paragraph of that widely read *Educational Leadership* article, in which he writes:

> It seems to me, therefore, that what is left of this discussion are three declarative statements: (a) We can, whenever and wherever we choose, successfully teach all children whose schooling is of interest to us; (b) We already know more than we need to do that; and (c) Whether or not we do it must finally depend on how we feel about the fact that we haven't so far. (Edmonds, 1979, p. 23)

By the mid-1980s, a consensus about the in-school factors that account for school effectiveness began to emerge around five characteristics—(1) strong instructional leadership by the principal; (2) a clear focus on basic skill acquisition; (3) high, but efficacious, expectations for student learning; (4) a safe and orderly school climate;

and (5) frequent monitoring of student learning. These findings did not dismiss the major findings of the 1966 Coleman Report with its emphasis on factors external to schools as the major determinant of student achievement. Rather, the effective schools research points out that although poverty makes creating an instructionally effective school difficult and time consuming, the evidence is clear—it can be done and has been done, time and again.

Although the study of effective schools has continued, those five characteristics, or correlates, have held steady. However, occasionally two additional correlates have been included—high-quality parental involvement and opportunity to learn / time on task. Additionally, new summaries and meta-analyses of the effective schools research are available. I have found two of these to be particularly helpful: *What Works in Schools* by Marzano (2003) and *What Effective Schools Do* by Lezotte and Kathleen M. Snyder (2011).

In *What Works in Schools*, Marzano (2003) identifies five school-level factors that positively affect student achievement.

1. A guaranteed and viable curriculum
2. Challenging goals and effective feedback
3. Parent and community involvement
4. Safe and orderly atmosphere
5. Collegiality and professionalism

Whereas Marzano (2003) relies heavily on statistical meta-analysis, Lezotte and Snyder (2011) take a more descriptive approach. They provide an in-depth description of school practices under seven effective schools correlates.

1. High expectations for success
2. Strong instructional leadership
3. Clear and focused mission

4. Opportunity to learn or time on task

5. Frequent monitoring of student progress

6. Safe and orderly environment

7. Positive school-home relations

I've found the summaries of the effective schools research by Marzano (2003) and Lezotte and Snyder (2011) to be particularly useful to school practitioners. Both books go beyond a general description of findings from various effective schools studies and provide a more in-depth description of the *practices and procedures* that effective schools implement to bury each effective schools correlate deep within school culture.

A Summing Up

As I wrote earlier, by this time in my career I had become particularly interested in the topic of high expectations for student success. Initially, my interest in high expectations focused on the effect of teachers' expectations on student achievement and behavior. Of course, I was aware of the emerging school effects research and that most studies identified high expectations as a major correlate of an effective school. What I did not realize was that the effective schools research would become a new road I would travel on my professional journey.

Serendipitous. This is the only word that comes to mind when I reflect on my deep interest and involvement in the effective schools movement. Like many others, I was surprised by Edmonds's sudden death at such an early age. I was aware of his growing partnership with Larry Lezotte in a number of new and important effective schools research projects, so I could only imagine the impact Edmonds's death was having on Larry, both personally and professionally. What I had not anticipated was a telephone call I received one evening soon after.

Larry called that evening to talk with me about a project that he (and Ron Edmonds) had committed to undertaking in Jackson, Mississippi. The general plan involved a commitment on the part of the Jackson city school system, which was led by Superintendent Robert (Bob) Fortenberry, to invest $5 million over a period of five years to implement each of the five effective schools correlates. Edmonds's death meant that Larry would now have to put the details of the project together by himself in a relatively short period of time.

More specifically, Larry called to ask if I would work with him to implement the practices and concepts associated with the high expectations correlate. This particular correlate would have an early emphasis, since the importance of high expectations for student learning would affect the overall culture of the district, as well as the other four correlates. It was obvious—at least to Larry and me—that the correlates of effective schools were not independent of each other; they were interconnected with the high expectations correlate cutting through and impacting the ultimate effectiveness of everything that would be done to increase student learning in Jackson.

I saw this as a wonderful opportunity. First, I had the highest regard for Larry—not only professionally but personally as well. Second, this was going to be a huge project over a number of years. I recalled that the superintendent, Bob Fortenberry, had testified before Congress about the plight of inner-city black children, particularly in the South, and his passion and commitment to change the culture of Jackson's schools, which were mostly black and mostly poor, were evident.

Soon afterward, Larry and I went to Jackson and began our work with the educators. It was a remarkable experience for me. Although I was teaching graduate classes at Middle Tennessee State University, my work in Jackson, as well as other places such as Chicago and Long Island, provided an authenticity to my teaching and writing. I particularly enjoyed and learned a great deal from our work with the principals. If my memory is correct, there were roughly fifty schools in the system, so, obviously, the cultures and achievement levels within the district varied widely from school to school.

In the years I worked with Larry in Jackson, I developed some wonderful friendships. My friendship with Larry grew deeper, and my regard for his work was enhanced. Larry and I expanded our work together as he worked tirelessly to extend the impact of the effective schools movement. More specifically, Larry started an organization, the National Center for Effective Schools Research and Development, and created a group he called Fellows to help lead the effective schools movement. I was flattered that Larry asked me to serve with that original group and was so pleased when, in the second year, Larry invited Rick DuFour to become a Fellow.

I also developed a budding friendship with a young principal named Gary Matthews. Years later, Gary contacted me to work with the districts in which he worked as he moved up the career ladder. He first contacted me when he was assistant superintendent in Spring Branch, Texas, a suburban area of Houston. I went there on multiple occasions. He later served as superintendent in places such as St. Augustine and Baton Rouge, to name just two, and he always asked me to assist in his efforts to embed the effective schools correlates in each district. My visits to work for Gary in Spring Branch had a multiplier effect, since Houston is surrounded by many small towns. My work in Spring Branch, coupled with the growing national prominence of the effective schools movement, meant that I was much in demand in both the Houston and the Dallas areas.

I also developed a friendship with and deep respect for Bob Fortenberry. Bob was a passionate and articulate spokesperson for the inner-city poor. Improving the lives of these children by improving their academic success was much more than an intellectual or tactical endeavor for him. He undertook the complex task of improving schools in Jackson—and beyond—with true fidelity. Bob and I did undertake a couple of consulting trips together and thus had the opportunity to get to know each other at a deeper level. I learned a great deal from him and value my time with him very much.

In retrospect, these years were hugely important to me, both personally and professionally. Simply *doing the work* with a broad range of practitioners provided me with insights regarding moving beyond communicating the correlates of effective schools to understanding the practices, concepts, processes, and leadership practices that were necessary to significantly improve schools.

And my writing increased—and hopefully, improved!—significantly during these years. When Larry created the National Center for Effective Schools Research and Development, he also began a monthly research report to which readers could subscribe. He asked me to critique one or more research studies each month. The format of these critiques was straightforward: (1) What did the researchers do? (2) What did the researchers find? and (3) What was the implication for school improvement? Writing these critiques (published frequently and disseminated to a large audience) increased my work in schools and school districts but also forced me to develop "habits of the mind"—the ability to examine research findings and connect them to specific aspects of school improvement.

However, the largest impact, by far, of the effective schools movement was on my partnership and friendship with Rick. During this period of my professional life, Rick and I expanded our work with schools, our writing, and our presentations at state and national meetings. More importantly, our personal friendship deepened and expanded to include our families as we began to visit each other on a more frequent basis.

On a professional level, Rick and I coauthored articles and a couple of books. One of our books, *Creating the New American School* (DuFour & Eaker, 1992), caught the attention of a state senator in

Idaho, which led to us working with schools throughout Idaho, particularly in Nampa and Caldwell. Perhaps our most rewarding work was with two specific organizations—the Association for Supervision and Curriculum Development (ASCD) and the Tennessee State Department of Education. For approximately ten years, Rick and I conducted summer leadership workshops for ASCD in different cities across the United States, focusing on the effective teaching and effective schools research and how to embed these findings into the day-to-day culture of schools.

We did the same thing with the Tennessee State Department of Education. I was serving as the dean of the College of Education at Middle Tennessee State University at the time and was friends with a number of leaders within the department of education. I was asked if I could arrange a meeting with a group from the department and Rick and me. The upshot was a contract for us to conduct a series of week-long leadership academies each summer in Murfreesboro, Tennessee, for school leaders from across the state. If my memory serves me correctly, we conducted these workshops for three or four summers.

While doing these workshops for ASCD and the Tennessee Department of Education was great fun for us, the greatest benefit came from preparing for these workshops, which deepened our thinking about how to translate research into practice. Our work—I was serving as a university dean at a large public university and had been engaged in the world of research, and Rick was serving as the principal of a large high school that was rapidly gaining national attention—represented a new kind of professional partnership, one that we took pride in throughout our careers. We thought of ourselves as *engaged scholars*.

In retrospect, it's obvious that the effective schools movement had a large and positive effect on our nation's thinking about improving schools. As with many, if not most, areas of new research, it would take years for the promise of the effective schools research to be accepted as conventional wisdom. Findings from the early studies were often either misunderstood or not understood at all.

For the misinformed, the findings were viewed as a direct attack on the primary findings of the 1966 Coleman Report. Simply put, for them, the effective schools research findings confirmed their commonsense belief that schools do matter. This view—that the effective schools researchers had proven that Coleman et al. (1966) and those who agreed with him were wrong—is a much too simplistic understanding of both the Coleman Report and the effective schools research. The issue is not who was right or who was wrong but, rather, what could be learned from each.

This misunderstanding about the effective schools research stems, I think, from a lack of understanding about big data and external factors versus small sample size and internal school factors. The 1966 Coleman Report is an excellent example of what is currently referred to as *big data*. Coleman and his team (1966) surveyed six hundred thousand students and sixty thousand teachers in four thousand school districts. When viewing data that are this large, one must remember that it's relatively easy to find *individual* schools within the data pool that are successfully educating poor students. Furthermore, it is likely that these individual schools share many, if not most, of the same in-school characteristics. This fact does not, however, discount the significance of socioeconomic status as a major factor for predicting the future academic success of students. One only has to analyze data from statewide test results to quickly see the relationship between social class and academic achievement.

I've always thought the effective schools research contributed to the discounting of the crippling effects that poverty plays within our public school system. This is no criticism of the research but, rather, of those who view the findings as a *simple recipe* for educating children of poverty. While time and again researchers identified the characteristics of schools that were successfully educating children of the poor, what was often missing was the fact that doing so was very difficult, often took a long time, and was dependent on outstanding leadership. While it is not uncommon to find schools of the middle and upper classes whose students are academically successful even though the quality of leadership is marginal at best, one is unlikely to find an effective school that serves children of poverty with weak and ineffective leadership. This fact leads to the very difficult issue of scale; it's one thing to find a few outstanding leaders of schools that are successfully educating children of the poor, but it's another to scale up the system and find literally hundreds, if not thousands, of such outstanding leaders.

And while the correlates of effective schools have been confirmed repeatedly, the early findings did not offer a *framework for implementation*. The acceptance and popularity of the effective schools research findings were due, in part, simply to the common sense of the movement. There is nothing controversial about the *effective schools correlates*, as they came to be commonly called. In fact, such characteristics would have been identified absent the research findings. On the other hand, there is a huge difference between widespread agreement on the characteristics of an effective school and widespread knowledge about how to embed those characteristics deep into school culture—especially on a large districtwide, statewide, or even national scale. The upshot of this problem was a focus on improving schools one at a time. While this approach was effective for a few schools, it didn't offer much for the students in other schools in which there was little or no school improvement effort underway.

These observations should not be taken in any way as discounting the contributions that the effective schools movement had and continues to have on our public schools. For me professionally, the effective schools research built on my experiences with the clinical supervision movement and the teacher effects research and provided both Rick DuFour and me with an intellectual and experiential foundation that would later serve as the cornerstone for our thinking about the Professional Learning Communities at Work process for improving student achievement.

CHAPTER 6

The Impetus of Professional Learning Communities at Work

In 1996, I was serving in the role of dean of the College of Education at Middle Tennessee State University, and Rick DuFour was the principal of Adlai Stevenson High School—a large, highly recognized secondary school in Lincolnshire, Illinois, a suburban area of Chicago. As I've noted previously, we had spent years consulting with school districts throughout North America, presenting at state and national conferences, and coauthoring articles and two books. We viewed ourselves as engaged scholars: practitioners who were absorbed in seeking research-based best practices to assist school improvement initiatives. More important, through the previous seventeen years of working and writing together, our personal friendship (and the friendship of our families) had deepened.

One day, my secretary rang that Rick was on the telephone. After chatting a bit (which always included Rick's witty sense of humor), he proposed that we coauthor a new book. We talked about our experience in working in a wide variety of school districts. We also discussed the fact that I had a career in higher education and an interest and experience grounded in the world of research, while he was a lifelong practitioner. We felt these divergent backgrounds put us in the position to create a commonsense, research-based framework for embedding best practices in schools for the purpose of improving student academic achievement. We saw the concept of schools functioning as a learning community as the most promising approach for such an endeavor.

The idea of organizations functioning as learning communities was not new at the time. Rick and I have never claimed that we were the first to coin the phrase *professional learning communities* or to call on schools to function as professional learning communities. We realized our work would be built on the work of others such as Milbrey McLaughlin (one of the first educators to use the phrase *professional learning communities*), Judith Warren Little, Shirley Hord, Fred Newmann and Gary Wehlage, Sharon Kruse, and Karen Seashore Louis, to name but a few.

Early in *Professional Learning Communities at Work* (DuFour & Eaker, 1998), we highlighted these researchers and writers and others who were early proponents of organizations and schools functioning as *learning communities* or *professional learning communities*. We highlighted the following in *Professional Learning Communities at Work* (DuFour & Eaker, 1998, pp. 23–24):

> Only the organizations that have a passion for learning will have an enduring influence. (Covey, 1996, p. 149)
>
> Every enterprise has to become a learning organization [and] a teaching institution. Organizations that build in continuous learning in jobs will dominate the twenty-first century. (Drucker, 1992, p. 108)
>
> The most successful corporation of the future will be a learning organization. (Senge, 1990, p. 4)
>
> Preferred organizations will be learning organizations. . . . It has been said that people who stop learning stop living. This is also true of organizations. (Handy, 1995, p. 55)

The new problem of change . . . is what would it take to make the educational system a learning organization—expert at dealing with change as a normal part of its work, not just in relation to the latest policy, but as a way of life. (Fullan, 1993, p. 4)

The commission recommends that schools be restructured to become genuine learning organizations for both students and teachers; organizations that respect learning, honor teaching, and teach for understanding. (Darling-Hammond, 1996, p. 198)

We have come to realize over the years that the development of a learning community of educators is itself a major cultural change that will spawn many others. (Joyce & Showers, 1995, p. 3)

If schools want to boost student learning, they should work on building a professional community that is characterized by shared purpose, collaborative activity, and collective responsibility among staff. (Newmann & Wehlage, 1995, p. 37)

We argue, however, that when schools attempt significant reform, efforts to form a schoolwide professional community are critical. (Louis, Kruse, & Raywid, 1996, p. 13)

What we did do, I think, is use our experience and backgrounds to develop a framework for describing *what occurs* in a high-performing school that functions as a professional learning community—day in and day out. And we set out to describe, in detail, the *practices and processes* school leaders could utilize to transform more traditional school cultures into high-performing professional learning communities. This is why we added the *at work* designation to the term *professional learning community*. For us, the phrase *at work* would be the central focus of our new book about schools that function as professional learning communities and our future efforts to improve schools.

As we began to brainstorm what such a framework would look like, we soon realized that we needed to add a new connection—a new dimension—to thinking about improving schools; that is, we wanted to merge findings of best practice from educational research with aspects of best practice from organizations outside the educational arena. We wanted to capture the power of best practices from the broader world of research in organizational development and leadership, rather than limit ourselves to the world of education.

I've never quite understood why educators are reluctant to embrace best practices, when appropriate, from outside our field. Rosabeth Moss Kanter (1997) observed that successful people are constantly looking for fresh perspectives, even from outside their own narrow field of specialization or interest. As we began our initial draft, we made an early commitment to learn from those outside of education. We relied heavily on writers and researchers such as Warren Bennis, James Champy, Stephen Covey, Terry Deal, Peter Drucker, John Gardner, Rosabeth Moss Kanter, John Kotter, James M. Kouzes, Burt Nanus, Tom Peters, Barry Z. Posner, Peter Senge, Robert Waterman, and many others. I should especially emphasize the work of W. Edwards Deming. Like most other students of organizational development and leadership, we were greatly influenced by his pioneering work, particularly his work related to the power of collaborative teaming.

My earliest remembrance of the phrase *learning community* is in an unpublished paper I read while at the University of Tennessee. The gist of the paper was that for organizations to flourish in our rapidly changing world, they must function as *learning* organizations. Otherwise, they will be left behind. (Two excellent examples are Blockbuster Video versus Netflix, and BlackBerry versus smartphones. Both Blockbuster and BlackBerry stubbornly refused to learn and embrace best emerging practice.)

While educators and noneducators alike were increasingly using the terms *learning community* and *professional learning community*, there was no widespread agreement on a precise definition. What was a professional learning community, and how did it work? We soon realized that we would have to be clear regarding our own understanding of the term *professional learning community* before we could use the term with the larger public. Repeatedly, in our writing and in our work, we have taken heed to Mike Schmoker's (2004) observation that "clarity precedes competence" (p. 85).

Professional Learning Communities Defined

As we began our early discussions, we soon realized it was not enough to simply declare that developing the ability of school personnel to function as a professional learning community offered the most promising strategy for sustained, substantive school improvement. We needed to focus on the meaning and implications of the three central words—*professional, learning,* and *community*.

Rather than simply use the term *learning community*, we decided to purposefully focus on the underlying meaning of the word *professional.* There is an expectation that a member of a profession seeks and utilizes the latest and best practices of his or her craft. In fact, failure to do so can become grounds for malpractice. It is not enough that a member of a profession has advanced training in a specialized field; the expectation is that he or she remain current in the field's evolving knowledge base (DuFour & Eaker, 1998).

At first glance, the implications of the word *learning* within the context of a professional learning community might seem obvious; that is, the focus should be on student learning. However, we viewed the word in a much broader and more powerful sense: a school in which everyone, both students and adults, was engaged in *perpetual learning for the purpose of continuous improvement.* This is a powerful idea since it implies that the core purpose of a school is to enhance the performance levels of students by enhancing the performance levels of adults—continuously!

Such a sharp focus on continuous learning cannot be accomplished in a school that relies on and is organized around the work of individuals—hence the word *community*. We realized that a dependence on individuals is not a sufficient structure or culture for a school that values the continuous learning of both students and adults. Schools—and society in general—had simply become too complex. Early in *Professional Learning Communities at Work* (DuFour & Eaker, 1998), we wrote that in a professional learning community, "educators create an environment that fosters mutual cooperation, emotional support, and personal growth as they work together to achieve what they cannot accomplish alone" (p. xii).

In the 2000s, the use of the term *professional learning community* spread to the point of practically losing all meaning. Increasingly, schools across North America were referring to themselves as PLCs, although their practices were wildly divergent and, in many cases, reflected little evidence of change. In 2006, we provided even sharper clarity for the term by defining a *professional learning community* as:

> Educators committed to working collaboratively in ongoing processes of collective inquiry and action research to achieve better results for the students they serve. Professional learning communities operate under the assumption that the key to improved learning for students is continuous, job-embedded learning for educators. (DuFour, DuFour, Eaker, & Many, 2006, p. 217; DuFour et al., 2016)

Enhancing the clarity regarding what a professional learning community is and, equally important, what it is not, has been an ongoing challenge. In an effort to provide clarity to the terms associated with the practices that are commonly found within a school that functions as a professional learning community, we developed a glossary of key terms and concepts as part of *Learning by Doing: A Handbook for Professional Learning Communities at Work* (DuFour et al., 2006).

In our writing and our work, we have emphasized the importance of leaders working to ensure a common vocabulary and a common understanding of the term *professional learning community* and the associated concepts and practices.

Characteristics of a School That Functions as a Professional Learning Community at Work

Recognizing the validity of Michael Fullan's (2005) observation that "terms travel easily . . . but the meaning of the underlying concepts does not" (p. 67), it became obvious that providing sharp definitions would not be enough. What would actually occur in schools that function as high-performing PLCs? What would such schools do differently from their more traditional counterparts? What are their basic characteristics?

In our initial discussions and earliest drafts, Rick and I realized that describing the characteristics of a professional learning community—adding specificity to the idea of a school functioning as a PLC—would need to be one of our first tasks. And we realized we needed to synthesize the writing, research, and practices of educational organizations, as well as those outside of our profession, if we were to paint a clear picture.

After much reading, thinking, discussing, and drafting, we described the following characteristics of a PLC (DuFour & Eaker, 1998).

1. **Shared mission, vision, and values:** We had been impressed with Warren Bennis and Burt Nanus's (1985) book, *Leaders: Strategies for Taking Charge.* We realized if a school was to function as a true professional learning community, leaders must build a solid foundation based on a common purpose and a shared sense of values.

2. **Collective inquiry:** We also recognized that it is impossible to be a learning community without an emphasis on

inquiry. A professional learning community differs from a group of curious individuals in its focused inquiry into best practices as a collective endeavor. In a school that functions as a professional learning community, the purpose of seeking new knowledge is clear—to improve student learning—and it's recognized that inquiry is enhanced when undertaken as a collaborative effort.

3. **Collaborative teams:** The idea of collaboration certainly wasn't a new idea. On the other hand, experience had taught us that collaboration was often simply for the sake of collaboration and often lacked a clear purpose. Equally important, we had learned that collaboration by invitation would not work. We proposed that the basic organizational structure of a school that functions as a professional learning community must be centered on the use of collaborative teams—teams of teachers who teach the same or similar content. Experience had also taught us that teams often lack a clear direction regarding what to do and a clear sense of *why*. In a professional learning community, teams engage in collaborative learning in order to improve student learning within a culture of continuous improvement.

4. **Action orientation and experimentation:** We wanted to communicate that high-performing PLCs reflect an action culture. We wrote that members of a professional learning community work collaboratively to "turn aspirations into action and visions into reality" (DuFour & Eaker, 1998, p. 27). This idea resonated so strongly with us that we would title one of our later books *Learning by Doing* (DuFour et al., 2006). For me, I think the pragmatic standard of "Does it have a positive effect on student learning? Does it help move us to the school we are seeking to become?" was grounded in my days of developing and promoting the consumer-validation process described previously. Palimpsest again!

For us, an action-orientated culture implied more than mere inquiry. It meant creating a culture that reflected a willingness to experiment, develop, and test new hypotheses—a culture in which experimentation was simply the way of doing things.

5. **Continuous improvement:** For us, the strand that ran through these characteristics was the idea that functioning as a professional learning community was not viewed as a series of tasks to be accomplished, but rather, as a way of doing the work to get better day in and day out: a journey that never ended.

6. **Results orientation:** Members of a professional learning community—whether an individual teacher, a team of teachers, or administrators and support staff—are obsessed with results. The questions that drive a professional learning community are, "Are the students learning?" "How do we know?" and "Are we moving toward the school we are seeking to become?" We felt Peter M. Senge (1996) summed up the importance of creating a results-oriented culture when he wrote, "The rationale for any strategy for building a learning organization revolves around the premise that such organizations will produce dramatically improved results" (p. 44).

Since the publication of *Professional Learning Communities at Work* (DuFour & Eaker, 1998), I have observed that some educators do not grasp the interconnectedness of these characteristics. Successful implementation of one characteristic requires *all* the others. Choosing to focus on only some of the characteristics will not work. Successfully becoming a PLC requires nothing short of a major cultural makeover of virtually every aspect of a school.

When Rick and I were framing the main ideas for *Professional Learning Communities at Work* (DuFour & Eaker, 1998), we knew that simply articulating the characteristics of a high-performing professional learning community, in and of themselves, would not be enough. We realized that for a school to successfully become a professional learning community, structural changes alone would not be sufficient. As a result, we began to focus our thinking and our early drafts on the issues related to school culture and the change process itself.

The Change Leader

As virtually every study of effective schools has shown, strong successful leadership is a prerequisite. While there is certainly no shortage of advocates calling for more effective educational leadership, a clear and consistent picture of what such leadership entails is harder to come by. However, one aspect of becoming a PLC is clear: school leaders must *successfully lead the change process*. Perhaps the greatest barrier to becoming a PLC is that while there may be widespread agreement, and even enthusiasm, regarding PLCs as a *concept*, there will often be deeper opposition to real change. This conflict has resulted in many schools proclaiming that they are PLCs while reflecting few, if any, of the structural and cultural changes embedded in the Professional Learning Communities at Work process.

The most basic reason for such a disconnect is obvious: change is hard! It is hard for us as individuals and even more so as a group, especially within an organization as complex as a school. Successfully leading change efforts requires exceptional leadership, passion, and persistence. If a leader seeks to successfully reculture a school into a PLC and, at the same time, seeks to be universally loved, that leader is likely to experience disappointment. Conflict is sure to rear its ugly head. In fact, we wrote that "the absence of conflict, particularly in the early stages of change, suggests that the initiatives are superficial rather than substantial" (DuFour & Eaker, 1998, p. 50). After some three decades as an administrator in a wide variety of roles,

I've learned the issue facing those in leadership positions is not how to avoid conflict, but rather, how to deal with it and embrace it as simply part of the change process.

If the change process is difficult and conflict is inevitable, how can leaders transform school culture? We decided a sense of urgency was important—but not a sense of panic. We believed that it was possible to create a sense of urgency around an inspiring sense of purpose and view of the future! (We only had to reflect on Martin Luther King Jr.'s 1963 "I Have a Dream" speech to understand the power of articulating an inspiring future that is better than what currently exists.) We believed that the concept and practices of a PLC could provide a compelling vision of the future of America's schools and what they should and could become.

Cultural Shifts

While Rick and I certainly believed in the power of the PLC concept to reshape public schools, we also realized we would need to be specific describing the cultural shifts that would be required. We began to see the move from traditional school cultures to the culture of a PLC in three major shifts (which came to be known as the three big ideas of PLCs at Work).

From a Primary Focus on Teaching to a Focus on Learning

The first big idea of a *learning* community is a clear declaration that the fundamental purpose of schools is student learning, and student learning is enhanced by adult learning. At first glance, this idea might seem to be mere semantics. On deeper reflection, however, it becomes clear that if schools had a sharp focus on the learning of both students and adults, they would behave in fundamentally different ways and ask fundamentally different questions.

As Rick and I were writing our first draft of *Professional Learning Communities at Work*, we were continuing our work with assisting schools in their improvement efforts. We would frequently ask groups, "What is the fundamental purpose of schools? Why do schools exist?" It was not unusual to hear responses such as, "Schools are a place where students go to be taught," or "Schools are a place where teachers go to teach." Obviously, both teaching and learning happen within schools, but the fundamental difference is this: teaching is a means to an end, and the end is student learning. While teaching is the primary way through which students learn, it is not the fundamental reason schools exist.

One only has to reflect on our experience with our own children. Remember when they were small and would come home from kindergarten or perhaps the first or second grades? We did not give them a hug and ask, "What were you taught today?" or "How were you taught today?" Instead, we asked, "What did you *learn* today?"

Many, if not most, reform efforts—especially those initiated by state governments—have been focused on teachers and how they teach. For example, many states require administrators to observe classroom teachers and rate teachers' teaching against a checklist of effective teaching practices. I think this approach to improving student performance is widespread simply because it seems like such an obvious thing to do. After all, if the research on effective teaching tells us that certain teaching behaviors are more effective than others, wouldn't it make sense to synthesize these behaviors into a checklist and then use multiple teacher observations throughout the school year, each time rating teacher performance against the predetermined list of effective teaching behaviors? The assumption is that such a system will significantly improve student achievement. But what do the results actually show? Marginal, if any, widespread improvement.

Given my background in the teacher effects research, I was not surprised. Two things that most of the researchers who had seriously spent considerable time on this topic agreed on were: (1) there is no single way teachers should teach, and (2) the teaching effectiveness research findings should not be turned into a checklist for the purpose of teacher evaluation.

Remember, too, that Rick and I had spent years working with the clinical supervision process, the core of which involved classroom observations. Our experience informed us that while administrators should frequently be in classrooms, by and large, the more formal observations that involved a generic checklist were of little benefit. On more than one occasion, Rick would remind me—and groups he was speaking to—that his background was that of a high school history teacher, yet as principal he was expected to observe science teachers, English teachers, foreign language teachers, physical education teachers, as well as others. He thought it was crazy that he was expected to formally observe and evaluate an advanced placement chemistry teacher or a French III teacher who conducted the entire class in French.

We also reflected on the amount of time required by the multiple observations of every teacher expected by some states. The result is that principals and assistant principals spend a large portion of the school year making sure they finish their observations. The goal becomes simply to "get 'er done." We thought it would make much more sense for administrators to spend *quality* time with teacher teams, asking such questions as, "Are the kids learning, and how do you know? What are the biggest challenges you are facing as a team or an individual teacher? What do you need from me—how can I help?" We believed stretching the aspirations and performance levels of teams by focusing on questions related to student learning was an important way to stretch the aspirations and performance levels of students.

Practices that reinforce a focus on teaching rather than on learning are almost always the result of good intentions. Take, for example, the standards movement. The idea of standards regarding what students should know makes sense. However, the large number of standards coupled with ever-increasing expectations for enhanced rigor create a challenge for teachers. Additionally, many of the standards are broad and vague, and since state testing usually occurs in April, the school year has, in reality, been shortened. This environment puts great pressure on teachers to simply get all of the standards they are expected to teach *covered*—not necessarily *learned* but taught!

These conditions led us to conclude that the first big idea of a learning community must be a shift from a school culture that views successful teachers as those who use correct teaching methodologies and teach all of the expected standards to a culture that views successful teachers as those who ensure high levels of learning for all students—skill by skill, name by name. Again, we believed such a shift from a focus on teaching to a focus on learning would represent a major cultural change for schools and require fundamentally different practices.

The question that would drive leaders in a PLC would then be, What decisions, practices, and procedures are necessary to ensure high levels of learning for all students?—not, What teaching methodologies are you using in your instructional practices? Did you cover all of the standards?

From a Culture of Teacher Isolation to a Culture of Collaborative Teams

As we began to brainstorm the main ideas that would ultimately form the framework for *Professional Learning Communities at Work* (DuFour & Eaker, 1998), we recognized that teachers were not only being expected to teach more standards, at a higher level of rigor, in less time, with less support for public schools than ever before, they were being expected to do this in a culture of increased teacher accountability. And, most importantly, teachers were expected to achieve results by themselves. Simply put, we believed—and the evidence was clear—such school cultures were a recipe for failure. Little wonder that a significant number of new teachers will leave the profession within their first five years. They simply succumbed to despair.

We concluded that for schools to successfully ensure high levels of learning for all students by focusing on the learning of each student, skill by skill, a second major shift in school culture must occur—a shift from a reliance on the individual teacher to a focus on the work of collaborative teams. In our thinking, teacher teams are the engine that drives a PLC.

The idea of organizations utilizing collaborative teaming was certainly not new. When I was in the United States Marine Corps, I, along with my fellow marines, were reminded time and again that the marine rifle squad—twelve marines who worked together to accomplish their mission—was the backbone of the corps, and nothing could be worse than letting your fellow team members down. In more recent years, we had become very much aware of Deming's emphasis on the use of teaming in the world of business.

We started our work on *Professional Learning Communities at Work* in 1996. Two years prior, we had been impressed with *The Fifth Discipline: The Art and Practice of the Learning Organization* (Senge, 1990). Peter Senge (1990) contends that "history has brought us to a moment where teams are recognized as a critical component of every enterprise—the predominant unit for decision making and getting things done" (p. 354). As we reflected on this statement, we recognized that to be more exact, the sentence should have ended with "except in America's public schools, where reliance on the individual teacher remains the primary organizing principle."

Of course, others called for schools to capture and use the power of teaming. Authors Gifford Pinchot and Elizabeth Pinchot (1993) refer to collaborative teams as "the basic building block of the intelligent organization" (p. 66). Robert Dilworth (1995) proclaims teams were "the essence of a learning organization" (p. 252). Still others, such as Linda Darling-Hammond (1996) and Newmann et al. (1996), identify collaborative teaming as an important element in successful efforts to improve schools (DuFour & Eaker, 1998).

The efficacy of shifting school structures and cultures to that one that emphasized collaborative teaming seemed to be beyond debate. The scholarship was clear; what was missing was the *how*. We believed the Professional Learning Communities at Work process could be a valuable tool for practitioners who struggled with questions such as, How do we organize into teams? What should teacher teams do? and How can the work of teams best be monitored, supported, improved, and celebrated?

Addressing questions and issues such as those associated with collaborative teaming was a perfect way for us to demonstrate our belief in the merger of scholarship and practice. In many ways, Adlai Stevenson High School—where Rick was principal and receiving increasing national recognition—served as a laboratory for our thinking. But our ideas weren't limited to what we were reading or what Rick was implementing at Stevenson. We also had the benefit of our work with dozens of schools and school districts across North America throughout the previous twenty years. Based on our experience, we knew that in order to become high-performing PLCs, schools would need to embrace the cultural shift from relying on individuals to using collaborative teams.

From Good Intentions to a Focus on Results

If schools were to successfully function as PLCs, we felt they must reflect a shift in school culture from a focus on good intentions to a focus on results—improved student learning. Hope is not a substitute for substance, and good intentions, however strongly held, are not the same as results.

As Rick and I wrote, I would fly to Chicago and spend a day or so with him, usually working at Stevenson High School, or he would fly to Nashville, and we would drive over to the lobby of the Opryland Hotel. On other occasions, he would drive down to my home in Murfreesboro and spend a couple of days there. This is only relevant to the writing of the book in that our most productive times were not spent actually writing but in conversations that were part of our normal times together.

As we explored the need to shift school cultures from good intentions to a results orientation, I distinctly recall how we reflected on our own experiences as teachers. We talked about how schools were very good at proclaiming broad, motivational beliefs. For example, it was not unusual to read mission statements, banners, or slogans such as "[Generic High School]: Where Every Kid Is Special!" or "Preparing Students for the 21st Century!" or statements such as "Where All Students Can Learn," "A Focus on the Whole Child," or "Helping Students Reach Their Full Potential."

As teachers, we had served on many committees charged with developing a mission statement, usually in preparation for an accreditation visit. In fact, we believed such experiences were so common that it would be possible for a group of teachers to quickly craft a generic, universal, all-purpose mission statement that would suffice for all schools!

The point is this: we believed the vast majority of educators had good intentions for their schools and the welfare of their students. But we also felt that in most schools, there was little focus on the crucial questions of, Regarding improving student learning, how are we doing? What evidence do we have that more of our students are learning at higher levels? We recognized that we must first ensure more students—and adults—were learning more before we could fulfill a school's purpose of high levels of learning for all students.

Student and Adult Learning

Effective leaders possess a results orientation. They realize that planning and hard work are meaningless unless they lead to results. This is why educational leaders clarify and emphasize that a school's core purpose is learning. Unless everyone is clear on why the school exists in the first place, adult work will probably focus on the wrong things or on a multitude of things (hence, no focus at all). Effective leaders create a sharp focus on a school's core purpose by monitoring the learning of each student—and teams of adults—in a frequent and timely manner. In a PLC, this is attained through the use of formative assessments at every level.

I mentioned earlier that after high school, I attended Mississippi State University on a band scholarship. As this was a large Southeastern Conference university, the band performed at halftime during football games in huge stadiums, often on national television. The band director, Dr. West, did not wait until after the halftime performance to assess how we, as band members, performed. Certainly, such summative assessments occurred and were important, but his *primary* emphasis was monitoring our performance as we prepared for the halftime performance. In other words, he placed his emphasis on checking along the way, in order to ensure positive results.

The same can be said of successful coaches and leaders of all types of organizations. And the same is true of each of us in our personal lives. The fact is, people check on and pay attention to the things they care about the most. School leaders regularly communicate what they value the most by what they check on. If school leaders proclaim their fundamental purpose to be ensuring high levels of learning for all students, doesn't it make sense that leaders pay attention to the learning of each student, skill by skill, prior to summative assessments? What leaders pay attention to has a much more powerful impact on those within the school or school district than simply what is said.

The Use of Formative Assessments

Leaders of high-performing PLCs develop a results-oriented culture by utilizing the power of formative assessments to monitor student learning (and the work of adults) to drive continuous improvement. It is impossible to develop a results-oriented culture absent formatively assessing student learning on a frequent and timely basis. This use of formative assessments is embedded at all levels: from within individual classrooms to the top levels of decision making.

Numerous researchers have pointed to the power of students learning how to monitor their own learning—both individually and as part of a cooperative learning group. Of course, helping students develop self-assessment skills requires an organized classroom culture that emphasizes the use of such tools as student portfolios and team-developed *I can* statements that are directly linked to specific learning targets and essential learning outcomes. In turn, such a classroom culture requires teachers who have the skills to organize classroom routines and activities that support student self-assessment.

Of course, formative assessments aren't limited to student self-assessment. Members of a PLC capture the power of formative assessments by engaging teacher teams in developing, using, and analyzing the results of collaboratively developed common formative assessments. The use of common formative assessments that are linked directly to a guaranteed and viable curriculum and to a systematic school plan for providing additional time, support, or extension of student learning is perhaps the most powerful tool teacher teams can use to enhance student learning. The use of common formative assessments drives the work and decision making of teacher teams in a high-performing PLC.

District leaders should also use formative assessment strategies. Effective schools, districts, teacher teams, and individual teachers should constantly be using the results of formative assessments in order to monitor and adjust within the school year, rather than relying solely on the results of high-stakes summative assessments once a year. District and school leaders must model what they expect of others. If teacher teams are expected to develop and use formative assessment strategies, they should see the results of formative assessments being routinely used for decision making on a frequent and timely basis throughout the district.

Leaders also monitor goal attainment of adults on a formative basis. They check along the way to see how things are going, which teams need assistance, and which goals need to be adjusted due to unforeseen difficulties. In short, effective leaders monitor the products and tasks of adults during the journey, rather than wait to see if they show up at the end. Want to know what leaders truly value? See what they are checking on, inquiring about, and supporting.

It became increasingly clear that these three cultural shifts—from a focus on teaching to a focus on learning, from teacher isolation to collaborative teams, from a culture of good intentions to a sharp focus on results—would form the basic framework of our views on the cultural shifts necessary if schools were to function as high-performing PLCs.

A Summing Up

When Rick DuFour and I began thinking seriously about what schools would look like—what they would *actually do*—if they functioned as high-performing PLCs, we saw the issue as primarily one of changing school culture. We knew that the structure of schools would have to change, but we also agreed with Seymour B. Sarason (1996):

> To put it as succinctly as possible, if you want to change and improve the climate and outcomes of schooling both for students and teachers, there are features of the school culture that have to be changed, and if they are not changed, your well-intentioned efforts will be defeated. (p. 340)

We recognized that changing school culture—the assumptions, beliefs, and habits that constitute the norms of a school—is inherently difficult. Even so, it is the cultural norms of schools that shape how administrators, teachers, students, support staff, and parents think, feel, and act.

Because changing organizational culture is a complex, messy, and challenging task, most school improvement efforts have relied mostly on structural changes. The fact is, structural change is much easier than cultural change. This explains to a great degree why leaders most frequently turn to structural changes as the framework for improvement efforts.

School improvement reforms of the decades just prior to our writing *Professional Learning Communities at Work* (DuFour & Eaker, 1998) were based on the belief that structural changes in schools would drive cultural change. There is little or no evidence that the top-down high-accountability structural changes of No Child Left Behind (2002) or the more bottom-up structural changes of the site-based management approaches had any significant impact on the day-to-day culture of most schools. Visitors to schools in 1988 would witness essentially the same school cultures in 1998. Rick and I came to believe that this thinking must be reversed. We saw fundamental cultural changes as the primary impetus for driving structural changes in schools.

We weren't alone in our belief that cultural change should drive structural change—that by itself structural change was seldom, if ever, enough. Fullan (1993) had written, "Reculturing leads to restructuring more effectively than the reverse. In most restructuring reforms new structures are expected to result in new behaviors and cultures, but mostly fail to do so" (p. 147).

We also realized that while most everyone understood that school culture was important, there was little agreement about the

characteristics of effective school culture and even less agreement
on how school leaders could embed the requisite concepts and
practices into the day-to-day life of a school or district. While the
research findings of the effective schools movement had provided
valuable insights into the characteristics of an effective school, we
felt the impact of the effective schools research could be enhanced
if the research findings were extended through the cultural changes
inherent in the PLC concept. In *On Common Ground: The Power of
Professional Learning Communities*, Lezotte (2005), the widely recognized leader of the effective schools movement, noted:

> The concept of the professional learning community was
> not part of the school improvement lexicon when the
> Effective Schools journey began. It would have been eas-
> ier and more efficient to engage schools in the conversa-
> tions around the research if it had been. (p. 190)

We realized we would have to move beyond a call for cultural
change and articulate specific cultural shifts that would drive systemic school improvement. We found the framework for cultural
change within the words *professional, learning,* and *community.* These
three words formed the foundation for the Professional Learning
Communities at Work process. I am proud to say a sharp focus on
these three words, and their implications for practice, has remained
constant as the Professional Learning Communities at Work process
has become a national, and increasingly international, approach for
meaningful and effective school improvement.

The cultural shift from a focus on teaching to a focus on *learning* causes educators to question their basic beliefs about the core
purpose of schools. The question is simply this: are schools a place
where students go to be taught or a place where students go to learn?
While this might seem like a false dichotomy to many, for school
improvement efforts to have any hope of success, schools need
to make the cultural shift from sorting and selecting—which has

characterized schools from our nation's founding—to ensuring high levels of learning for all.

This shift requires another foundational cultural change: moving from a culture of teacher isolation to one of teacher collaboration, of *community*. The problem, as we saw it, was that most educators felt a culture of collaboration already existed within their schools. The mistaken belief that communication is the same as collaboration was prevalent. But as Rick was fond of saying, "There is a huge difference between *co-blabbering* and *co-laboring*." We felt the answer could be found in the use of collaborative teams as the cultural engine that would drive the work of a learning community.

Equally important, we felt schools must move from a culture of averaging opinions to a culture of seeking and utilizing best practices. We referred to this shift as embedding a culture of collective inquiry and a focus on results. We believed this shift went right to the heart of what it means to be a *professional* educator, a licensed practitioner. At the most basic level, we realized that simply because the majority of educators within a school want to engage in a particular practice doesn't make that a best practice. It simply means most people agree.

Focusing on school culture does not mean ignoring school structure. Changing the culture of a school doesn't lessen the importance of a school's policies, procedures, rules, relationships, and schedules. In *Professional Learning Communities at Work* (DuFour & Eaker, 1998), we tried to put both school culture and school structure in proper perspective. We contended that a PLC would be attentive to both school culture and school structure. One would not substitute for the other.

And we knew that cultural change would need constant attention. Creating a school culture reflective of a high-performing PLC requires hard work and attention. We concurred with Champy (1995), who had written, "Only a very strong, constantly cultivated

culture can prevent the weeds of mistrust, disrespect, and uncoop-
erativeness from taking over the garden" (p. 84). In other words,
shaping school culture was not a task to be completed but, rather,
an ongoing commitment (DuFour & Eaker, 1998).

Finally, as we began to form the Professional Learning Communities at Work process, we knew success would depend to a great
degree on specificity. In this regard, we detailed our strategies for
shaping school culture. They included (DuFour & Eaker, 1998):

> › Articulating, modeling, promoting, and protecting the
>   shared values and commitments that were collaboratively
>   identified

> › Systematically engaging staff in reflective dialogue that
>   asks them to search for discrepancies between the values
>   and commitments they have endorsed and the day-to-day
>   operation of the school

> › Inundating staff with stories that reflect the culture of a
>   Professional Learning Community at Work

> › Celebrating examples of shared values and commitments,
>   as well as progress in the improvement process, with
>   ceremonies and rituals (The link between the behavior that
>   is being celebrated and the specific value or commitment
>   that is being promoted must be clear and explicit, and it
>   should be everyone's job to identify individuals—both
>   adults and students—and teams that warrant special
>   recognition. Importantly, the strategies for recognition
>   and celebration should ensure lots of winners and occur
>   frequently, so that everyone in the school setting feels he
>   or she can be recognized for positive contributions to the
>   improvement process.)

Recognizing the importance of changing school culture is more than the affirmation of an idea; it is a call to action. At the most basic level, Rick DuFour and I viewed ourselves as research-based practitioners and the Professional Learning Communities at Work process as a road map for improving the academic achievement of all students.

CHAPTER 7

The Implementation
of Professional Learning
Communities at Work
Concepts and Practices

Afte the publication of *Professional Learning Communities at Work* (DuFour & Eaker, 1998), Rick and I continued working with schools and school districts in their efforts to improve student achievement. And with the addition of Becky DuFour to our team in 2002, we continued to write. The focus of our writing centered primarily on sharpening the case for schools functioning as PLCs.

We published *Getting Started: Reculturing Schools to Become Professional Learning Communities* (Eaker, DuFour, & DuFour, 2002), in which we further elaborated on the shifts required for moving from more traditional school cultures to school cultures reflective of a PLC. In *Whatever It Takes: How Professional Learning Communities Respond When Kids Don't Learn* (DuFour, DuFour, Eaker, & Karhanek, 2004), we joined with Gayle Karhanek to describe how successful PLCs can provide systems of focused and timely additional time and support for students who are experiencing difficulty in their learning. And, as editors, we developed *On Common Ground: The Power of Professional Learning Communities* (DuFour, Eaker, & DuFour, 2005), in which nine leading authorities on education joined us in making the case for schools functioning as PLCs.

However, as we were assisting school districts and continuing our writing, it became increasingly clear to us that the vast majority of educators did not need to be convinced of the efficacy of the PLC concept. After all, there is nothing in the idea of schools functioning as PLCs that is controversial or requires a commitment to large sums of money and other resources. We felt the case had been sufficiently made—not only by us, but also by many others—and the need had shifted from the *what* (a clear definition) and the *why* (the research supporting PLCs and the failure of past reform efforts) to the *how* (how to embed PLC concepts and practices in the day-to-day world of schools).

Our primary effort in this regard was to join with our friend and colleague Tom Many in writing *Learning by Doing: A Handbook for Professional Learning Communities at Work* (DuFour et al., 2006). Through three editions, *Learning by Doing* (DuFour et al., 2006, 2010; DuFour, DuFour, Eaker, Many, & Mattos, 2016) has been our implementation guide for school leaders seeking to reculture their schools into high-performing PLCs.

We argued that in order to reculture schools into PLCs and create a culture of continuous improvement, leaders simply needed to get started—to *do* the work of seeking and implementing best practices. In other words, we made the case that the most effective tool for adult learning was learning by doing, rather than the more traditional approaches of in-service training, college courses, book studies, and the like.

We had increasingly observed that many educators expressed strong support for the PLC concept but then failed to implement the associated practices. It was as if they believed *agreeing* and *taking action* were synonymous. We were struck by this problem: why don't schools do what they know—and say—makes sense?

In addressing this question, we were heavily influenced by *The Knowing-Doing Gap: How Smart Companies Turn Knowledge Into Action*, in which Jeffrey Pfeffer and Robert I. Sutton (2000) write about what they regarded as one of the great mysteries of organizational management: the disconnect between knowledge and action. They explore the question, "Why does knowledge of what needs to be done so frequently fail to result in action or behavior that is consistent with that knowledge?" (Pfeffer & Sutton, 2000, p. 4).

One of our primary goals for writing *Learning by Doing* (DuFour et al., 2006) was to help school leaders address the knowing-doing gap by describing purposeful, research-based practices that would move schools toward functioning as PLCs and, by doing so, help all students achieve at higher levels. I've found the following suggestions are beneficial to those who embark on the journey to become a PLC.

Getting Started and Getting Better

How should school leaders think about getting started on the journey to becoming a PLC? Doug Reeves and I, in *100-Day Leaders: Turning Short-Term Wins Into Long-Term Success in Schools* (Reeves & Eaker, 2019), make the case that leaders should begin by looking within themselves. In *Insight: Why We're Not as Self-Aware as We Think, and How Seeing Ourselves Clearly Helps Us Succeed at Work and in Life*, Tasha Eurich (2017) makes a powerful case that reflection and self-knowledge are at the core of what effective leaders must do.

Before leading others, leaders must examine their own beliefs, assumptions, and behaviors and think through the journey that lies ahead. What resources will we need on this journey? What are the key stops along the way? What potential hazards lie ahead, and how can they be overcome? How will I support those I am leading? These are but a few of the questions effective leaders must explore as they prepare.

Developing a Common Understanding and a Common Vocabulary

Reculturing schools to function as PLCs is a complex undertaking, a long and difficult journey, that requires fundamental incremental changes. While more than one route might be taken to arrive at the final destination, some things must be in place prior to departure. Following are a few actions leaders can take that will increase the likelihood of success—or at least make the journey smoother.

Develop a Small Guiding Coalition of Key Staff Members Who Will Help During the Early Stages of the Journey

It is unreasonable to think that one leader, regardless of how strong he or she might be, can reculture an entire school or district single-handedly. In *The Myth of the Strong Leader*, Oxford professor Archie Brown (2014) challenges the widespread belief that strong leaders who go it alone, overcoming all obstacles, are the most successful. In each edition of *Learning by Doing* (DuFour et al., 2006, 2010, 2016), we have stressed the importance of leaders identifying key staff members who will join in deep learning about PLCs and share the lead in bringing others along on the journey.

Develop a Plan for Building Shared Knowledge and a Common Vocabulary

Enhancing learning as part of the PLC process begins with enhancing adult learning. It's unrealistic to expect all the adults within a school or district to learn everything at once, so leaders and the guiding coalition must have a plan to build their knowledge base about high-performing PLCs.

Leaders must also plan for developing a common vocabulary of terms that will be used throughout the journey. (Visit **go.SolutionTree.com /PLCbooks** for a free, shareable online glossary.) Leaders have to be at least as knowledgeable as the people they are trying to influence.

Identify and Provide the Resources That Will Be Required for the Journey

During the early stages when it is critical for everyone to develop a common understanding of PLC concepts and practices, I have found certain resources to be essential.

> › *Learning by Doing* (DuFour et al., 2016): If becoming a PLC is a journey, I like to think of *Learning by Doing* as a leader's guidebook. Each chapter represents a stop on the journey and is organized around essential topics, including a case study, a section that describes how issues within the case study could have been handled more effectively, a *why* section that highlights the research base supporting the practices presented in each chapter, a tool to assess one's place on the journey, questions to guide the work that must be addressed at each stop, and dangerous detours and seductive shortcuts that those who undertake the journey are likely to encounter.

> › *The Power of Professional Learning Communities at Work* (DuFour, Eaker, & DuFour, 2007): This video series highlights the work of teams engaged in practices representative of a school that functions as a PLC. The series was filmed in eight diverse schools and features unscripted scenes of teams at work. The video is organized around the three big ideas of the Professional Learning Communities at Work process—a focus on learning, collaborative teaming, and a focus on results—and is accompanied by a presenter's guide.

> › *The Journey to Becoming a Professional Learning Community* (banner and booklet; Keating, Eaker, DuFour, & DuFour, 2008): This resource is particularly helpful as a visual aid depicting the journey to becoming a PLC and highlights the essential stops along the way. The heavy vinyl banner, which is approximately seven feet

long and two and a half feet wide, was the brainchild of
Janel Keating, our friend and colleague. In her role of
leading the implementation of PLC concepts and practices
districtwide, she realized that for many, it was difficult to
see how different tasks and activities are interconnected.
The resulting banner comes with two additional paper
banners on which to write the tasks that are being
undertaken at each key point along the way. The banners
also come with a short booklet with helpful hints for using
the resource.

> **PLC at Work Institutes:** I highly recommend that
  leaders arrange for key people within the school or
  district to attend a PLC at Work Institute. The institutes
  are especially helpful for providing a guiding coalition
  with a deeper insight into what it means to function as a
  PLC and with expert guidance for implementation. The
  institutes are staffed by experienced practitioners who have
  successfully led the implementation of the PLC process in
  their own school or district. Institutes are held across the
  United States and, increasingly, worldwide. An alternative
  is a Streaming Solution, in which a regularly scheduled
  institute is streamed live to schools or available sites. These
  events can be in real time or broadcasted at a later date. In
  either case, Solution Tree associates are on-site to assist.

> **The websites www.allthingsplc.info and www
  .SolutionTree.com:** Everything on the allthingsplc.info
  website is free; nothing is for sale. The website contains
  everything from blogs to research supporting PLC
  practices. Especially helpful is a list of over 150 PLC
  model schools that have significantly improved student
  achievement across all subgroups by implementing
  PLC practices. SolutionTree.com is another source for
  information and a wide range of resources, including

books, videos, institutes, professional development workshops, and the like. I view this site as the home for everything related to the Professional Learning Communities at Work process.

Connecting to the Why and Making the Work Personal

Developing a common understanding of the PLC concept and practices requires more than mere memorization. I've found most successful leaders are able to give the journey meaning by constantly connecting the specific tasks the team is undertaking back to the *why*—and the *why* always goes back to improving learning for all kids. The place to start is not with what needs to change but, rather, with why the school exists in the first place and why undertaking this journey is so important (Collins & Porras, 1994). I've found that educators are ready and willing to work very hard, even in adverse conditions, if they believe that what they are being asked to do will prove beneficial to their students.

Connecting to the why is even more powerful when it is made personal. As the superintendent of the White River School District in Buckley, Washington, Janel Keating is constantly asking, "Would this be good enough for our own children?" I've found that leaders who communicate this standard of care for every decision, every task, every unit, every lesson, and every interaction find the journey to becoming a PLC to be more meaningful for everyone.

Communicating Clearly at Every Step Along the Way

Changing the culture of any organization is difficult, but it is especially difficult in education because there are many diverse constituencies involved: the school board, administrators, faculty, support staff, students, parents, and the broader community. I've learned that when it comes to implementing the Professional Learning Communities at Work process, clear communication begins with the leader's deep understanding of the importance and implications of embedding a culture that is simultaneously *loose* and *tight*. Leaders must clearly communicate there are some things about which the organization will be *tight*, but within this tight framework, creativity and empowerment for decision making are encouraged and supported.

Rick DuFour and I were heavily influenced by *In Search of Excellence* by Thomas J. Peters and Robert H. Waterman Jr. (1982). As they studied some of America's best-run companies to determine what practices they had in common, the authors discovered all of the companies exhibited a culture that was both loose and tight. They wrote, "Organizations that live by the loose-tight principle are on the one hand rigidly controlled, yet at the same time allow (indeed insist on) autonomy, entrepreneurship, and innovation from the rank and file" (Peters & Waterman, 1982, p. 318).

Since both top-down and bottom-up efforts aimed at school culture and outcomes had clearly failed, the idea of and research supporting a simultaneous loose-tight culture made a lot of sense to us. The question became, Tight about what? In *Learning by Doing* (DuFour et al., 2006, 2010, 2016), we highlighted six elements of a PLC about which leaders should be tight—and these must be clearly articulated and connected with the why:

1. Educators work collaboratively rather than in isolation, take collective responsibility for student learning, and clarify the commitments they make to each other about how they will work together.
2. The fundamental structure of the school becomes the collaborative team, in which members work interdependently to achieve common goals for which all members are mutually accountable.
3. The team establishes a guaranteed and viable curriculum, unit by unit, so all students have access to the

same knowledge and skills regardless of the teacher to whom they are assigned.

4. The team develops common formative assessments to frequently gather evidence of student learning.

5. The school has created a system of interventions and extensions to ensure students who struggle receive additional time and support for learning in a way that is timely, directive, diagnostic, and systematic, and students who demonstrate proficiency can extend their learning.

6. The team uses evidence of student learning to inform and improve the individual and collective practice of its members. (DuFour et al., 2016, p. 14)

It's important to remember that people learn what is valued through what leaders monitor tightly and celebrate. The old adage applies: what we do speaks louder than what we say!

Communicating, however, is not the same as communicating *clearly*. I have two suggestions for communicating clearly. First, avoid educational jargon as much as possible. Certainly, most ideas, concepts, and practices associated with the Professional Learning Communities at Work process can be communicated in everyday conversational language. When reading the economist John Kenneth Galbraith's (1981) autobiography, I was struck by his assertion that even a subject as seemingly complex as economics can be communicated without resorting to jargon: "There is no idea associated with the subject that cannot, with sufficient effort, be stated in clear English" (p. 535). I've found the same is true for the field of education, but I've also learned that using plain English requires thoughtful effort and self-discipline.

Second, when communicating key points, communicate in writing. As I mentioned earlier, I have been blessed with many friendships in my life. One longtime friend who had a significant impact on me, both personally and professionally, was Richard Marius. In addition to teaching a popular course on William Faulkner, Richard headed Harvard's Expository Writing Program for eighteen years. When Richard was visiting in Tennessee, we would try our best to have what we jokingly referred to as power breakfasts. What made the breakfasts memorable for me were the long conversations that accompanied them. One particular comment Richard made influenced my own leadership practice, and I frequently share his observation with others who are assuming leadership responsibilities. When discussing why expository writing was such an important part of the Harvard undergraduate curriculum (at that time, expository writing was the only course required of all students), Richard explained, "Writing is the pencil sharpener of the mind."

It is almost impossible to clearly communicate the key concepts and practices associated with the Professional Learning Communities at Work process by relying on verbal communications alone. Janel Keating and I, in *Every School, Every Team, Every Classroom* (Eaker & Keating, 2012), suggest sending emails to everyone within the school or district setting to describe each key step along the journey. (Examples are included in the book's appendix.) As I assist school leaders in the implementation process, I recommend that such emails be organized around the format in figure 7.1.

There's one last point: just because we communicate—even if we communicate frequently, clearly, and in writing—that does not mean everyone understands. Communication occurs only when the message *sent* is the same as the message *received*. Leaders must engage with people at every level to learn the degree to which they understand what the school or district is trying to do and why.

Developing the Cultural Foundation of a Professional Learning Community

It's been my experience that many who undertake the journey to becoming a PLC often choose to engage in some parts of the process and ignore others. One frequently skipped component is the process

From: _____

To: *[The entire school or district community]*

Subject: *[Specify collaborative teaming; a guaranteed and viable curriculum; common formative assessments; a systematic plan for additional time, support, and extension of learning; or other such subject.]*

What do we mean by *[subject]*?

[Provide a short, clear definition of the subject.]

Why is this important for our school or district?

[Include a brief paragraph of the research supporting the use of this practice. Each chapter of Learning by Doing *contains a section titled* Why *to draw from.]*

What have we done so far?

[Share with everyone what has already been done to embed this practice within the school or district. For example, you might write, "After our initial training session, each principal has been directed to organize his or her school into collaborative teams consisting of teachers who teach the same or similar content and to direct each team to develop a draft of their norms regarding how they will work together as a team."]

What are our next steps?

[People need to see how things fit. Such information is particularly helpful when used in conjunction with the PLC journey road map.]

FIGURE 7.1: *Format for communicating clearly in email.*

of developing a solid foundation of shared mission, vision, values, and goals that will support a culture of continuous improvement.

When Rick and I were developing our first drafts of the ideas in *Professional Learning Communities at Work* (DuFour & Eaker, 1998), we had much discussion about why such topics as mission and vision are so often left unaddressed. We concluded it is simply because educators—particularly teachers—have had such bad experiences in the past. Because of their experiences, many, if not most, teachers basically view the process of developing mission and vision statements as meaningless.

Educators are asked to serve on committees to revise a school's mission and vision statements (usually associated with an accreditation visit). After many meetings and much discussion, the new mission and vision statements look very much like the previous statements and rarely, if ever, affect practices within the school in any appreciable way. For most, it seems the goal simply is to have a written mission and vision statement. I believe people's attitudes are primarily influenced by their experiences. If so, it is little wonder that many teachers view revisiting topics such as mission and vision as essentially a waste of time.

As Rick and I began to finalize our outline for *Professional Learning Communities at Work*, I think we both realized that developing a school's philosophical foundation would be a major focus of our efforts. In our earlier book *Fulfilling the Promise of Excellence* (DuFour & Eaker, 1987), we wrote about the fundamental role that a shared vision and values play in school culture and how vision and values can be used in a practical way to improve student learning. In *Professional Learning Communities at Work* (DuFour & Eaker, 1998), we expanded our thinking and determined that mission, vision, values, and goals were the pillars of the foundation of a PLC.

It seemed to us there were two issues related to developing a solid foundation of mission, vision, values, and goals. First, it was necessary to articulate a clear definition and provide a clear explanation of why each pillar of the foundation was important and each interconnected with the others. Second, we felt it was essential to provide insights we had gained from our work in schools about how to make the foundation pieces meaningful and useful.

The Mission of Our School: Why Do We Exist?

While the fundamental purpose of a school might seem obvious to most, in fact, there is less agreement than we might think. Some administrators think school is just a place where students go to be taught. To many, a school's mission is represented by broad, universal statements that are actually useless when it comes to driving behavior. Consider: "The mission of our school is to honor the dignity and worth of all students and assist them to develop their full potential in order to become contributing members of a global society." While few would disagree with the idea that recognizing a child's worth is important, such statements do little to provide direction.

Yet Rick and I recognized the importance of a clear, articulate declaration of a school's fundamental purpose. And we weren't alone in our belief. Collins and Porras (1994) had observed:

> Contrary to popular wisdom, the proper first response to a changing world is *not* to ask, "How should we change?" but rather to ask, "What do we stand for and why do we exist?" This should never change. And *then* feel free to change everything else. Put another way, visionary companies distinguish between their core values and enduring purpose (which should never change) from their operating practices and business strategies (which should be changing constantly in response to an ever-changing world)." (p. xiv)

Earlier I remarked on the fact that our thinking about school improvement was heavily influenced by Newmann and Wehlage. In 1995, Newmann and Wehlage wrote, "There is no point in thinking about changes in structure until the school achieves reasonable consensus about its intellectual mission for children" (p. 195). For us, there was little doubt about the importance of a meaningful, accurate statement of a school's fundamental purpose. The challenge was how to articulate that statement effectively.

My experience has been that leaders spend far too much time on developing a mission statement. After all, the *fundamental* purpose of schools is fairly obvious—to ensure high levels of learning for all students. A school might tinker with this core statement and make it sound a little more exciting. For example, the White River School District has declared "To ensure high levels of learning for all students for success beyond high school" as their core mission, their core purpose.

The issue is not so much the exact wording but the fidelity with which the words are used. Any mission statement will only have an impact to the degree to which it is used in meaningful ways. As Pfeffer and Sutton (2000) remind us, merely clarifying or reaffirming their mission will not improve results. In many schools, developing a mission statement has served as a substitute for meaningful action. Merely drafting a new mission statement does not automatically change how people act. Merely writing a mission statement does nothing to close the knowing-doing gap.

The key is how the mission statement is used. For example, in a results-oriented culture such as a PLC, the obvious question is, Are the kids learning, and how do we know? Monitoring student learning on a frequent and timely basis and using data to drive decision making are the most powerful ways to embed a mission of learning throughout a school or district. In short, ensuring all students are learning, kid by kid, skill by skill, must be at the core of any school's mission.

Our Vision of the Future: What Kind of School or District Do We Hope to Become?

I repeat: a school's mission statement must be *used* in order to have any meaningful impact at all. Perhaps the most important way it can be used is by linking the school's mission to its vision of the future—that is, What must our school become if we are to achieve our core purpose of ensuring high levels of learning for all kids?

As with articulating and reinforcing a school or district's core purpose, the language that is used in sharpening a vision of the future is critical. It's not a good idea to proclaim, "We're going to get a committee together to update our vision statement." Compare an approach such as this with the process that Becky DuFour used when she became principal at Boones Mill Elementary School in Franklin County, Virginia. Becky met individually with every faculty and staff member. During each conversation, she focused on two questions. The first was, "What are the best things about this school?" Notice that Becky opened with the positive aspects of the school's current reality. Second, she asked, "How do you think this school should be significantly different; what would you like to see changed?" The advantage of such language is that it reflects the kind of dialogue that typically occurs in schools, and it leads to answers that are much more specific and realistic.

Any process for articulating a vision of what a school or district seeks to become has to address how it currently exists. In the twenty years that Rick and I worked together assisting schools prior to writing *Professional Learning Communities at Work* (DuFour & Eaker, 1998), we began the process of helping schools describe the school they were seeking to become by asking them to paint a portrait of their school using data.

What would an accurate portrait reveal? An artist selects certain colors; our school portrait selects specific data on, for example, student achievement, student engagement, discipline, survey results, and demographics. (*Learning by Doing* [DuFour et al., 2016) includes a form titled A Data Picture of Our School that contains indicators under each category.)

Engaging in this kind of process sharpens an understanding of the school as it currently exists—in order to then focus on how the school should be significantly different in the future. It is much easier to get from point A to point B if we know where point B is and what it would look like if we saw it. But in many schools, more effort is put into describing point B than having a clear and accurate understanding of point A—the starting point of current reality (DuFour et al., 2008).

Describing the school or district you seek to become should involve more than averaging opinions. A useful vision of the future is the result of *informed* decision making. Rick and I suggested organizing a task force to examine what could be learned from the effective schools research and research from the best-run organizations. In this way, articulating a vision of the future becomes a form of staff development. As I mentioned previously, improving student learning begins with adult learning.

Once the group has a clear picture of the current reality, a sense of how various members of the school or district community would like the school or district to be significantly different, and an understanding of organizational effectiveness, the process of writing can begin. Rick and I found it helpful to start by describing how various aspects of the school culture would look in an excellent school. For example, when Rick led this process at Stevenson High School, they wrote vision statements describing the curriculum, instruction, and assessment; an emphasis on the individual student and equity and access for all; the work within a PLC; a culture of learning; and community engagement. (The vision statement of Adlai Stevenson High School is included in the appendix of *Revisiting Professional Learning Communities at Work* [DuFour et al., 2008].)

Such specificity makes a vision document useful. Stevenson avoided broad statements such as "Our vision is to become a world-class school for the children in our community." When Martin Luther King Jr. proclaimed that he had a dream, he didn't stop there. He *described* his dream, articulating his vision of the future of America.

Many benefits can accrue from a vision statement that describes the school or district's future. Following are three (DuFour & Eaker, 1992).

1. Describing the school you would like to see in the future can be motivational. People generally want things to be better. A shared vision of an ideal future can be compelling. When people collectively develop a shared vision of the future, they become motivated to make the vision a reality.

2. A shared vision that is widely used gives those within the organization a sense of direction. It serves as a direct link to the why—"We are doing these things because they will help move us toward the kind of school we, collectively, envisioned."

3. A collaboratively developed and clearly articulated vision can serve as a call for action. A vision can serve as the first step in developing an agenda for the future.

Excellent organizations are built on a common understanding of where the organization is headed and why various initiatives are being undertaken. Schools are no exception. Before schools can make significant progress on the journey of continuous improvement, they must first develop a clear picture of where the journey is headed—a vision of the future.

Shared Values and Commitments: How Must We Behave to Achieve Our Vision?

I think that most leaders who undertake the journey to becoming a PLC will find that although clarifying a school's core purpose (why it exists) and developing a shared, clearly articulated vision of the future are necessary, by themselves they are insufficient. As I wrote earlier, many, if not most, teachers believe mission and vision statements are useless because they have not seen their impact on the day-to-day life of their school. Addressing the question, How must we behave, both individually and collectively, if we are to achieve our vision of the future? causes educators to shift their focus from more philosophical musings to specific commitments to act in specific ways.

Shared values and commitments can guide the daily work of a school. If everyone knows where the school is headed and why, the need for countless rules and policies is diminished. Educators in a school that has clearly articulated values and shared commitments enjoy much more autonomy, creativity, and empowerment than those who work in a school governed by excessive rules (DuFour et al., 2016).

Clearly defined commitments can also enhance the effectiveness of leaders. Most school leaders depend heavily on authority derived from their position as the ultimate tool for change. While positional power can have an impact on behavior, it is limited, can disappear quickly, and more often than not, lacks inspiration. On the other hand, when a school has agreed on a set of values and commitments that will move the school toward its vision of the future, the leader becomes armed with moral authority: "I expect certain behaviors because, as a school, we made these commitments to each other."

Shared values and commitments serve as the spark that causes us to "start doing" and then "get better"—*continuously*!

A word of caution: clearly communicating a school's core values and commitments requires much more than verbal or even written communication. Many businesses offer a prime example. It's not uncommon for customers to wait in long lines to pay or return a defective item and, at the same time, observe a sign stating the business's commitment to customer service. In short, we determine what is truly valued in any organization—including schools—by what we see people doing much more than by what they proclaim.

I distinctly remember talking with Rick about this. He had taken an early flight from Chicago down to Nashville, and we were spending the day brainstorming and writing at a restaurant in the Opryland Hotel near the airport. As we talked about the disconnect between what leaders say they are committed to doing and what others actually witness them doing, we decided to develop an audit to help illuminate what behaviors communicate. We included the communication audit in *Professional Learning Communities at Work* (DuFour & Eaker, 1998) as well as in many of our other books.

> **What do we plan for?** Planning is the institutionalization of what we value. Planning communicates what has a high priority within the organization. In short, planning sends the message, "This is so important to us that we are making plans to see that it happens."

> **What do we monitor?** It is difficult to convince others that something is important if it is never monitored. As a person who has spent over four decades in higher education, I can attest to this fact. Nowhere is the disconnect between what is professed as a core value and what is actually monitored more evident than at a university that proclaims the importance of excellent teaching but pays far more attention to faculty's publication record.

> **What questions do we ask?** What questions is the organization struggling to answer? Questions communicate priorities and point people in a particular direction:

> > All learning organizations are driven by the persistent questioning of the status quo and by a constant search for a better way to fulfill the organization's purpose more effectively. For schools, the focus of the driving questions must be enhanced student achievement. (DuFour & Eaker, 1998, p. 109)

> **What do we model?** Leaders communicate much more effectively through the behaviors they model than by what they say. John W. Thompson (1995) argues that the modeling behavior of leaders is "the single most powerful mechanism for creating a learning environment" (p. 96).

> **How do we allocate our time?** Another important way by which an organization communicates its core

values is through the allocation of time. The time that is devoted to an issue tells people what is truly valued. Two examples stand out. If a school proclaims it values collaborative teaming, leaders must provide adequate time for meaningful and productive collaboration to occur on a systematic and regular basis within the school day. And if a school proclaims it values the learning of all students, leaders must provide adequate time for students to receive additional time and support within the school day when students struggle with their learning.

> **What do we celebrate?** Just as what gets monitored sends a strong message about what is truly valued, so does what is celebrated. It is common for both students and adults to observe the disconnect between what is proclaimed as a core value and the behaviors that are recognized and celebrated. For example, in many high school cultures, celebrations related to athletics far surpass those for improved learning. Focused, purposeful, and frequent celebrations for stellar examples of a school's core values offer a powerful tool for leaders of professional learning communities.

> **What are we willing to confront?** I've never viewed *confrontation* as a four-letter word. The issue is not "Should leaders confront?" but rather, "What should leaders confront, and how should they go about it?" In order to communicate the core values of a school in an unequivocal way, violations of the school's core values must be confronted. Nothing erodes the credibility of a leader faster than an unwillingness to confront behavior that is incongruent with the core values for which the organization has proclaimed it stands (Burns, 1978).

> **How can we keep it simple?** One of the most overlooked ways to clearly communicate what an organization values is keeping the message simple: "The message of change

must be simplified and amplified. Metaphors, analogies, logos, and examples can present verbal pictures of a change initiative more effectively than pages of text" (DuFour & Eaker, 1998, p. 115).

As with collaboratively developed mission and vision statements, collaboratively developed, widely shared values and commitments can have a positive impact on schools seeking to function as PLCs— if such values and commitments are clearly articulated and used. Shared values that are linked directly to a school's core purpose to ensure high levels of learning for all students and to a school's vision of its future state—if done so with fidelity—produce several benefits.

As we outlined our thoughts about the benefits of shared values and commitments, Rick and I concurred with James M. Kouzes and Barry Z. Posner (1987) in their observation that clarity of organizational values can foster strong feelings of personal loyalty, facilitate consensus about key organizational goals, encourage professional behavior, promote strong norms about working hard and caring, and reduce job tension and stress (DuFour & Eaker, 1998).

Additionally, shared values can reduce the need for excessive rules and policies:

> If members of a school know what they are trying to create and are using the values as guiding principles for their actions and decisions, there is little need for the ubiquitous rule book that is meant to cover all possible situations in a school setting. (DuFour & Eaker, 1998, p. 98)

And perhaps most important, shared values and commitments provide direction. They can move a school focus from articulated aspirations to specific actions. I like to think of the development of shared commitments as an if-then process. *If* the mission and vision of our school reflect an emphasis on the learning of all students, *then* we must all commit to such collective behaviors as a guaranteed and viable curriculum, monitoring the learning of each student skill by skill on a frequent and timely basis, systematically providing additional time and support for students who experience difficulty in their learning, and so forth, within a collaborative culture.

Collaboratively developed commitments provide an internal focus and a more effective system of accountability. They are essential to changing school culture. Shared commitments, if used in meaningful ways, can become the threads that bind individual behavior into a collective and focused whole.

The value statements of Adlai Stevenson High School (those of the school board and administrative team, school faculty, support staff, students, and parents) can be found in the appendix of *Revisiting Professional Learning Communities at Work* (DuFour et al., 2008).

Goals: What Steps Will We Take, and When Will We Take Them?

Of course, everything cannot be done at once. An effective goal-setting process is a powerful tool for setting priorities. Goal setting determines not only what must be done first but also the specific steps that must be taken and a timeline for them.

Ironically, virtually everyone agrees on the importance of setting meaningful goals while simultaneously agreeing that goal setting can be a useless waste of time. I have worked in organizations in which the primary goal of most people was simply to get their goals turned in! I suspect others have had a similar experience.

I emphasized earlier that a PLC relies heavily on a meaningful process of collective inquiry—the collaborative search for best practices. There is a solid body of research that supports effective goal setting. I think Ken Blanchard's (2007) observation is an excellent summary:

> Goal setting is the single most powerful motivational tool in a teacher's toolkit. Why? Because goal setting operates in ways that provide purpose, challenge, and meaning. Goals are the guideposts along the road that make a compelling vision come alive. Goals energize people. (p. 150)

Collaboratively developed goals that are monitored on a frequent and timely basis support a results-oriented culture and create a sense of mutual accountability. As James Champy (1995) observes, "Vision is the rhetoric of inspiration . . . while goals are the rhetoric of accountability" (p. 54). In short, goal setting only has an impact when goals are actually *used* as a tool to drive improvement efforts.

As Rick and I were forming our thinking about effective goal setting for inclusion in *Professional Learning Communities at Work*, it became clear that more specific criteria were required. Ultimately, we wrote that schools that are undertaking the journey to becoming a PLC should establish written goals that are:

- Clearly linked to the vision.
- Limited in number to ensure focus.
- Focused on the desired outcome rather than on the means to achieve the outcome.
- Translated into clear, measurable performance standards.
- Monitored continuously.
- Designed to produce short-term wins.
- Understood and accepted as significant by all parties. (DuFour & Eaker, 1998, p. 102)

In the decade that followed the publication of *Professional Learning Communities at Work* (DuFour & Eaker, 1998), we expanded our knowledge base and experience base regarding effective goal setting. By 2008, when Rick and I, along with Becky DuFour, wrote *Revisiting Professional Learning Communities at Work*, we had settled on the SMART goal acronym (Conzemius & O'Neill, 2005, 2013). We suggested that schools seeking to function as a PLC should set goals that are:

> Strategic and specific
> Measurable
> Achievable
> Results oriented
> Time bound

In 2016, I revisited goal setting with my close friend and colleague Deb Sells in *A New Way: Introducing Higher Education to Professional Learning Communities at Work*. We wrote that while the particulars might vary, in effective goal setting, goals are (Eaker & Sells, 2016):

> › Data driven and collaboratively developed
>
> › Set for both short-term and long-term ends
>
> › Focused on results rather than activities to achieve results
>
> › Limited in number
>
> › Monitored, encouraged, supported, and celebrated

Checking on progress toward goal attainment must occur more frequently than once a year. Monitoring goal attainment on a frequent and timely basis is an important way that leaders listen, learn, and provide ongoing support. As Deb and I write, "Effective leaders use monitoring to send the twin messages of 'This is a high priority for us' and 'How can I help?'" (Eaker & Sells, 2016, p. 111).

The Pillars Together

The pillars (mission, vision, values and commitments, and goals) that form the foundation of a PLC are interconnected, each supporting the others. Leaders of a PLC do not pick and choose the pillars they wish to address; each pillar is essential. When working with schools or school districts, I frequently use the graphic in figure 7.2 to show how the foundational pieces of a PLC are interconnected and how, together, they drive the work that is to come.

Capturing the Power of Collaborative Teaming

Collaborative teams are the primary structural and cultural organizational concept that drives the work within a PLC process. If schools are to significantly enhance the learning levels of all students, they must break free from the traditional culture of teacher isolation and instead rely on high-performing collaborative teams

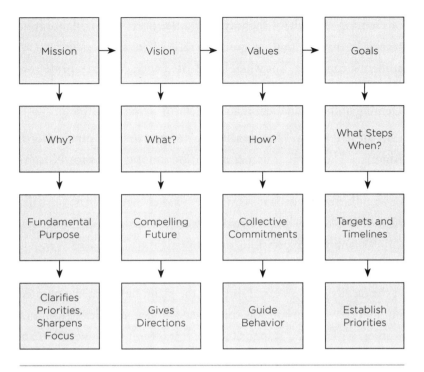

FIGURE 7.2: *The foundational pieces of a PLC interconnect.*

as the central organizing principle and the cultural norm (Eaker & Sells, 2016).

Collaborative teaming is utilized by virtually all organizations throughout the world and has been for decades—with the exception of America's public schools. Most schools are still characterized by a culture of teacher isolation. Teachers are expected to successfully teach more standards at higher levels of rigor in less time with declining resources and support in a culture of increased accountability for student learning by working individually, by themselves. Such structures and cultures are a recipe for failure.

As a young doctoral student at the University of Tennessee, I became familiar with W. Edwards Deming's work and the concepts commonly referred to then as *Japanese management*. Academicians and the American business sector alike were enamored with the ideas of Deming, especially the power of *quality circles*—collaborative teams. In my doctoral program, the idea of quality circles was an academic construct, but when I graduated and accepted a professorship at Middle Tennessee State University, I witnessed the impact of Deming and the Japanese management movement firsthand.

In the late 1970s, Nissan made the decision to build cars in North America. There was much competition among states for Nissan's new automobile plant. Rutherford County, Tennessee, the home of Middle Tennessee State University, was chosen. When construction of the Nissan plant began, I learned that my neighbor Ken Cruckshank was responsible for its oversight.

As construction neared completion, Ken invited me to take a look at the facility. As we walked through the plant, he repeatedly pointed out that the entire plant was constructed around the idea of teams of workers with similar responsibilities. It was built to allow each team to collaboratively analyze the quality of their work as the work was being done. This tour provided me with a firsthand look at Deming's ideas of quality circles and how collaborative teaming was such an integral part of the Japanese management framework.

I remember reading Peter Senge's (1990) *The Fifth Discipline: The Art and Practice of the Learning Organization* and being struck by the emphasis he placed on collaborative teaming. He pointed out that the use of teams was so widely utilized by organizations of all types the world over that it was hardly discussed anymore. I couldn't help but think that he should have added, "Except in America's public schools, where teachers are expected to do an almost impossible job by themselves!"

The Structure of Collaborative Teams

Much thought should be given to how teams are structured. While there is no one right way for teams to be organized and conditions vary from school to school, three broad organizing principles should drive decision making.

First, teacher teams must be composed of teachers who teach the same or similar content. Mathematics teachers need to collaborate with other mathematics teachers, science teachers need to collaborate with other science teachers, and so forth. (This principle holds true for organizing district support staff as well; teams should be composed of staff who engage in the same or similar work.)

Implementing this principle requires flexibility. The key is finding structures that work. Often this means that at times teacher teams meet with different colleagues. For example, twice a month, the entire mathematics department might meet, and during the two remaining weeks, teachers who teach the same courses meet. Leaders must engage faculty in a process that leads to an initial organizing structure for teams but, as the year progresses, be willing to tweak teams and schedules based on feedback from teachers and student performance data.

The structuring of teacher teams presents a particular issue for teachers who are the only ones teaching a subject or course. For example, it is not unusual for an elementary school to have only one music teacher. In our work, we refer to these teachers as *singletons*. Many schools have solved the singleton problem by creating virtual teams using technology. Others have worked with the central office to create times when all the singletons within the district who teach the same course can meet. (For more ideas and options regarding team structures, including singletons, see *Learning by Doing* [DuFour et al., 2016] and the AllThingsPLC website [www.allthingsplc.info].)

Second, teachers must have unencumbered time to meet. I've found that teams need a minimum of one hour per week. It is unreasonable to think that schools can develop a meaningful collaborative culture without providing adequate time for teams to do the work that is expected of them. In most cases, this means that the school's master schedule will need to be adapted or changed completely. Fortunately, changing schedules is doable and doesn't require extra funds. (Again, additional ideas for how to provide time for teams to meet can be found in *Learning by Doing* [DuFour et al., 2016] and on the AllThingsPLC website [www.allthingsplc.info].)

Third, leaders must take the initiative and organize the school into teams. Obviously, this requires input from teachers and careful thought and deliberation, but it must begin with top-down leadership. Rick and I quickly realized that collaboration by invitation will not work.

When Rick became principal at Adlai Stevenson High School, he was determined to create a collaborative culture. At his first faculty meeting, he enthusiastically announced that creating a collaborative culture was going to be one of his top priorities. He said that he would support any teachers who wanted to collaborate. If teachers wanted to team-teach a topic or course, he would make it happen. If teachers wanted to join together in an action research initiative, he would support it. His commitment to creating a collaborative culture at Stevenson was met with loud applause. One teacher remarked, "Finally, we have a leader who values teacher collaboration!" At the end of the year, Rick had not received a single request from teachers to collaborate. We learned that collaboration was something that teachers wanted, but it required a collaborative structure.

The second year as principal, Rick organized Stevenson into collaborative teams. Organizing a district or school into collaborative teams must be a thoughtful, deliberate act, and the use of teams must be connected back to the why—Why are we organizing into teams? Everyone needs to clearly understand what is meant by the term *collaborative teams*, the research supporting teaming, what has been done so far regarding the use of teams, and the next steps that will be taken, such as training and support.

The entire school or district must be organized into teams. In short, the use of collaborative teams must simply become "how things are done here—day in and day out." At the district level, the foundational team is the superintendent and the school board. The central office leadership should be a team, and the support personnel (transportation, food service, clerical, administrative services, maintenance, and so on) should function as a team. It's very important that principals also be organized into teams. In smaller districts, all of the principals can form a team, and in larger ones, the elementary principals might be one team and the middle school and high school principals another. In very large districts, they might be organized by divisions.

The same idea should be carried out in individual schools. The entire organization—not only teachers—should be organized into collaborative teams. And appropriate, effective, and timely training and resources must be embedded in the teaming process.

Finally, a word should be said about selecting team leaders. This must be a thoughtful and deliberate process. The selection of team leaders is, I think, a prime example of what Pfeffer and Sutton (2000) refer to as the knowing-doing gap—the disconnect between what those within organizations know to be best practice and what actually occurs. While there is virtually unanimous agreement that effective leadership is critical for success, the selection of team leaders is often given little thought. I have been in many high schools in which much more attention was given to the selection of assistant coaches than to the selection of department chairs or team leaders.

People will likely be asked to serve as team leaders with little or no understanding of exactly what the position entails, so clearly defined expectations are critical. Collaboratively developed position descriptions can be useful, if they are not too tight. It is much better to include the types of activities and tasks team leaders are generally expected to manage rather than a rigid checklist. (A sample team leader position description can be found in Eaker and Keating's [2012] *Every School, Every Team, Every Classroom.*)

The Work of Collaborative Teams

I've discovered it is not unusual for school or district leaders to organize teachers into collaborative teams but then provide them with little or no direction. If leaders are not prepared to direct the work of teams, it is better to simply avoid collaborative teams. Of course, this raises the central question, What *is* the right work of collaborative teams in a PLC?

Schooling is a complex endeavor. Recognizing this fact requires that leaders focus team expectations on the right work and provide training and examples. The overarching work of teams must focus on enhancing the learning levels of all students, skill by skill, name by name. And this process begins with teams collaboratively developing units of instruction.

While the formats of instructional units will vary from team to team, the issues, questions, and topics that are the focus of team collaboration are the same or very similar. For example, White River School District relies on a graphic to drive unit planning within each teacher team (figure 7.3).

In the graphic, notice the bookends. They should be the same; that is, what students are expected to know or be able to do (the standard or essential knowledge or skill) should be the same as the items on the summative assessment. Each book on the bookshelf represents a topic that teacher teams should address as they collaboratively develop their common unit plans.

As teams are collaboratively planning common units, they are sharing ideas, strategies, materials, and their professional experience and expertise. Teachers are not left alone to figure things out by themselves. While improving student learning is difficult, it is not nearly as lonely or overwhelming for a teacher who is a contributing member of a high-performing collaborative team. Time and again, I have heard teachers say, "I felt overwhelmed as an individual teacher, but I believe *we* can do this—and do it well." Teachers' professional

Unit Planning: A Conceptual Framework for Teams

Relationship Between Power Standards, Common Formative Assessments, Checks for Understanding, Additional Time and Support, and Common Summative Assessments

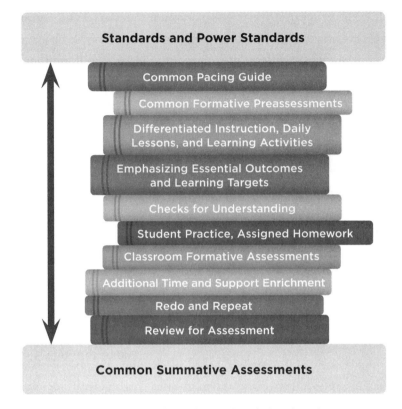

Standards and Power Standards

Common Pacing Guide

Common Formative Preassessments

Differentiated Instruction, Daily Lessons, and Learning Activities

Emphasizing Essential Outcomes and Learning Targets

Checks for Understanding

Student Practice, Assigned Homework

Classroom Formative Assessments

Additional Time and Support Enrichment

Redo and Repeat

Review for Assessment

Common Summative Assessments

Multiple checks for understanding during the unit
Performance • Product and Rubric Scoring • Paper and Pencil • Observation

Source: Adapted from Ainsworth & Viegut, 2006.

FIGURE 7.3: *A conceptual unit-planning framework for teams.*

satisfaction is enhanced by being part of a collaborative team focused on the right work and by seeing their students incrementally learning more as a result of their efforts.

When Rick and I wrote *Professional Learning Communities at Work* (DuFour & Eaker, 1998), we realized that if the core purpose of schools was to ensure high levels of learning for all students—and if the school or district leaders really meant it—then the work of teacher teams had to center around a few basic questions. We viewed these questions from an if-then perspective.

If we really mean it when we say we want to focus on the learning of each student, skill by skill, then wouldn't we have to be crystal clear about what students are expected to learn? Wouldn't this be the most basic question requiring our attention? And if we are clear about what students should know and be able to do as a result of each course or unit of study, then wouldn't this lead to the rather obvious question, How will we know if students have learned it? Since virtually everyone recognizes that students learn at different rates and in different ways, if we know some students will struggle with some skills and concepts, then how will we respond to these students who haven't learned? I've always felt this commonsense focus on these critical questions accounted, to a great degree, for the widespread acceptance of the PLC at Work process.

Notice that in this process, the attention is on three fundamental questions associated with improving student learning. By the time we wrote *Revisiting Professional Learning Communities at Work* (DuFour et al., 2008), we had added a fourth question based on our work in schools. It became apparent to us that many, if not most, schools did not have a plan for addressing the question, How will we respond to students who have learned, who already demonstrate proficiency? We recognized that schools shouldn't simply expect all students to learn at *some* level but, rather, at ever-increasing *high* levels. Many students earn high grades but are still learning under their potential. We added this fourth question to help schools extend student learning.

Of course, the real day-to-day work of teacher teams requires drilling deep into the work associated with each of these four critical questions. For example, regarding the question of what is essential for each student to know or be able to do, teacher teams must clarify and agree on the basic meaning of an essential learning expectation. Many state standards are far too broad or vague. So, teams must determine the most essential learning expectations for all students, and most importantly, determine what each essential learning expectation looks like in student work if the expectation is met. Agreeing on what essential learning should look like in student work enables teachers to sharpen their planning of common homework assignments, supports specific feedback, informs teacher teams regarding the formatting of common formative assessments, and helps move the teams toward a more standards-based form of grading and reporting of pupil progress.

A hallmark of high-performing teams is specificity. Teams are constantly drilling deeper. Highly effective teacher teams will break each essential learning into learning targets. In elementary settings, these learning targets are translated into "I can" statements for the students and their parents. The "I can" statements drive student portfolios and assist students in learning how to self-assess their progress and identify next steps. These statements are also the anchor for common homework assignments. Discussions about the "I can" statements and how parents can support their children's learning should be a major focus of parent-teacher meetings. Of course, student portfolios containing "I can"-type statements can be effective at the secondary level also; they are simply more sophisticated.

In each yearly teaching cycle, teacher teams sharpen the units taught previously. After teaching each unit, teams keep notes for the following year. In the White River School District, this is accomplished using a unit reflection form. In each subsequent year, the teams examine the previous year's unit reflection form and student learning data, then tweak the unit to become more effective. This cyclical process enables teacher teams to become students of the standards.

Rick, Becky, and I tried to avoid the term *pacing guide*. We were aware that pacing guides can, if used improperly, become too restrictive, too in lockstep. On the other hand, we recognized the importance of teacher teams "chunking out" the yearly calendar around the essential outcomes that students were expected to learn. We suggested that teacher teams collaboratively plan an academic year by first focusing on how much time would be needed to effectively teach each essential outcome. After building this time into the yearly planning calendar, the team could sprinkle in the less-critical learning expectations. This point is important: teams must collaboratively plan a yearly academic calendar by first allocating time for the most essential student knowledge and skills but still leave time for teaching things of lesser importance. It is important that the team not fill up every single minute of allocated time; don't screw the unit calendar down too tight!

Developing Common Formative Assessments

Many years ago, when I met Barbara Eason-Watkins, she was an elementary school principal on the south side of Chicago. (Barbara would later become a key leader in the district office of the Chicago public school system.) She was an amazingly effective principal, and she told me that she frequently asked herself, her teachers, each team, everyone, "Are the students learning, and how do you know?"

When outlining the first draft for *Professional Learning Communities at Work*, it seemed obvious to us that once teacher teams become crystal clear about what students should learn, they turn their focus to the question, Are the students learning? And they recognize that in order to answer this question, they must monitor student learning on a frequent and timely basis. In a PLC, the primary tool teacher teams use to monitor student learning is collaboratively developed common formative assessments.

Some key terms require emphasis. *Collaboratively developed* requires that these assessments are created by the teacher teams that will be teaching the unit. They are not commercially developed or developed by teachers from across the district. Rick and I felt that the process of teams developing common formative assessments was one of the most effective staff development exercises in which teachers could engage.

Common requires teacher teams to develop and use the same formative assessments. It's important to emphasize that the common assessments are not the only assessments teachers use, but they are the *primary* assessments teacher teams will use to frequently monitor the learning of each student, skill by skill, during each unit.

Ensuring a clear definition and understanding of *formative* requires special attention. By the early 2000s, much attention was being paid to the power of formative assessments to positively impact student achievement. Rick Stiggins (2005) contrasts formative assessments and summative assessments by noting that summative assessments are assessments *of* learning, while formative assessments are assessments *for* learning. Dylan Wiliam (2011) writes that an assessment is formative "to the extent that teachers, learners, or their peers elicit evidence about student achievement to make decisions about the next steps in instruction that are likely to be better, or better founded, than the decisions they would have taken in the absence of that evidence" (p. 43). Doug Reeves (2000) uses the analogy of an autopsy versus a checkup to highlight the difference between summative and formative assessments. While autopsies (summative assessments) might provide information to others, they cannot improve your health. On the other hand, medical checkups (formative assessments) can be a powerful tool for improving one's health.

The power of common formative assessments lies in the collaborative analysis of results and the decisions that are made to further the learning of each student. Improved student learning only occurs to the degree that teacher teams collaboratively analyze the results of each formative assessment using a predetermined protocol to assess the learning of each student, skill by skill. (An example of a team-developed protocol can be found in *Every School, Every Team, Every Classroom* [Eaker & Keating, 2012].)

Developing practices, processes, and procedures in which common formative assessments simply become a way of life within a school or across an entire district is a complex, difficult, and incremental undertaking. However, the resulting improvement in student achievement can be striking. Collaboratively developed common formative assessments are an essential element of the PLC at Work process. Schools accrue many benefits by regularly using common formative assessments as an integral aspect of the work of each team. Following are a few such benefits from *Learning by Doing* (DuFour et al., 2016).

> **Common formative assessments enhance efficiency for teachers:** Once the assessments are developed, they don't have to be redeveloped each time a unit is taught. The teams simply review the assessments and make whatever adjustments need to be made. Individual teachers do not have to repeat the same tasks over and over.

> **Common formative assessments are more equitable for students:** We've all heard the refrain "It just depends on the teacher." This comment is especially relevant regarding assessments. Common assessments enhance equity since the quality of student work is analyzed against the same criteria using the same formats.

> **Common formative assessments are a powerful tool for ensuring the guaranteed curriculum is being both taught and learned:** Common formative assessments promote consistency among teachers, and they are a powerful tool for providing timely, accurate, specific, and consistent feedback to both students and teachers.

> **Common formative assessments inform the practice of individual teachers:** Common formative assessments

provide teachers with a basis of comparison as they learn, student by student, skill by skill, how the performance of their students is similar to or different from the performance of other students who took the same assessments. The collaborative dialogue that follows is a powerful way to enhance teacher learning.

> **Common formative assessments build a team's capacity to achieve their goals:** The likelihood of goal attainment is enhanced by formative assessments. When teacher teams collaboratively analyze the results of commonly developed formative assessments, they are better able to identify and address problem areas with enhanced specificity.

> **Common assessments facilitate a systematic, collective response to students who are experiencing difficulty in their learning:** Because the results of common formative assessments are analyzed collaboratively, student by student, skill by skill, teams are able to provide targeted time and support for both groups of students who are experiencing the difficulty with the same skills or concepts and individual students whose problems are unique.

> **Common formative assessments are a powerful tool for improving the professional practice of educators:** Teacher practice is positively impacted when teachers see their colleagues consistently getting better results against the same standard, using the same assessments. There is power in the peer pressure that comes from being a member of a high-performing team whose results are transparent.

Implementing team-developed common formative assessments is challenging. I have found the following suggestions can help move the process of developing and using common formative assessments forward.

> Beginning the process of writing and analyzing the results of common formative assessments requires planning and forethought. Consideration must be paid to making sure everyone has a common understanding of what is meant by a *common* and *formative* assessment. Teams will need training and resources, and in particular, teams will need high-quality examples of common formative assessments. (Schools that are listed under See the Evidence on AllThingsPLC [www.allthingsplc.info/evidence/www .allthingsplc.info] are committed to sharing examples of their work with other schools seeking to implement PLC at Work procedures, processes, and practices.)

> Particular attention must be given to the question of how broadly and rapidly the inclusion of collaboratively developed common formative assessments should occur. I have seen smaller schools begin the development process schoolwide, in every subject, course, and unit. Likewise, I have seen schools take a more measured approach, beginning in a few subjects. Many schools choose mathematics as the place to start since the discipline is more naturally sequential than many other subjects. Deciding how widespread the initial undertaking should be calls for sound professional judgment. My friend and colleague Janel Keating is fond of saying she and her team in White River address this problem by asking, "How much, how hard, and how fast?"

> Frequently, we're asked how many common formative assessments should be developed for each unit. There is no set number. The size and complexity of each unit will dictate how many common formative assessments a team should develop. After teaching a unit, teams should make notes regarding whether the number of common formative

assessments was too many or too few and ways they could be improved next time the unit is taught. I believe it is preferable to give shorter, more frequent common formative assessments than a few long assessments.

> Teams should pay particular attention to the formats of their common formative assessments. The formats should be determined by two things. One, when units were collaboratively planned, what was student work expected to look like if essential skills and concepts were learned? And two, what formats will students see on high-stakes summative assessments? When students take a high-stakes summative assessment, it should not be the first time they have answered questions in those particular formats. In short, teams should constantly and consistently work toward aligning each standard or essential learning with what student work should look like on deliberate student practice and toward aligning the formats of the common formative assessments with the formats of the high-stakes summative assessments students are likely to encounter.

Learning by Doing (DuFour et al., 2016) contains additional tips for developing common formative assessments, including:

1. Recognize that common formative assessments might create teacher anxiety.
2. Remember that common formative assessments are only one element of an effective and balanced assessment process for monitoring student learning.
3. Remember districts can play a role.
4. Create shared understanding of the term *common formative assessment*.
5. Embrace the regular and routine use of protocols and team tools.
6. Use assessments as a means rather than an end.
   (pp. 150–157)

The most important suggestion, however, is simply this: *use* the results of common formative assessments. While the process of developing common formative assessments can sharpen teachers' understanding of what students should learn and what they should practice, unless teachers use the results of the assessments, the process will have little impact on student learning.

The results of the common formative assessments must be used to identify the skills or concepts with which each student demonstrated proficiency, along with the skills and concepts with which individual students are struggling. The identification of learned and unlearned skills or concepts becomes the blueprint for teams making focused, deliberate decisions regarding additional time, support, or extension of learning for each student, name by name.

In addition, the results of the common formative assessments provide meaningful data for teams, as well as individual teachers, with which to reflect on their instructional effectiveness. The results are a powerful tool teams should use to move beyond *feeling* whether a unit went well to making more data-driven reflections. This collaborative data-driven reflection is an important way that teachers learn from one another—all for the purpose of continuous improvement.

Providing Systematic Additional Time, Support, and Extension of Learning

One of the most obvious examples of the knowing-doing gap is the disconnect between knowing that students learn at different rates and in different ways and structuring schools within a framework in which students are expected to learn at the same rate and suffer penalties, such as low grades, if they fail to do so. Educators have a clear choice: they can organize their schools around the idea that every student will be given the same amount of time to learn, resulting in varying levels of student achievement, or they can organize their schools to hold what is essential for each student to learn constant and create systems for varying amounts of time of student learning. Leaders of traditional schools choose the former, while leaders of PLCs make a conscious effort to choose the latter.

Rick and I would often ask principals, "How does your school respond when students struggle with their learning?" Most frequently, they responded by saying there was no *school* response and pointing out individual teachers who went to extraordinary lengths to help kids with their learning. In other words, there was no *school* response; there were only *individual teacher* responses. While I agree that many teachers go to great lengths to help students, this raises a few important issues—issues that must be addressed if we are serious about enhancing the learning of *all* students.

We should recognize that there is only so much an individual teacher can do. Even the best teachers will soon hit a ceiling when it comes to helping students. Individual teachers cannot change the school schedule, hire tutors, or create labs or other support systems to provide students with additional time and support.

More problematic is the fact that some teachers simply do not believe it's their job to go above and beyond more traditional approaches to teaching. The refrain is, "It's my job to teach, but it's their job to learn. And if they choose not to learn, they must suffer the consequences." Some offer an even more problematic response: "We have to avoid spoon-feeding these kids. I'm preparing them for the real world. In the real world, you don't get to turn in late work or redo mistakes." The worst response? "These kids simply don't have the ability, and there's nothing I can do about that."

While it's true that a school is a social organization composed of individuals with a wide range of beliefs and assumptions, if these kinds of responses are not addressed, schools become lotteries; success is determined simply by the teacher to whom students are assigned. In other words, in traditional schools, luck plays a huge role in student achievement.

And, of course, some of these beliefs are based on assumptions that are simply untrue. I have been an administrator for decades, and in the real world that I've worked in, when I was late or did something incorrectly, I still had to complete or redo the work. Rick frequently used the Internal Revenue Service (IRS) as an example. If you fail to turn your taxes in by midnight on April 15 and later attempt to pay, the real world of the IRS will not say, "Oh no! We don't take late payments! Just keep your money!" Most people in the real world still must do the work even if it's late and redo it if it is incorrect.

So, what is the answer? In the PLC at Work process, the answer is a systematic plan to provide students with additional time and response when they experience difficulty with their learning. Such schools also develop plans to extend the learning of students who demonstrate proficiency. Schools that function as high-performing PLCs create structures and cultures in which students are engaged in a more rigorous and challenging curriculum and are provided the additional time and support to be successful in their studies. In other words, leaders of PLCs create systems that stretch the aspirations and performance levels of all students—and all adults.

Occasionally, I am asked, "But isn't it unfair for some students to get more time than others?" My response usually is a statement I heard many years ago (often attributed to Aristotle): "There is nothing so unequal as the equal treatment of unequals." If we really believe students learn at different rates and in different ways, don't we have a moral, as well as practical, obligation to ensure school structures and cultures are aligned with what we know about how students learn?

A systematic plan to collaboratively develop such structures and cultures should reflect specific characteristics. First, leaders must be clear about what is meant by *a systematic plan*. *Systematic* means it is a schoolwide plan that is collaboratively developed, and the additional time, support, or extension of learning occurs within the school day, regardless of the teacher to whom a student is assigned. It is a formal, written plan.

A systematic plan must also be *timely*. That is, schools must not wait too long to provide additional time, support, or extension of learning. A rough rule of thumb is this: interventions should begin no later than the third week of school, and in some cases, they should begin immediately.

The collaborative analysis of big data can be valuable in this regard. When collaborative teams analyze student learning data longitudinally, subject by subject, skill by skill, patterns of student learning emerge. In addition to perhaps altering their instructional strategies, it only makes sense that teams go ahead and plan for additional time and support for those skills or concepts in which many students struggle each year.

Many secondary schools, such as Adlai Stevenson and Grant Community High School in Fox Lake, Illinois, work closely with their feeder middle schools to identify students who will need immediate help when they begin their high school experience. These students are provided additional time and support in such skills as test taking, note taking, writing, or algebra to enable them to hit the ground running when they arrive at the high school.

The plan must also be *flexible*. Avoid labeling students. Most students do not need to be placed in a program; they simply need some help on a specific essential skill or concept. They move in and out of additional time and support as needed. An effective plan does not try to correct everything with which students might be struggling. The plan only addresses those skills and concepts that were identified by the team as essential.

If the teams have identified a specific skill or concept as essential, it follows that the plan for additional time, support, or extension of learning must be directional rather than invitational. Teams and individual teachers must not *encourage* students to get assistance or give them the *opportunity* to do so; they must *direct* them to do so.

Some schools make the mistake of pulling students out of core instruction to receive additional assistance. When students are pulled from core instruction, they are likely to fall further behind. There may be instances in which a student is experiencing such extreme difficulty that he or she will need to be placed in an alternate program rather than in core instruction. But, the vast majority of students must not miss core instruction in order to receive additional assistance with their learning.

Having a collaborative, systematic plan to provide additional time, support, or extension of learning doesn't necessarily mean the plan is effective. Coupled with the plan must be a system for monitoring its effectiveness. And in a PLC, the cornerstone of determining effectiveness is answering the question, What is the impact on student learning? Enhancing the impact of a plan for additional time, support, and extension of learning on student achievement typically involves improving specificity in both identifying and assisting specific skills and concepts and on the schedule, processes, practices, and procedures that are in place to match student needs with support.

As with most aspects of a PLC, the key to developing an effective plan for additional time, support, and extension for learning is to get started *but then get better*. I've found that it is not uncommon for school leaders to let their quest for perfection keep them from getting started. There will always be problems and issues associated with any initiative. The fact is, things cannot be improved until they are first begun. Leaders must recognize that the few people who will point out the obvious difficulties with any plan to provide students with additional time and support are often just stating the obvious: "I don't want to change."

This is a perfect time to demonstrate a commitment to simultaneously loose and tight leadership. Leaders communicate *tight* by moving ahead with the collaborative development of a plan to provide additional time and support because the school's mission is to ensure high levels of learning for all students. Yet the leadership practice is also *loose* in moving forward by continually seeking feedback and frequently adjusting along the way. Remember, continuous improvement is a journey that never ends!

Getting Started, Getting Better, Drilling Deeper

I've found that many teachers have a rather cynical view of new initiatives—and understandably so. Generally speaking, our attitudes result from our experiences. For many teachers, their experiences with new initiatives have been that they come and then rather quickly go away—one new initiative after another. As a result, initiative fatigue sets in, and teachers develop an attitude of "This too shall pass."

How can school leaders assist in keeping teachers and support staff focused on the right work that is most likely to have a positive impact on student success? The answer lies in persistence, limited initiatives, and continuous improvement. As Rick and I drafted *Professional Learning Communities at Work*, we emphasized that successful implementation of PLC practices would provide teachers with new experiences, and over time, new attitudes would emerge.

As PLC practices are embedded in structures and culture, effective leaders continue the process by increasing specificity and drilling deeper into the work of improving student learning. Enhancing specificity is accomplished by frequently monitoring and improving team products and processes within the context of close examination of student learning data. It is a process of continuously tweaking "how we do things" day in and day out and drilling deeper to aspects of schooling that are seldom examined yet have a significant impact on student achievement.

Examining Routine Practices

As the journey to becoming a PLC gets underway, the disconnect between some routine practices and the commitment to improve student learning will emerge. Deep examination of these practices, coupled with collective inquiry into better practices, becomes an important aspect of the continuous improvement journey. Close examination of routine practices can be difficult but not avoided.

In my many years of working in schools, I've often witnessed routine practices that hinder student learning and contribute to student failure. Some of the most obvious practices—practices that are deeply embedded in the culture of most traditional schools—are rarely examined. One of the most obvious examples is the practice of averaging grades to report student progress. As districts, schools, and teams drill deeper into gaining shared knowledge about specific practices that support or hinder student success, they will move away from averaging student learning and move toward reporting student progress on specific learning standards. Examining grading will inevitably lead to a re-evaluation of the often thoughtless ways in which zeros are used or homework is weighted in determining grades. In many schools, decisions about grading practices are left to individual teachers; in a PLC, they are the result of collective inquiry and agreed-on ways of doing things that support, rather than hinder, student learning.

As schools drill deeper into the impact of various routine practices that influence student learning, they should engage in deep, rich discussions about the impact of unequal ranges between grades. For example, in most schools, students can move from a grade of B to a grade of A by overcoming ten or fewer points. The same is usually true between other grades—except the grade of F. Students in the F range have to overcome a much larger deficit to move to a higher grade. Many schools have switched to a four-point scale, the kind universities have used for years.

Designing the Schedule

The impact of a school's daily schedule should not be overlooked. Throughout my professional career, I have repeatedly heard the refrain "I'm afraid that won't work in our school; our schedule won't allow it." Think about that statement! Other than start and end times, and perhaps lunch or some other factor that is unique to a specific district or state, everything else regarding the schedule can be examined and likely changed.

When collaboratively examining a school's schedule, it usually comes down to this singular question, Is our school's daily schedule designed to enhance student success, or is the schedule primarily for the happiness of the adults? In a high-performing PLC, the school schedule will support a minimum of one hour (or period) per week within the school day for teams to meet, one hour per week for the school leadership team (the principal and team leaders and appropriate others) to meet, and a specified time for additional time, support, and extension of learning within the school day, regardless of the teacher to whom students are assigned.

Monitoring Efforts and Celebrating Success

Drilling deeper involves frequently monitoring the impact of our efforts and celebrating success that occurs along the way. When Rick and I began to draft *Professional Learning Communities at Work* with an emphasis on cultural change, we devoted much of our thinking to the role celebration plays, or can play, in organizational culture. We wrote of several benefits from using celebration, ceremonies, rituals, and stories to create a culture reflective of a PLC:

- The recipients of the recognition feel noted and appreciated.
- It reinforces shared values and signals what is important.
- It provides living examples of the values of the school at work and encourages others to act in accordance with those values.

- It fuels momentum.
- It is fun. (DuFour & Eaker, 1998, pp. 142–144)

We offered readers some tips for the frequent and meaningful use of celebration and recognition to foster cultural change.

- Explicitly state the purpose for attending to the need for celebration.
- Make celebration everyone's responsibility.
- Establish a clear link between public recognition and the advancement of vision and values.
- Create opportunities for lots of winners. (DuFour & Eaker, 1998, pp. 144–146)

Remember, while practitioners are typically not in the position to implement changes in traditional compensation systems, they do have the power to develop creative systems of informal rewards, recognitions, and ceremonies that both express appreciation and signal to everyone what is valued.

The larger point is this: schools that begin the journey to function, with fidelity, as a PLC will get started and then work collaboratively to make research-based, data-driven decisions in order to continuously get better. On their journey, they will collaboratively drill deep into policies, practices, and procedures that are left unexamined in more traditional schools. And they will frequently monitor the effects of their efforts and celebrate incremental improvement, both of students and adults, regularly and in multiple and meaningful ways.

A Summing Up

When *Professional Learning Communities at Work* (DuFour & Eaker, 1998) was published, the phrase *at work* reflected our philosophical foundation that we best learn by *doing*. This doesn't mean practitioners should ignore research—to the contrary. I always believed that actually doing the work of a high-performing PLC, day in and day out, meant a constant search for best practices—practices that actually impacted student learning in a positive way. I've learned that the most effective leaders of PLCs are those who can effectively connect research and best practices to how people behave.

I've viewed the two decades following the publication of *Professional Learning Communities at Work* as years of experimentation—my personal journey of learning by doing. Actually, learning by doing—experimenting—is a centuries-old tradition. In Walter Isaacson's (2017) biography *Leonardo da Vinci*, he emphasizes that Leonardo placed a high value on personal experimentation. He notes that in 1490 Leonardo proclaimed that rather than simply reading of the works and thoughts of others, he would rely on a far worthier thing: experience. More recently, Jeffrey Pfeffer and Robert Sutton (2000) in *The Knowing-Doing Gap* explore what they considered to be one of the great mysteries of organizational life: why does the knowledge of what needs to be done so frequently fail to result in behaviors that are consistent with what is known?

My feelings about the importance of getting better by doing the work—getting started and then getting better—are reflected in our book *Learning by Doing* (DuFour et al., 2006):

> How odd then that a professional who pays homage to the importance of learning by doing is so reluctant to apply the principle when it comes to developing the collective capacity to meet the needs of students. Why do institutions created for and devoted to learning not call upon the professionals within them to become more proficient in improving the effectiveness of schools by actually doing the work of school improvement? Why have we been so reluctant to learn by doing? (p. 1)

Although throughout my professional career I had spent a great deal of time in the preK–12 setting, I began to spend more time in school districts, working and learning of ways to embed PLC at Work concepts and practices throughout an entire district. In other words, I sought to learn more but also to sharpen my thinking about what was already known. In this effort, I was blessed to meet Janel Keating, who had become assistant superintendent in the White River School District in Buckley, Washington.

I first met Janel in 2001 when she attended a Professional Learning Communities at Work Institute in Vancouver, Washington. At that time, she was a new principal at Mountain Meadow Elementary School in the White River School District. Having never been a principal, she was using *Professional Learning Communities at Work* (DuFour & Eaker, 1998) as her go-to resource.

A few years later, I met her again at an institute in Everett, Washington. However, this time, she was presenting a few breakout sessions for the participants. Her presentations were informative, practical, useful, and engaging. Demands from school districts were rapidly increasing, and Janel was one of the first practitioners to be asked to work as a PLC at Work professional development associate.

By this time, Janel had moved to the central office, serving as the assistant superintendent for teaching and learning. A short time later, she would move to the superintendent's position. Janel viewed the PLC at Work concepts and practices as the most promising framework to improve student learning districtwide, and she asked me if I would serve as a resource to help her and the district on their school improvement journey. This began a friendship, not only with Janel, but also with many in the district, that has lasted well over a decade. Not only did I gain a new friendship, but the district served as a laboratory for Janel and me to sharpen our knowledge base about implementing the PLC at Work process districtwide.

Few aspects of White River's structures and cultures were left unaffected by Janel's leadership. PLC at Work concepts and practices were embedded in everything that affected teaching and learning, either directly or indirectly. She worked tirelessly with the school board, instituted a late start on Monday mornings for team meetings, reconfigured the district office staff ensuring that principals were part of the district leadership team (which included teachers also), and provided requisite training, support, and examples—just to highlight a few of the changes she led. Importantly, the work throughout the district, by both adults and students, was frequently monitored, improved, and celebrated.

Because of the enhanced learning that was occurring in White River, Janel and I began co-authoring articles and books. In 2012, Janel and I published *Every School, Every Team, Every Classroom: District Leadership for Growing Professional Learning Communities at Work*. A companion book, *Kid by Kid, Skill by Skill: Teaching in a Professional Learning Community at Work* was published in 2015. As word of the work of White River spread, requests from others to visit the district and observe teams in action increased dramatically, and Janel became one of Solution Tree's most sought after professional development associates.

Soon after the first Professional Learning Communities at Work Institutes, Jeff Jones quickly recognized that in order to respond to requests from districts and schools, Solution Tree would need to create and grow a cadre of practitioners who had successfully implemented PLC at Work concepts and practices to serve as professional development associates. This pool of highly skilled experts has grown incrementally, currently numbering in excess of 150.

Rick, Becky, and I continued our writing and working with Jeff on ways to meet the growing demand for PLC at Work products and services. The expanded number of PLC at Work books was enhanced by Douglas Rife accepting the position of president of Solution Tree Press. Not only did Douglas become my professional colleague, he also became one of my dearest friends. We learned that we shared many of the same interests in both travel and reading. Suffice to say, the quality of my life, both personally and professionally, has been enhanced by my relationship with Douglas.

Rick, Becky, Jeff, Douglas, and I realized that not only were our professional development associates talented presenters, but they also had the potential to become successful writers. With the assistance of the Solution Tree Press staff, many of the PLC at Work associates became highly regarded authors. This expansion of associates into the publishing arena coupled with the increased number of PLC at Work Institutes led to the growing familiarity of, and demand for, PLC at Work concepts and practices nationally and, increasingly, internationally.

As my writing and presenting on the PLC at Work process expanded, so did my responsibilities at the university as dean of the College of Education. We implemented a number of initiatives, requiring an academic major for all students enrolled in our teacher education programs and raising the grade point average for admittance. We developed professional development centers with neighboring school districts to both enhance the quality of teachers to whom we would assign student teachers and provide professional development for preK–12 educators. I, along with others in the college, worked hard to establish close relationships with the Tennessee State Department of Education and legislative leaders. I was particularly blessed to develop close relationships and friendships with Jane Walters, the commissioner of education; Andy Womack, the chair of the Senate Education Committee; and State Representative John Bragg, the chair of the House Finance Committee.

I have often been asked how I was able to do so much work in the preK–12 setting while working full-time as dean of the college. The answer is simple: I worked for presidents and vice presidents who not only allowed me to work in public schools but also actually supported and encouraged me to do so. The last president for whom I worked, Dr. Sidney McPhee, asked if I would serve as his interim executive vice president and provost. I responded that I would be pleased to serve in that role, but I would not be interested in doing so on a permanent basis. The year and a half I served as vice president and provost was one of the most fulfilling professional experiences of my career. It was capped off with the publication of *A New Way: Introducing Higher Education to Professional Learning Communities at Work* in 2016, co-authored with my colleague and friend Debra Sells.

One of the most important things I learned in the years following the publication of *Professional Learning Communities at Work* (DuFour & Eaker, 1998) is that becoming a high-performing PLC—one that has a systemic and significant impact on student learning—is difficult. And, one of the most difficult things is simply getting started. There are lots of reasons to keep doing the same thing year after year, the main one being that it is simply easier not to change.

People often say to me, "Bob, I really believe the professional learning community concept would have a positive impact on our school, but we are just so busy right now with so many things going on. The time just isn't right." I respond by asking if they can remember a time when they weren't busy or overwhelmed. The fact is, the time will never be right. The issue isn't so much whether the work will be hard. Yes, the work will be hard, but it will be the *right* work!

Another objection I hear is, "Professional learning community practices require real collaboration—a culture of trust—and we just don't have that right now. Everybody isn't on board." Again, can you remember a time when everyone *was* on board, especially if the concept and practices would impact how adults think and act? The key is to get started, create small wins, and frequently publicly recognize and celebrate incremental improvements along the journey. Remember, there is little one can say on the front end that will convince everyone to get on board. Commitment follows experience, not the other way around.

Getting started requires effective top-down leadership. It is unreasonable to think that the PLC at Work practices will simply bubble up from the staff. While getting started requires effective top-down leadership, once the staff begin to develop their products—such as team norms, a guaranteed and viable curriculum, common formative assessments, and plans for additional time, support, and extension of learning—they will have ownership of their work and begin to take pride in the fact that their work is having a positive impact on student learning. Bottom-up leadership will begin to emerge. Successfully implementing PLC at Work processes and practices depends on both top-down and bottom-up leadership. But, as I wrote previously, successful bottom-up leadership is dependent on effective top-down leadership.

CHAPTER 8

Absolutely Indispensable: Passionate and Persistent Leadership

Learning about, and even believing in, the practices inherent in the PLC at Work process will be of little value unless it causes people to act. Causing people to act requires leadership, and at its core, effective leadership requires deep knowledge, specificity, passion, and unwavering persistence.

As Rick was fighting lung cancer, we had many opportunities to reflect not only on our four decades of friendship but also on what we had learned on our professional journey together. We had come to believe effective leadership was the one indispensable factor for sustained significant school improvement. We had worked for nearly forty years in districts and schools, and when we reflected on why some school-improvement efforts took hold and others did not, we came to the conclusion that the distinguishing factor was almost always leadership.

Putting forth the notion that effective leadership is critically important may seem as if I'm simply recognizing the obvious. And, I suppose in many ways, I am. Leadership is an interesting concept in that virtually everyone affirms that effective leadership is very important, but there is much less agreement on what it is—what effective leadership practices look like in a district, school, or team.

Foundational Inquiry Into Leadership and Organizational Development

Compared to other areas of inquiry, the formal study of leadership and leadership practices is relatively recent. Prior to the 1900s, leadership was viewed through the lens of personal characteristics. The leadership practices of individuals—particularly military leaders and politicians—who were generally viewed as highly effective leaders were analyzed and described. While the resulting descriptions made for interesting reading, common themes could not be found among those being studied.

I recently watched two movies. One was *Patton* (McCarthy & Schaffner, 1970), and the other was *Won't You Be My Neighbor?* (Neville, Capotosto, Ma, & Neville, 2018) about Fred Rogers of television's *Mister Rogers' Neighborhood* fame. George Patton is recognized by many as a great military leader, while Fred Rogers is recognized as a leader who revolutionized children's television. I couldn't help but wonder if there are two more diverse examples of effective leaders than George Patton and Fred Rogers.

And yet, the idea of viewing leadership through the lens of personal traits makes some sense to most of us since in our own lives we've had experiences with individuals whose leadership behavior impacted us in some meaningful way. My professional (and personal) journey is no exception. Even though I can name many leaders who made a significant impact on my life, each had very different leadership traits. While studying leadership through the lens of personal characteristics is interesting, as a research methodology, it is not useful.

The Search for Efficiency

The Industrial Revolution of the early 1900s ushered in many dramatic changes. Harvard historian Jill Lepore (2018) writes, "Industrialism brought great, glittering wealth to a few, prosperity to the nation, cheaper goods to the middle class, and misery and want to the many" (p. 362). One thing that didn't change with the Industrial Revolution, however, was the quest for ways to increase profits. In the industrial age, increasing profits meant increasing efficiency. Increasing efficiency meant more effective management practices, and *management* gradually became synonymous with *leadership*. Warren Bennis and Burt Nanus (1985) would later make the distinction between management and leadership, concluding, "Managers are people who do things right and leaders are people who do the right things" (p. 21).

The underlying intellectual framework for the age of efficiency was based on a simple idea: by increasing efficiency through more effective management techniques, the speed of production could be increased, which, in turn, lowered per-unit costs, thus increasing profits. This rather simplistic approach to enhancing profits through enhancing efficiency created an entirely new field of study, and no one had a larger impact on this new area of study than Frederick Winslow Taylor (1911).

Born in 1856 in Germantown, Pennsylvania, Taylor went to work in the Midvale Steel Works in Philadelphia in 1878. He began his career at the steel works as a laborer, but when he left in 1890, he held the title of chief engineer. He became interested in determining how to maximize the efficiency of people and machines. In 1911, Taylor authored the best-selling book *The Principles of Scientific Management*. At the heart of Taylor's (1911) scientific management system were his time and motion studies. In the studies, efficiency experts observed each step of production in order to calculate the fastest rate at which a unit of work could be completed. These findings could be used to set minimum worker production rates per task and determine ways to increase production rates.

Generally speaking, Taylor's scientific approach to enhancing efficiency emphasized increasing the rate of per-unit production, rigid discipline on the job, minimal interpersonal contact among workers, and strict application of incentive pay systems (Owens, 1970).

As improbable as it might seem to us today, *Taylorism*—as the quest of efficiency was popularly called—swept the country. The search for efficiency even reached into family life with the introduction of the study of home economics (Lepore, 2018). Perhaps the best example of the extent to which Taylorism impacted American society was set by Henry Ford. In addition to organizing his automobile production plant on scientific management principles, he exerted control over the home lives of his mostly immigrant workers by creating a Sociological Department, along with founding an English School to Americanize immigrant workers. Interestingly, the school was organized to use the same efficiency techniques as the factory. The organizers of the English School saw the school and the factory as one in the same, declaring: "This is the human product we seek to turn out, and as we adapt the machinery in the shop to turning out the kind of automobile we have in mind, so we have constructed our educational system with a view to producing the human product we have in mind" (Lepore, 2018, p. 384).

As Rick and I were drafting our outline for *Professional Learning Communities at Work* (DuFour & Eaker, 1998), we engaged in lengthy conversations about both the structure and the culture of many, if not most, American schools. While other aspects of society had moved past Taylor's (1911) principles of scientific management, schools still clung to the most basic of Taylor's ideas. We felt this was especially true of America's secondary schools with their rigid schedules, teacher isolation, emphasis on sorting and selecting students, and periodic plans to incentivize teacher pay through various merit pay schemes tied to student achievement. And we felt Taylorism continued to influence the view of effective school leadership. In many districts, the emphasis seemed to be on efficient management, as opposed to effective leadership. These discussions about the nature of public schools, the remains of Taylorism, and the leadership behaviors that would be needed to reculture schools into high-performing PLCs played a huge role in both our writing and our working with schools across North America, especially regarding the need to change the fundamental culture of schools and districts.

From Efficiency to Psychology: The Hawthorne Effect

While Taylor's (1911) principles of scientific management dominated the thinking about effective management behaviors in the early 1900s, the last half of the 20th century witnessed a focus on psychological factors that influenced productivity. This human relations movement had its beginning at the Western Electric plant in Hawthorne, Illinois.

The Western Electric Company studies were conducted at Western Electric's Hawthorne plant between 1924 and 1933. Work at this particular plant involved assembling telephone relays, among other things. Although an impressive group of researchers was involved in the studies, perhaps the most well-known were Elton Mayo and Fritz Roethlisberger. Using a classic research model involving experimental groups and control groups, researchers began to manipulate the workplace conditions of the experimental group. Various changes were made in creating work schedules, providing rest breaks, allowing and encouraging teamwork, providing company lunches, providing cleaner working conditions, and removing obstacles from the workplace. However, the Western Electric studies are best known for the illumination studies (Eaker & Friziellie, 2018).

The illumination studies focused on the effects differing illumination conditions had on productivity. Researchers increased and decreased lighting conditions within the workplace. Surprisingly, productivity increased in all cases—even with the control group. Worker productivity improved when lighting was increased and, likewise, when it was decreased. Researchers concluded the explanation for increased productivity had to be due to factors beyond the physical manipulation of the workplace environment (Western Electric Company, 1924–1933).

Seeking further explanation, researchers conducted a wide range of interviews with participants in both the control group and the experimental group—ultimately interviewing more than twenty thousand employees. The findings were groundbreaking at the time. Researchers concluded the increased productivity was due, primarily, to the motivational effect of workers feeling special by simply being part of the research studies. Because workers were being asked about their feelings and their views of the work environment as part of the interview process, they were made to feel important and their views valued (Western Electric Company, 1924–1933). (As a side note, one result of the Western Electric studies was that future researchers would have to contend with the Hawthorne Effect—the very fact that being a participant in a study can affect participant behavior and responses.)

An additional outcome of the interviews was the conclusion that management generally held workers in low regard. Elton Mayo referred to this as the *rabble hypothesis*—the belief that society was made up of a horde of unorganized individuals whose only concerns were self-preservation and self-interest (Eaker & Friziellie, 2018).

After the Western Electric Company (1924–1933) studies, no longer were effective management and leadership viewed exclusively through the lens of Taylor's scientific management. An entirely new field of study was opened—the study of human psychology—as a major contributing factor in effective leadership, motivation, and organizational development.

The Ohio State and University of Michigan Leadership Studies

The early efficiency studies, such as the Western Electric Company (1924–1933) studies, sparked an increased focus on the study of leadership, organizational development, and the social studies in general. Whereas the early studies regularly used the word *manager*, many of these new studies focused more specifically on *leadership* behavior. Two of the most significant of these studies were the Ohio State and University of Michigan studies.

The Ohio State leadership studies, which began in 1945, focused on various aspects of leadership behavior. Eventually, the findings were grouped into two distinct dimensions of behavior. One was labeled *initiating structure* and the other *consideration*. The initiating structure dimension referred to the degree to which leaders were task oriented—working toward achieving organizational goals. The other dimension, consideration, referred to the degree to which leaders were sensitive to their subordinates. The consideration dimension focused on such areas as establishing relationships, being sensitive to the feelings of others, and building trust.

Interestingly, the researchers concluded that these two dimensions, initiating structure and consideration, were distinct and separate. A particular score in one dimension did not necessarily correlate, either positively or negatively, to the score attained in the other dimension (Hersey, Blanchard, & Johnson, 2001).

Research into leadership behavior also began in 1945 at the University of Michigan with similar purposes as the Ohio State studies. The Michigan studies identified two clusters of leadership behavior: production orientation and employee orientation. These findings mirrored the Ohio State findings in that the production-oriented leadership behaviors focused on the more technical aspects related to completing various tasks associated with production, while the employee-oriented behaviors focused on relationships (Hersey et al., 2001).

Taken together, the findings from these two studies deepened the understanding of specific leadership behavior. They extended the insights that had been gleaned by Elton Mayo and his colleagues in the Western Electric studies by validating the fact that leadership behavior does indeed involve both a task dimension (getting the job done) and a relationship dimension (the importance of interpersonal relationships). This two-dimensional way of viewing leadership behavior would form the framework for future leadership research for years to come.

Abraham Maslow and the Needs Hierarchy

In 1954, Abraham H. Maslow published his seminal work, *Motivation and Personality*. Maslow (1954) postulated that human behavior is driven by the urge to satisfy basic and psychological needs, and he arranged these human needs into his classic needs hierarchy.

The most basic human needs are reflected at the base of the hierarchy. These are the basic *physiological* needs that are required to sustain life—things such as water, food, shelter, and clothing. After these needs are met, the next level of needs emerges: the need for safety and security.

Once the basic survival needs and the need for safety and security are met, *psychological* needs emerge. According to Maslow (1954), the first of the psychological needs is social in nature—the need to belong, to be included. Once this need is met, the need for esteem emerges. This involves the need to feel important, to be recognized. At the top of Maslow's (1954) needs hierarchy is the need to feel self-actualized. I've always found it difficult to adequately articulate exactly what Maslow (1954) meant by this term. I personally like Paul Hersey, Kenneth Blanchard, and Dewey Johnson's (2001) definition:

> Self-actualization is the need to maximize one's potential, whatever it may be. A musician must play music, a poet must write, a general must win battles, a professor must

teach. As Maslow expressed it, "What a man can be, he must be." Thus, self-actualization is the desire to become what one is capable of becoming. (p. 38)

Douglas McGregor and Theory Y Leadership

Following the clues gleaned from the Western Electric studies regarding how human psychology and motivation impact worker behavior, leadership studies shifted to an emphasis on group dynamics and worker morale. Leaders were encouraged to pay attention to worker inclusion, interpersonal relations, and the feelings of others. Robert G. Owens (1970) observes, "Managers and administrators in industry, business, the military—all kinds of organizations, including schools—were admonished to pay attention to 'the human side of the enterprise'" (p. 27). Owens's (1970) use of the phrase *the human side of the enterprise* was no mere accident. In terms of influence, Douglas McGregor's (1960) *The Human Side of Enterprise* was one of the most important books on organizational development and leadership in the last half of the 20th century.

Building on the groundbreaking findings of the Western Electric studies and Maslow's (1954) view of human motivation, McGregor (1960) set out to redefine what it meant to be an effective organizational leader—the basic assumptions upon which leadership behavior should be based. At the heart of McGregor's (1960) thesis is the disconnect between the assumptions that management generally holds regarding workers and what is known about human motivation. He represented this disconnect in his classic Theory X and Theory Y framework.

I've always felt McGregor must have been greatly influenced by Elton Mayo's articulation of the rabble hypothesis. Mayo had surmised that management typically had a dim view of workers (Western Electric Company, 1924–1933). McGregor (1960) built on Mayo's view by adding specificity. He proposed that much of management

behavior was the result of assumptions that management held regarding workers, which he labeled Theory X assumptions:

1. Work is inherently distasteful to most people.
2. Most people are not ambitious, have little desire for
    responsibility, and prefer to be directed.
3. Most people have little capacity for creativity in solv-
    ing organizational problems.
4. Motivation occurs only at the physiological and sec-
    urity levels.
5. Most people must be closely controlled and often
    coerced to achieve organizational objectives. (McGregor,
    1960, p. 60)

(As an aside, Rick and I frequently talked about how, sadly, Theory
X assumptions could still be observed in some classrooms, schools,
and district offices.)

McGregor (1960) felt that Theory X assumptions, while widely
held by management, did not reflect the new knowledge about
human motivation—particularly, the pioneering work of Maslow
(1954). Theory X assumptions did not recognize the power of psychological needs and their implications for human motivation.
McGregor (1960) proposes a different set of assumptions, which he
referred to as Theory Y assumptions:

1. Work is as natural as play, if the conditions are favorable.
2. Self-control is often indispensable in achieving organ-
    izational goals.
3. The capacity for creativity in solving organizational
    problems is widely distributed in the population.
4. Motivation occurs at the social, esteem, and self-
    actualization levels, as well as at the physiological and
    security levels.
5. People can be self-directed and creative at work if
    properly motivated. (Hersey et al., 2001, p. 60)

Importantly, McGregor (1960) recognizes that not all employees will behave in ways that make Theory Y assumptions and the accompanying behaviors appropriate for everyone. In other words, Theory X is not necessarily wrong and Theory Y is not necessarily right. McGregor (1960) recognizes that while Theory Y assumptions were much more in line with the knowledge base regarding human behavior, some people need to be directed and controlled. However, the long-term goal should be to help such people grow so their behavior will allow the manager's (leader's) behavior toward them to reflect Theory Y assumptions.

It's difficult to overstate the importance of McGregor's (1960) *The Human Side of Enterprise.* Not only did it reject the widespread autocratic management assumptions and practices that were prevalent at the time, McGregor's (1960) work also laid the foundation for future thinking about leadership behavior based on a two-dimensional model of thinking. On the one hand, leaders need to have the competencies that will ensure tasks are completed on time and of a high quality, and on the other hand, leaders need to have the interpersonal skills to motivate workers in ways that capture the power of higher-order psychological needs.

Leadership Theory and Professional Learning Communities at Work

The study of leadership that gained momentum during the 20th century formed the basis for the importance Rick and I placed on leadership as a prerequisite for systemic and significant school improvement. As we began to draft *Professional Learning Communities at Work* (DuFour & Eaker, 1998), we knew that functioning as a high-performing PLC required fundamental changes in school cultures, and we also knew that changing organizational culture required effective and persistent leadership.

Fortunately for us, the last two decades of the 20th century witnessed an increased interest in the study of leadership and organizational development. There was an explosion in the number of books, articles, and research studies, and we relied heavily on the ideas and findings of writers and researchers from both within and outside public education.

I previously noted the importance of Peters and Waterman's (1982) *In Search of Excellence* as the basis for the necessity for leaders of PLCs to develop a simultaneously loose and tight culture. We had also been heavily influenced by Bennis and Nanus's (1985) *Leaders: Strategies for Taking Charge* as we began to write about the need for leaders of PLCs to build a solid foundation of shared mission, vision, values, and goals.

We both knew the difficulties leaders faced as they undertook the task of changing district or school culture. Our own experiences had provided us with valuable practical insights into the leadership behaviors that were necessary for leading such cultural shifts. We added to this practical knowledge base the findings from respected researchers and writers such as Seymour Sarason (1996) and his work on both school culture and leading organizational change.

I had gotten to know Terry Deal after he moved to Vanderbilt University from Harvard, and he wrote the introduction to our book *Fulfilling the Promise of Excellence: A Practitioner's Guide to School Improvement* (DuFour & Eaker, 1987). Rick and I were impressed with Terry Deal and Allan Kennedy's (1982) *Corporate Cultures: The Rites and Rituals of Corporate Life*, particularly their work regarding rituals and celebrations, and drew heavily on their ideas as we wrote about how leaders can effect cultural change.

Regarding specific leadership behaviors, our thinking was heavily impacted by *The Leadership Challenge* by Kouzes and Posner (1987), particularly their focus on the importance of shared vision and values. Their work also reinforced our thinking about the important relationship between effective leadership and collaboration. And, like Deal and Kennedy (1982), they emphasized the importance of leaders recognizing contributions by showing appreciation for individual excellence and celebrating values and victories (small wins).

In retrospect, as we were developing our leadership ideas related to the PLC at Work process, perhaps we were most influenced by Senge's (1990) *The Fifth Discipline: The Art and Practice of the Learning Organization.* Previously, I wrote of the importance we placed on Senge's (1990) assertion that successful organizations of the future would need to be *learning* organizations. After reading and discussing *The Fifth Discipline* (Senge, 1990), we realized that a major shift in our thinking about leadership was taking place.

Throughout our careers as administrators, the emphasis had been on the importance of educational leaders being strong *instructional leaders*. We realized this emphasis was misplaced. For educational leadership to be effective, leaders needed to be *learning leaders*— leaders who led the creation of school and district cultures that emphasized the learning of both students and adults. And, notably, Senge's (1990) work also reinforced our ideas about the importance of team learning.

More recently, we have learned that effective leadership can lead to significant improvement much more quickly than was previously thought. In *100-Day Leaders* (Reeves & Eaker, 2019), my friend and colleague Doug Reeves and I cite numerous examples of dramatic accomplishments in relatively short periods of time—accomplishments ranging from the writing of the United States Constitution to the presidential and legislative enactments of the first one hundred days of Franklin D. Roosevelt's administration that saved the country from the ravages of the Great Depression. In short, we have learned that significant positive gains can be made in a relatively short period of time if leaders do the right things for the right reasons in the right ways.

A Summing Up

For Rick and myself, the question wasn't simply what we could learn from researchers and writers about effective leadership practices—although we valued and relied on the thinking of others very much. For us, ultimately, the central leadership question was, What do effective leaders of the PLC at Work process do?

Rick, Becky, and I joined with Gayle Karhanek (DuFour et al., 2010) in writing *Raising the Bar and Closing the Gap: Whatever It Takes*. Our initial intent of the book was to describe how schools across North America had successfully implemented processes and practices to provide additional time and support for students who experienced difficulty with some aspect of their learning, as well as how these schools extended the learning of students who demonstrated proficiency. However, by the time we had completed our draft, we realized that by studying these diverse schools in diverse settings we had uncovered common leadership patterns, especially at the district level, that positively impacted the successful reculturing of each of these schools into high-performing PLCs.

The first of these patterns, and the pattern that impacted subsequent leadership behaviors, was that in each case the leader, whether it was the superintendent at the district level or the principal at the school level, accepted responsibility for embedding PLC at Work concepts and practices throughout the organization. By *taking responsibility*, I mean that these leaders behaved in specific and similar ways to ensure certain things began to occur, either districtwide or schoolwide.

In virtually all cases, the leaders realized they could not lead the effort to become a PLC by themselves. They surrounded themselves with a small guiding coalition. Importantly, they selected these people with great care, making sure that each person was widely respected and had the ability to influence others. The first order of business of the leader and the guiding coalition was to learn together. They learned about the PLC at Work process—the key concepts and practices reflective of a high-performing PLC. And, they learned a common vocabulary of key terms associated with PLCs.

Importantly, they explored ways the guiding coalition could effectively enhance an understanding of and an interest in the PLC at Work process. One way they did this was by always connecting concepts and practices back to the why—and the why was always to enhance the learning levels of *all* students. (For a deeper insight into the importance of emphasizing the why, see Simon Sinek's [2009] *Start With Why: How Great Leaders Inspire Everyone to Take Action*.) These leaders recognized the goal was not to become a PLC but, rather, to increase student learning. The PLC at Work concepts and practices were communicated as a means to an end, not as an end in and of itself. In other words, the why was always connected to the students and their learning.

At the district level, we found successful leaders' efforts focused on the work of the principals. In this regard, the PLC at Work process was simply reflecting the findings of multiple effective schools research studies. Simply put, principal behavior matters—a lot! The emphasis on principals was reflected by organizing the principals into a learning team or teams, depending on the size of the district. If an individual school was beginning the journey to becoming a PLC, the principal actively sought other principals who were successfully implementing the concepts and practices of a PLC to gain insights about what works and what doesn't. We found that many of these principals took advantage of the website www.allthingsplc .info and connected with other principals electronically.

The work of the principal teams generally focused on three things: (1) anticipating issues and questions, (2) sharing learning data, and (3) practicing and rehearsing the work that was being undertaken. This meant the nature of principal meetings was drastically changed.

Once the principal and the guiding coalition gained sufficient knowledge and commitment necessary for the journey to begin, the district leadership directed principals to organize their schools into collaborative teams of teachers who taught the same or similar content, making sure that a constant reference was made to the why—in order to achieve better results. Two points were critical. One, collaboration by invitation will not work, and two, everyone must be part of a collaborative team. For singleton teachers, this meant connecting with others in creative ways. Successful principals understood that teachers only teach in isolation because either they want to or they are allowed to.

Much attention was given to the selection of team leaders. The overarching standard was who would most likely do the best job of successfully leading the team. It was understood that after gaining input from others, selecting team leaders was the principal's responsibility. In some districts, district leaders had collaboratively developed a position description for team leaders.

Principal leaders also developed a school leadership team. This team was composed of the principal and team leaders. They met weekly and focused on the same three things as the districtwide principal teams—anticipating issues and questions, sharing learning data, and practicing and rehearsing the work that was to be undertaken by the teacher teams. Effective district-level leaders viewed the principal team as the key link between the district office and the school, and effective principals viewed the school leadership team as the key link between the principal and the teacher teams.

One of the most important leadership behaviors we discovered was leaders *directing* the work of teams. This was a classic example of the simultaneously loose and tight concept. Leaders were tight about the work of teams but loose in how they did their work.

The power of collaborative teams lies in what teams do, not merely that they collaborate. The first thing teams were directed to do was develop team norms—how the team would work together day in and day out. If implementing the PLC at Work process was a districtwide initiative, principals were expected to share with other principals within the district the team structure within their school, whom they had selected as team leaders and why, and the norms each team had developed. Additionally, the principal teams modeled the importance of norms by developing their own shared norms or commitments.

One of the most critical leadership behaviors was ensuring that appropriate training and resources were provided. Effective leaders understood it made little sense to expect people to accomplish specific tasks without the prerequisite training and resources necessary to be successful. This training was especially important as teams began to engage in work associated with the four critical questions of learning: (1) What do we want students to learn in each subject, course, and unit? (2) How will we know if they've learned it, student by student, skill by skill? (3) How will we respond when students experience difficulty in their learning? and (4) How will we respond when students demonstrate proficiency; how will we extend their learning? Each successful leader we encountered understood that focusing the work of teams on these four questions was difficult and complex, but the secret was to get started and get better.

Leadership, by its very nature, involves a degree of multitasking. Reculturing schools into PLCs is no exception. As leaders engaged in the process of organizing into teams, directing teams, and providing training and resources for teams, they were also engaged in two additional efforts. They were leading the process of clarifying and communicating a clear sense of shared mission, vision, values and commitments, and goals. And they were working with principals to develop a systematic schoolwide plan to provide additional time, support, and extension of learning for all students within the school day, regardless of the teacher to whom students were assigned. These two tasks were difficult, and both required training, resources, and examples. However, the most important requirements were the passionate and persistent leadership to get started and then get better.

As the work of embedding the concepts and practices of the PLC at Work process was underway, the leadership role shifted to monitoring and improving the work of individuals and teams. District leaders clearly communicated that it was the responsibility of each principal to stretch the aspirations and performance levels of each team.

The more effective leaders recognized that adults, like students, learn at different rates and in different ways. This meant it was unrealistic to think that each team would experience the same degree of success at the same time. Successful leaders understood the importance of being firm and consistent regarding expectations but flexible in providing feedback and assistance to each individual team. One of the leaders, Janel Keating, referred to this as "relentless pressure, gracefully applied."

Each of the leaders we encountered in these successful districts or individual schools had captured the power of frequent and meaningful recognition and celebration of incremental success—of both students and adults. They created lots of winners and frequently and publicly celebrated successes. In particular, they celebrated the work of individuals and teams and gains in student learning and behavior, even if the gains were rather small. The leaders understood the power of communicating, "Here's evidence we're getting better as a result of our hard work! Way to go! Let's keep it up and get even better results!"

Last, each of the leaders we contacted had made a commitment to limit initiatives. Embedding PLC at Work concepts and practices was not viewed as one of many initiatives to improve student learning; rather, it was viewed as *the* initiative. In this regard, the leaders diligently and purposefully connected work within the district back to the four critical questions of learning and to the larger question of *why*—to improve student learning.

CHAPTER 9

Connie Donovan Revisited

A s we were writing *Professional Learning Communities at Work* (DuFour & Eaker, 1998), Rick and I realized the readers would be interested in details—what would people actually be doing in a school that had embedded the concepts and practices of a PLC? To address this question, we included a scenario titled The Connie Donovan Story. The scenario follows a new teacher at a school that had implemented the PLC at Work process fully and with fidelity. Although the name of the teacher was fictional, the school and the experiences of Connie Donovan were real.

I think it is fair to ask, "What has been learned about implementing Professional Learning Communities at Work concepts and practices since 1998?" And I think it's fair to respond that the basic assumptions and concepts have remained the same. On the other hand, the practices have been enhanced, extended, and refined. I cannot think of a more effective way to describe a highly effective PLC at Work school in 2018 as opposed to in 1998 than revisiting the Connie Donovan story and including new learnings that have evolved over the past two decades.

The School as a Professional Learning Community: A Scenario

Connie Donovan approached her first teaching assignment with all the anxiety and nervous trepidation of any first-year teacher. She had been assured during her interview process that her new school operated as a learning community that valued collaboration. She had been impressed when the principal emphasized that she was being employed as a contributing member of a teacher team, not as an individual teacher. And the team had been very involved in the interview process.

Nevertheless, the memory of her roommate's introduction to the teaching profession the year before was still fresh in her mind. Poor Beth had been assigned to teach one of the most difficult remedial courses in her school, and her classes were filled with students who had failed the course in the past due to a variety of problems. Her orientation had consisted of a review of the employee manual and an overview of the teacher's contract by the principal on the morning of the day before students were to arrive. Then she was given the key to her room, the teacher's edition of the textbook, and her class roster.

The following day, she faced her 135 students for the first time. Her nine weeks of training as a student teacher had not prepared her for the difficulties she encountered, and there was no support system to help her. She did not know how to respond to student misbehavior and apathy, and she had told Connie tearfully that she felt she was losing control of her class.

Connie had watched Beth work far into the night, preparing lessons and grading papers, but each week, Beth only seemed to become more discouraged and overwhelmed. Weekends offered no respite. Beth's teaching position had been contingent on her willingness to serve as cheerleading sponsor, and Fridays and Saturdays were spent supervising cheerleaders.

By March, she had decided that she was not cut out for teaching. She dreaded each day and frequently called in sick. By the end of the year, she had admitted to Connie that she felt like she was hanging on by her fingernails.

Knowing this story as she did, Connie was relieved to get a phone call that summer from Jim, a veteran member of the faculty of her new school. Jim was a member of the team that had interviewed Connie for her position and a member of the team to which she would be assigned. He congratulated her on her appointment to the social studies department, explained that he would be serving as her mentor during her first year, and invited her to lunch to make introductions and answer any questions she might have. Her anxiety was diminished somewhat when Jim told her that the school provided two full days of orientation and another three days for the faculty teams to work together before students arrived.

The new teacher orientation was nothing like what Beth had described. After introductions, the principal, Dr. Silvia Goodwell, spent the morning explaining the history of the school. She carefully reviewed the school's vision statement, pointing out that it had been jointly developed by the faculty, administration, community members, and students. She explained that the statement described what the school was striving to become, and she highlighted recent initiatives that had begun in the school's effort to move closer to the ideal that was reflected in the school's vision document. She then divided the new teachers into small groups and asked them to identify any points within the vision statement they felt needed clarification. The emphasis the principal gave the vision statement made it clear to Connie that it was a major focus for the school.

Connie spent the afternoon with her department chairman (also referred to as the team leader) and Jim. Jim shared with Connie the departmental norms—commitments the team had collaboratively developed regarding how the team would work together as a high-performing collaborative team. There were a limited number of norms, but Jim emphasized that everyone on the team was expected to honor the team norms and support each other in their efforts to improve student learning. Connie noticed that the last norm addressed how the team had collaboratively agreed to address team member behavior that was incongruent with the team's norms. The steps ranged from the team leader simply giving the team member a heads-up about his or her behavior all the way to asking the principal to intervene with the teacher.

The department chair and Jim provided Connie with an overview of the entire scope and sequence of the social studies department's curriculum. They also provided her with descriptions that teachers had developed for each course, and they reviewed the essential outcomes all students were expected to achieve in the courses she was teaching. Jim explained further that these outcomes had been determined collectively by the teachers after considerable discussion and a lengthy review of the state's goals in social studies, the report on student achievement in social studies by the National Assessment of Educational Progress, and the curriculum standards recommended by the National Council for the Social Studies and the National Center for History in the Schools.

Perhaps the thing that impressed—and pleased—Connie the most was the fact that the department chair and Jim showed her how to access the unit plans that had been collaboratively developed previously for the course she was assigned. Connie's anxiety was greatly diminished, to say the least. She noticed that although the unit plans had been collaboratively developed, she still enjoyed considerable individual freedom regarding the teaching methods she would use.

Jim explained that the unit plans reflected the school's simultaneously tight and loose philosophy. The school and the department were tight about what students should learn and the use of common formative assessments that had been collaboratively developed but loose regarding each teacher's choice of *how* to teach. The emphasis was on results. The department chair chimed in, adding, "At our school and in this department, the question, Are the students learning, and how do we know? drives pretty much everything we do." Connie was impressed by the fact that after each unit was taught the team would analyze student learning data and reflect on the effectiveness of each unit, making notes regarding how the unit could be improved the next time it was to be taught. Connie began to realize that she was not left alone to develop unit plans over and over. She was even more surprised to learn that every team's unit plans were on the school's central server so that all teachers had access to each team's unit plans.

Finally, they reviewed the vision statement for the social studies department that the teachers had developed. They discussed the department's improvement goals and priorities and explained to Connie how she could engage her fellow teammates regarding materials, teaching ideas, and helpful hints.

On the second day of orientation, the principal introduced the president of the teachers' association, who distributed and explained the faculty value commitment statements. These statements had been developed by the faculty to give direction to the daily work of teachers. The association president pointed out the link between the value commitment statements and the school's vision and explained that every group in the school—the board of education, administration, support staff, students, and parents—had articulated similar statements of the commitments they were prepared to make to improve the school. Connie heard the association president remark, "Our collective commitments serve as the sinew that binds everyone's behaviors and attitudes together."

The rest of the morning was spent hearing from representatives from the different support services available to teachers—the deans, the director of the media center, the technology coordinator, the pupil personnel department, the special education department, and the tutors from the resource centers. Each speaker emphasized that his or her function was to help teachers. That afternoon, Connie's mentor helped her set up her classroom, asked what she hoped to accomplish on the first day and during the first week of class, and offered a few suggestions based on her responses.

When the entire faculty arrived the next day, Connie was surprised to see that the morning was devoted to a celebration of the start of the new school year. At the opening meeting, the principal announced milestones—weddings, births, engagements, advanced degrees, and other important events that faculty members had experienced over the summer. Each announcement was met with warm applause by the faculty. The principal then stressed several themes from the vision statement and reminded teachers of the priorities they had established for that school year. Each new faculty member was introduced to the group by his or her mentor and then given a faculty T-shirt. The rest of the morning was spent enjoying a festive, schoolwide brunch, complete with skits and entertainment presented by members of the faculty and administration. Connie was surprised and pleased to learn that this back-to-school celebration was an annual tradition planned and orchestrated by a faculty committee.

That afternoon, the teachers split into teaching teams to discuss how the team would handle its responsibilities. Connie realized that many teachers were on more than one team. For example, Connie was a member of a content team that met one period per week and an interdisciplinary team that met less frequently. The interdisciplinary team included, in addition to Connie, an English teacher and a science teacher. Together the three of them would be responsible for seventy-five students. These students were assigned to Connie and her two colleagues for a three-hour block every day and would remain with the same three teachers for two full years.

Connie was excited about this assignment. She believed in the benefits of an integrated curriculum. She felt the long-term relationships with students would be beneficial, and she welcomed the idea of working closely with two colleagues who shared the same students. She was also enthusiastic about the fact that the teachers were free to schedule the three-hour block as they saw fit. (Connie realized this was another example of the school's simultaneously loose and tight culture.) Free from the limits of a fifty-minute period, Connie thought she could offer some interesting simulations and mock trials for her students. She spent the rest of the day working with her colleagues to strengthen their first interdisciplinary unit, referring to notes that were made after the last time the unit was taught.

On the next day, Connie worked with her other team—the United States history team. All teachers responsible for teaching the same course were members of a team for that particular course. In addition to team norms, the teams developed common course descriptions, articulated the essential outcomes for the course, established the criteria for assessing the quality of student work, and developed common assessment instruments. The history team spent considerable time reviewing and grading examples of essays that students had written the year before.

Connie was particularly impressed with the emphasis the team gave to agreeing on what student work would look like if a student learned the essential knowledge or skills. She found this particularly helpful in both understanding what the department emphasized and identifying the criteria for evaluating student work. And, indirectly, knowing what student work should look like helped her sharpen her thinking about student practice and feedback. By the end of the morning, the teachers were very consistent in the way they applied the departmental criteria to grading student work. Connie realized the grading was toward a standard, as opposed to averaging scores during a fixed period of time.

That afternoon, the team analyzed student performance according to the common assessment instruments from the previous year, identified areas where students did not meet the desired proficiencies established by the team, and discussed goals and strategies aimed at improving student performance during the coming year. The discussion helped Connie understand what students were to accomplish, how they were to be assessed, and where they experienced difficulties in the past. She found the discussion to be invaluable and made a point to pay particular attention to areas in which students had experienced difficulty.

She spent part of the third day of teacher preparation working with her teams and discussing with her mentor a few ideas she planned to use in her opening comments to students the next day. Finally, she spent the rest of her day examining the profiles of her new students. She quickly noticed the guidance counselor had provided a heads-up regarding particular students who might need immediate additional time and support with their learning.

Once the school year was underway, the new teachers continued to meet at least once each month for ongoing orientation. Sometimes teachers with particular interests or skills would talk to the group about activities in their classes. One of these sessions helped Connie solve a problem she was having structuring individual accountability into cooperative learning activities. Other times, the principal provided new teachers with an article or case study and asked them to react to the item in their personal journals. These reflections then became the basis for the group's discussion. The sessions always included an opportunity to ask questions. As the year progressed, Connie found her meetings with the other new teachers helped her develop a sense of camaraderie and shared experience with them.

By the third week of school, Connie had become concerned about one of her history students who seemed unwilling to work. Although he was not disruptive, Matthew seemed detached in class and rarely turned in any work. Connie spoke to him after class one day to express her concerns and to discuss possible ways of engaging him in the classroom activity. When the conference failed to bring about any change, Connie discussed the problem with Jim.

Jim suggested alerting Matthew's student support team (SST). Connie learned that teachers were not the only ones in the school to work in teams. A counselor, dean, and social worker also shared responsibility for the same group of students. When Connie explained her concerns to Matthew's counselor, the SST decided to seek information from all of his teachers. It soon became evident that the behavior pattern that Matthew demonstrated in Connie's classroom was evident in all of his classes.

The SST decided it was time to convene a parent conference to review Matthew's status with both his parents and his teachers. At the conference, the teachers jointly developed strategies that would enable Matthew's parents to be aware of his assignments. The parents promised to monitor their son carefully to ensure he would keep up with his work.

Jim trained Connie in the school's approach to classroom observation and teacher evaluation before the department chairman and principal began the formal process with her. She became comfortable having him observe her teaching and found her debriefing sessions with him to be very helpful. He explained that all the mentors had been trained in analyzing teaching and providing constructive feedback.

Connie expected the principal to be more directive in the teacher evaluation process and anticipated she would receive some kind of rating at the conclusion of her conference with the principal. She was wrong on both counts. The principal asked probing questions: Why did you decide to teach this content? How does it fit with the major outcomes of the course? How did you know students had the prerequisite knowledge and skills to be successful in this unit?

Why did you use the instructional strategies you selected? How do you know if each student achieved the intended outcomes? What patterns do you see in your teaching? What worked and what did not work in this lesson? If you were to teach this lesson again, would you do anything differently? By the end of the conference, Connie realized that she had done most of the talking and that the principal was simply providing prompts to encourage her to reflect on and articulate her conclusions about her teaching.

Connie was surprised to discover the number of action research projects in progress in her department. For example, teachers were divided on the question of ability grouping. Some argued that remedial classes created a climate of low expectations and were harmful to students. They called for students to be grouped heterogeneously. Others argued that remedial classes offered the best strategy for meeting the individual unique needs of students who had experienced trouble with social studies in the past.

The teachers subsequently agreed to put their respective theories to the test. Remedial students were randomly assigned either to heterogeneous classes or to remedial classes, and the teachers agreed on the assessment strategies they would use at the end of the year to see which approach was more effective.

In another project, some teachers volunteered to increase their class size by 25 percent in order to reduce their teaching assignment from five sections to four, thus leaving more time for joint planning. Once again, teachers in the experimental and traditional classes agreed on the criteria they would monitor to determine the effectiveness of each approach. Connie couldn't help but to reflect that this was what a true learning community looked like—teachers learning collaboratively through collective inquiry and action research in order to enhance the learning of each student, skill by skill, name by name.

She soon learned that action research was not limited to her department; in fact, each department had various action projects underway. She also learned the school had established a special entrepreneurial fund offering teachers opportunities to develop grant proposals for projects to improve the school. After a review by a faculty committee to determine which proposals offered the greatest promise, the school board provided funding for the implementation of those proposals. It was obvious to Connie that experimentation played an important part in the culture of her new school.

Reflection and dialogue were also essential to the workings of the school. She remembered the principal emphasizing the school promoted a culture in which teachers reflected on their instructional effectiveness and students reflected on their own learning. For example, all teachers benefited from peer observation. Teachers created reading clubs that reviewed and discussed books and major articles on teaching, learning, organizational and school improvement, and leadership. Faculty members participated in a portfolio development project based on the criteria identified by the National Board for Professional Teaching Standards. Connie was excited to learn the board and the principal would support, with finances and assistance, each teacher ultimately gaining National Board Certification. And, each teacher who successfully achieved National Board Certification would receive a bump in his or her annual salary. The teachers who had previously gained National Board Certification formed a support team to assist teachers who were undergoing the process.

Department meetings typically opened with a teacher sharing a strategy or insight with colleagues and then responding to questions. Connie was impressed with the lively give-and-take of these discussions. She noticed that teachers felt comfortable probing and challenging one another's thinking. Although the phrase *professional learning community* was used sparingly, Connie realized that her experiences reflected collaborative professional behavior.

It was soon very evident that ongoing professional growth was expected and supported at this school. The district offered three areas of concentration—authentic assessment, student-centered learning, and multiple intelligences. Teaching teams agreed to pursue one of these three professional growth initiatives for at least three years. In past years, other topics had been studied. Connie's interdisciplinary team had already opted for authentic assessment. Each school year, five half-days and two full days had been set aside for concentrated focus on these topics.

The faculty members had committed themselves to making a concerted effort to integrate technology into the curriculum. They had agreed to adjust other budget areas in order to fund a full-time technology trainer. This trainer not only offered a regular schedule of technology classes for all staff during their preparation periods, she also provided one-on-one, just-in-time training when individual staff members identified a need. With the trainer's help, Connie learned to log onto a social studies teachers' group on the internet. She enjoyed asking questions and soliciting ideas from colleagues around the world. She was somewhat surprised to learn of the power of virtual teaming. Reflecting on this one day, she shared with a friend how her school really valued a collaborative culture; she was a member of her larger department team, her subject-specific team, her interdisciplinary team, and her virtual social studies team.

Each teacher in the school was asked to develop an individual professional growth plan in an area they felt they needed to improve. Teachers were expected to review the results of their students' performance on the team's common formative assessments and reflect on areas of instructional improvement that might enhance student performance.

Connie realized she needed to learn more ways to differentiate instruction in her classroom, as well as effective question strategies. She worked with her department chair to develop a plan for investigating these topics. The chairman provided her with articles summarizing the research on differentiated instruction and questioning strategies, and the principal recommended she observe several teachers who were particularly skilled in these areas. During the next several weeks, Connie implemented some of the strategies she had either read about or observed firsthand. She also requested feedback on her questioning techniques from Jim after he had observed her teaching. And, she was most surprised when the principal informed her of a differentiating instruction conference that the school would pay for her to attend if she chose to do so.

In addition, the district offered a series of workshops and courses that were tied to district goals. Most of these classes were taught by local teachers or administrators. Connie took the course on questioning strategies, as well as courses on differentiating instruction and classroom management. She was happy to learn that she received credit on the salary schedule for doing so.

The district not only encouraged teachers to be active in their professional organizations, but it also contributed toward the membership fee of approved organizations. Connie joined both the National Council for the Social Studies and its state affiliate. The principal, department chairperson, and Connie's colleagues frequently distributed copies of journal articles they found interesting, and team and department meetings were often devoted to the discussion of the ideas in the articles. The district also published its own professional journal once each year, comprised exclusively of articles written by teachers in the district.

The district's partnership with a local college served as another stimulus of reflection and productive interchange. Undergraduate students in education were frequent observers and often served as teacher aides in the school. They had many questions after they observed a class. University staff often advised teachers in setting up action research projects. School staff reciprocated by participating in the research of the university. Professors frequently taught units in the high school, and many of the undergraduate and graduate education courses were team-taught by university staff members and a teacher from the district. Late in the year, Connie was invited to share reflections on her experience as a first-year teacher with a class of college students as they prepared for their student teaching assignments.

Connie had been surprised when, shortly after she had accepted her teaching position, the personnel office asked her to complete a survey on her experience as a teaching candidate. As the year went on, she realized that surveys soliciting feedback were frequently used throughout the district. The principal and department chairpersons distributed surveys to the staff for feedback on their performance. Teachers could choose from a variety of survey instruments that gave students the opportunity to comment on the teacher and the class. All seniors were asked to complete a survey reflecting on their high school experience, and the school conducted a phone survey of randomly selected students one year and five years after their graduation to assess their high school experience and to determine their current status.

Parents were surveyed annually to determine their impressions of the school, and the principal and members of the school board participated in neighborhood coffees throughout the district to seek feedback and answer questions from members of the community. Teachers completed annual surveys for assessing the school's improvement efforts and identifying areas for improvement. They also completed self-evaluation forms on how effectively their teams functioned. It was clear that seeking and using feedback on performance were the norm both within the school and throughout the district.

Connie noticed that it was not uncommon for the principal to share and celebrate improvements on the survey results at faculty meetings. He usually did this by showing longitudinal data on some kind of graphic. Connie began to grasp the significance of celebration based on improvement in different types of data. Once she asked the principal about this, and he talked with her at length about the importance of creating small wins and then publicly recognizing and celebrating improvement.

Connie considered her common planning time with the members of both her interdisciplinary team and her history team to be her most valuable resource. The members of the interdisciplinary team used some of their time to refine integrated curriculum units and to discuss how to apply what they were learning about authentic assessment. Much of the time was spent discussing the students they had in common, identifying individuals who seemed to be having problems, and developing unified strategies for helping those students—especially utilizing the school's pyramid of interventions system.

The history team did not share the same students, but they did share the same content, and it was with her content team that Connie engaged in most of her planning. She found collaboratively planning for each unit to be particularly useful and, in fact, enjoyable. In thinking back on her experience as she developed common unit plans with her team, Connie realized that in many ways the planning work was simply common sense. The work of the team as they planned units of instruction was framed within four questions: What is essential for all students to know and be able to do as a result of this unit? How will we know if they have learned it? How will we respond to students who haven't learned the material? And, how will we respond to students who have demonstrated proficiency?

Developing unit plans around the four questions reflected a rather routine process. The team retrieved the unit plan that was taught the previous year along with the notes that were kept on the Unit Reflection Form. The team began discussing how the unit needed to be tweaked for this year's instructional cycle. The teachers were happy to share materials and ideas with Connie. It was unbelievably helpful that she did not have to create each unit on her own for the very first time.

In planning each unit of learning, the team paid particular attention to clarifying the outcomes that were essential for all students to learn as a result of the unit. The team agreed on what student work would look like if students learned the intended knowledge or skills. The team used this information to plan for common homework assignments. The team spent considerable time reviewing the common formative assessments for each unit. Connie quickly realized the common formative assessments were the engine that drove the work of the team.

These collaboratively developed, teacher-made assessments were the primary way teachers monitored student learning on a frequent and timely basis. Connie noticed the assessments were fairly short and only addressed the learning outcomes the team had agreed were essential. The longer units included more common assessments, while shorter ones had fewer. Attention was given to the formats of the common formative assessments. The team discussions ensured the assessment formats were aligned with the expectations regarding what student work should look like if students were successful, with the summative end-of-unit assessments, and with high-stakes normative assessments such as state assessments, SAT or ACT, advanced placement exams, and the National Assessment of Educational Progress. The team benefitted from the sample test items that had been collected and analyzed through the years.

The team spent considerable time collaboratively analyzing the results of the team's common formative assessments. Connie understood the purpose of the formative assessments was to provide information regarding the learning of each student, skill by skill, for the team in order to improve student learning. These discussions went smoother than Connie had expected due to the fact the team had developed a protocol for analyzing formative assessment results.

The protocol was simple and straightforward. The team first reviewed the essential outcomes of the unit, and collaboratively analyzing the assessment results, the team identified the items in which each student did well. There was a brief discussion about the instructional practices that led to these successes. Next, the team identified the skills with which students struggled. Connie had never really thought of it before, but she began to realize the importance of identifying skills with which individual students struggled, as opposed to identifying the problems that students missed. She learned that three students might miss the same problem but struggle with entirely different skills or understanding within the same problem.

The team discussed the specific steps that would be taken to provide each student who struggled with additional time and support. And students who had demonstrated proficiency were targeted for ways their learning could be extended or deepened. Of all the positive things about the school during her first year of teaching, Connie was most impressed with the school's plan for providing students with additional time, support, or extension of learning.

Soon after she arrived at her new school, Jim had explained to her that the school had collaboratively developed a systematic plan to assist students who were experiencing difficulty with their learning and to help students who were proficient move beyond proficiency. He pointed out the school was committed to not only providing additional time and support to help students learn but also to ensure students were not under-learning.

Connie was impressed by the fact that there was a schoolwide systematic plan to provide assistance to students. There was a recognition that there was only so much an individual teacher could do to assist students with their learning. The plan was sequential; that is, there was a strategy that was tried first, and if the student was still struggling, the plan called for a next step. For students who were still struggling, the plan had another step. Importantly, testing for special education or a special program was the last step, the step that was taken when everything else had been tried.

Other aspects of the plan also impressed Connie. The plan called for timely intervention—no later than the third week of school. And, it was directional, rather than invitational. There was a specific time within the school schedule for additional time, support, or extension of learning so that students did not miss core instruction to receive help with concepts or skills with which they were struggling. She had also noticed the attention that was given to monitoring the effectiveness of the plan. Jim had told her the idea had been to get the initial plan in place, then continually make it better. Connie realized this seemed to be the basic approach behind every initiative within this school.

In addition to providing assistance to support student learning—student by student, skill by skill—the team used the analysis of data from the common formative assessments to reflect on their planning effectiveness and their instructional effectiveness. It was particularly helpful for Connie since she was a new teacher to learn that teachers whose students had performed well were willing to share their instructional strategies and materials with other team members.

The last step of the protocol called for the team to fill out the short End-of-Unit Reflection Form on which the team made notes about how the unit might be improved the next time it would be taught. This form was kept by the team and was used for their planning purposes the next time the unit would be taught. The cumulative data from both the formative and summative assessments were used as the primary basis for the team's setting of improvement goals each year.

Connie felt there was never enough time to do everything that was required, but she appreciated the efforts the school had made to provide teachers with time to plan, reflect, and collaborate. In addition to the teacher planning days at the start of the year, the five half-days and three full days set aside for professional development, and the common preparation periods allocated for teaching teams, teachers were given two hours every two weeks for planning and conferencing. This was possible because a few years earlier the faculty agreed to extend the school day by ten minutes each day in exchange for a two-hour block every other Wednesday when teachers could work together on joint projects. The principal emphasized the importance of collaboration by assuring the faculty substitutes would be provided for any team that needed more time to complete its work. The principal had also enlisted a group of parent volunteers who would assist the group as needed.

That spring, teaching teams were invited to develop proposals for summer curriculum projects. The proposal form called on each team to describe what it wanted to accomplish, how the project related to departmental and school visions, and what the project would produce. Connie's interdisciplinary team submitted a proposal for creating two units that linked American literature, United States history, and scientific principles. After their plan was approved by the faculty committee that reviewed project proposals, the team members coordinated their calendars to find a week during the summer break when everyone would be available.

On three different occasions during the year, Connie participated in small-group discussions on proposals developed by different school improvement task forces. The task forces—composed of teachers, parents, and students—were convened to generate strategies for addressing priorities that had been identified by the school, primarily from the result of data and survey analysis. One task force submitted a proposal to increase student participation in co-curricular activities. Another offered strategies for teaching students to accept increasing responsibility for their learning as they advanced from their freshman to senior years. The third proposed a systematic way of monitoring each student's academic progress and responding to any student who was in danger of failing.

Each proposal included the criteria with which the long-term impact of its recommendations should be assessed. Connie learned that every teacher in the school was expected to participate in these improvement task forces from time to time and that one of the primary responsibilities of each task force was to build a consensus in support of the recommendations. It became apparent that the proposals often had to be revised several times before consensus could be reached.

At the end of the school year, Jim asked Connie to reflect on her overall experience. She acknowledged that not every lesson had gone well and that there had been days when she was frustrated and perplexed. Teaching had turned out to be much more difficult and complex than she had ever imagined. She had expected that her enthusiasm for history would be contagious and that her students would learn to love the subject just as she had.

She now had to acknowledge that some did not seem to care for history at all, and she wondered why she had been unable to generate their enthusiasm. She had been certain that she would be able to reach every student, and when one of her students elected to withdraw from school saying, "This school sucks!" she questioned why she had been unable to connect with him. She admitted she did not understand where her responsibility for student learning ended and the student's responsibility began. She often asked herself if she was doing too much or not enough to help each student succeed in her class.

She had been quite certain she knew all the answers when she decided to become a teacher, but as she worked through her first year of actual experience, she felt as though she had more questions than answers. It was not until the second semester that she came to realize that good teaching is driven by such questions. She gradually came to a clearer understanding and appreciation of the section of the school's vision statement that said, "We will be a school that is noted for two characteristics: our commitment to promoting the success of every student and our continuous discontent with the immediate present." In her school, the process of searching for answers was more important than actually having answers.

It was clear that every teacher was called on to reflect each day, "How can I be more effective in my efforts to be a positive influence in the lives of students entrusted to me?" Yet, it was equally clear that teachers were never to conclude that they had arrived at *the* definitive answer to any fundamental question. The year had been exhilarating and exhausting, fun and frustrating, but at its end, despite all the unanswered questions, Connie was certain of one thing—her life would be spent teaching!

Would It Be Good Enough for Our Own Children?

I think the vast majority of parents would want their own children to attend a school such as the one Connie Donovan experienced. In 2002, Janel Keating moved from Idaho to a small town south of Seattle to become a first-time principal. She faced a difficult challenge since the school was one of the lowest-performing elementary schools in the state of Washington. In just three years, the school had improved dramatically, to the point that parents were clamoring to send their children to the school and teachers were seeking to transfer to the school. The school was described by one journalist as the Nordstrom of American public education because of its commitment to customer (parent and student) service. Most important, student performance in mathematics and language arts improved significantly, from the bottom quartile to the top quartile on state achievement tests.

When she was being interviewed about this remarkable turn-around, Janel did not mention the term *professional learning communities*. The PLC at Work concept was simply the process she used to embed best practices into the collaborative culture that had been embedded within the school's culture. Instead, she pointed out that her daughter, Taylor, was two years old when she accepted the principalship. She knew that Taylor would be attending the elementary school in just a few short years. Janel said, "I just wanted to create a school that would be good enough for Taylor."

When I first heard Janel's remark, I thought it reflected a larger truth regarding school improvement. I believe most parents know the kind of school they want for their own children. They want safe schools, schools in which students are not only physically safe but psychologically secure as well. They want their children to attend a school in which their children are made to feel special. And importantly, they want their children to learn at high levels. The question, then, is this: if this is the kind of school we would want for our own children, shouldn't we want such schools for all students? In short, wouldn't we want our own children to attend a school that functioned, day in and day out, as a high-performing PLC? And wouldn't teachers find it professionally rewarding to teach in such a school?

School cultures such as the one Connie Donovan experienced will not result from mere good intentions. They must be created. Changing a school culture from a focus on teaching to one that reflects a relentless focus on the learning of each student, skill by skill, requires effective, passionate, and persistent leadership. The same is true for a cultural shift from teacher isolation to collaboration in which teachers are contributing members of high-performing teams within a larger collaborative school culture. And, a cultural shift from good intentions to a sharp focus on results requires a strong commitment to research-based, data-driven decision making. I believe the evidence gained is clear: the PLC at Work process offers our best hope for significant, sustainable, affordable, and attainable school improvement.

We know enough to create highly effective schools for all students, and there are many, many examples of schools across North America, and increasingly around the world, that have successfully recultured their schools into highly effective PLCs. We have reached a point in time in which the knowledge base regarding how to develop effective schools for *all* students is so strong and so consistent that it should be an embarrassment not to do what we know works. Don't we, as a profession, have an obligation to erase the knowing-doing gap that exists in many of our nation's schools and classrooms?

The issue is not a lack of knowledge but a lack of leadership and will. Shouldn't every district and every school make a public commitment to parents, students, faculty and staff, and the larger community that every school, every team, every teacher, every lesson, every decision, and every interaction will meet the standard of care that is reflected in the question, Would this be good enough for our own children?

A Summing Up

I realize that what we know about the efficacy of PLC at Work concepts and practices is an extension of the work of countless others in years past. My own summing up about how to improve schools is really a summing up of what I've learned about the power of effective classroom observation, research on effective teaching practices, dissemination and professional development, effective schools research, and research on learning communities. Palimpsest? Absolutely!

A Life Fulfilled

By Jeffrey C. Jones,
Chief Executive Officer, Solution Tree

B ob Eaker, Rick DuFour, and I met for the first time in Mont-Tremblant, Québec, Canada, in August 1998. My business partner and I had purchased a small company called National Educational Service (now Solution Tree) in January 1998. The previous owner of the company, who was then serving as president, chose Mont-Tremblant as the site for the first Professional Learning Communities at Work Institute. Why? No one is quite sure. Nonetheless, Bob, Rick, myself, two or three staff members, and ninety-one registrants were there to witness the beginning of what has arguably become the most sustained movement in K–12 professional development in the United States—possibly the world. It was also the beginning of a truly unique friendship and partnership between Bob, Rick, and myself.

I came to National Educational Service with a background in fundraising and marketing in higher education. In that work, the donor is always right (within reason, of course). He or she has the assets and will decide where to distribute them. My job was to make sure donors knew all the options and opportunities, manage the internal processes, and then get out of the way. After all, the fundraiser isn't the one who gets his or her name on the building. As I sat in the back of the room during each institute session in Mont-Tremblant, I viewed Bob and Rick at work in much the same way as a major donor; what they shared, their assets, came from their experiences and vast knowledge—their intellectual property. My predecessor at National Educational Service had a different approach to running the company; he thought he knew a better way for Bob and Rick to deliver their content. It didn't take long for me to realize that my style of working with authors was going to be very different; I had no idea how to do what Bob and Rick were doing. They were the experts, and that mindset would guide my approach.

What was very clear to me during our stay in Québec was that I liked these guys right from the start. Bob and Rick exuded a very personable style of calm and comfort in their coaching. Bob, a country gentleman with a background in higher education and educational research, was every bit the teacher as he communicated with educators and brought them into the discussion. Rick, with a background as a highly successful practitioner, was a more authoritative presence, leaving no doubt that the process they described would increase student achievement. It also became obvious to me during the institute that the Professional Learning Communities at Work process made a remarkable amount of sense and was easy to understand, but it was a lot harder to change the culture of schools and to implement the process. This realization was perhaps the impetus for what was to come in the development of PLC from a concept into a movement.

Starting a Movement

When I was asked to write this piece—to take time to reflect on the more than twenty years of working with Bob—it was hard to wrap my mind around how this concept of professional learning communities that began with researchers and higher education leaders became a practice that is nearly mandated to implement in all schools. Early researchers took business practices and applied them to K–12 public school systems, showing why it *would* work. But there wasn't a movement until Bob and Rick put those practices to work at Adlai E. Stevenson High School, along with other schools with which they had consulted during the previous decade, one at a time, building, molding, scaffolding, tweaking, and collaborating on those practices for over twenty-five years before writing the premier practitioner book on PLCs: *Professional Learning Communities at Work: Best Practices for Enhancing Student Achievement.* This first book truly launched a movement of not only the PLC process but of practitioners publishing quality work around action research.

When I reflect on my journey with Bob and Rick from our first meeting in Mont-Tremblant to today, I recall three monumental meetings and one specific institute that ended up shaping the future, putting us on a trajectory personally and professionally that really none of us anticipated fully.

Taking a Collaborative Journey: Life After Stevenson, 2001

"Life After Stevenson" was the title at the top of the two pages I handed to Rick in his office in September 2001. Rick was retiring as superintendent of Adlai E. Stevenson and was going to marry Ms. Rebecca Burnette and move to Virginia. I knew he wanted to do professional development, he liked the institute, and he was beginning to enjoy writing more and more. I have never been short on ideas when it comes to someone else creating the content, so my list was extensive and maybe a little overwhelming to a guy who was so love struck that all he really wanted to do was get to Virginia. He cherry-picked the items he felt he could undertake during his transition year. That year, he and Bob addressed maybe a third of what was on that list. They didn't take any items off the list altogether, and we eventually accomplished all those goals and then built on them. This approach is indicative of what happened for years after: my annual lists kept coming, and as a team, Bob, Rick, and Solution Tree tackled those items that moved us foreword, and tabled some for later that didn't seem to be right for that time.

Building the Team: Stone Mountain, Georgia, 2003

In 2003, Bob and I met at an event held by the Georgia Department of Education, where he was presenting. By this time, I had created a detailed visual of the model for expanding our offerings around the original PLC at Work book with different strands using our core products of books, videos, events, professional development, technology, other presenters, and so on. To Bob, it must have seemed like pie in the sky and really nice of this young man to share his wild ideas. I also told Bob that we wanted to build an associate pool that would represent their work and that by creating new content, with them and others, I was confident this would work much like an annuity for him and thus his work would continue to grow and sell for years and years. Once again, I am sure Bob was thinking, "Nice dream, Jeff."

Bob and I brainstormed and discussed each idea I shared, generating even more ideas and opportunities. I asked if he and Rick would consider writing books with other well-respected authors, like Michael Fullan and Douglas Reeves. Bob then shared with me the concept in higher education called a "book of readings" in which many authors came together with a chapter or paper on a specific topic, creating an anthology of ideas. BRILLIANT! This idea spawned the best-selling book *On Common Ground: The Power of Professional Learning Communities*, featuring Roland Barth, Rebecca DuFour, Richard DuFour, Robert Eaker, Barbara Eason-Watkins, Michael Fullan, Lawrence Lezotte, Douglas Reeves, Jonathon Saphier, Mike

Schmoker, Dennis Sparks, and Rick Stiggins, and edited by Rick, Bob, and Becky. This book not only brought a field of well-known and respected authors together but it set the stage for a PLC at Work Summit with each of these authors presenting and giving us as a company the opportunity to showcase what we could do.

Also in 2003 was the beginning of our partnership with Rebecca DuFour who joined the team as an institutes keynoter and presenter. At the time, I was doing all of the emcee work and would introduce her as "The charm and grace of the PLC process." Her first keynote was at the Professional Learning Communities at Work Institute in Lincolnshire, one of the three Professional Learning Communities Institutes held that year. Bob and I were standing in the back of the auditorium to watch her inaugural keynote. Midway through, I looked at Bob as he turned to me and said in his charming Southern drawl, "Oh my, Jeff. What are we gonna do?" Becky was so nervous we thought she might just freeze. She stood as straight and stiff as can be and got a bit tongue-tied a few times. But by the end, she was much more relaxed, her personality began to shine through, and she was off on her journey to becoming one of the finest keynoters I have ever seen, winning the hearts and minds of everyone who knew and watched her.

Creating Lasting Friendships: Hawaii Professional Learning Communities at Work Institute, 2004

I am not sure who suggested it first, Bob, Rick, or me, but somehow the idea of a Professional Learning Communities at Work Institute in Hawaii came up. Becky was part of the team, and Bob's wife, Star, and my wife, Margaret, had met before, so it seemed only right to have Star and Margaret be the event staff, I'd handle the logistics and emcee work, and we would put on an event there. So in February 2004 we hosted over three hundred attendees, which paid all the bills;

and, since we were already there, heck, why not go to Kona for a few days and play tennis, putt-putt golf, relax, and just hangout? It was a perfect venue to really get to know each other, and our working partnership began to grow into a truly great friendship. We returned to Hawaii two more times over the years, and also took vacations together; these were some of the best vacations of my life.

Traveling Side by Side: The Brawn Behind the Brains

To date, Solution Tree has published twenty-seven books authored or edited by Rick, Bob, and Becky; created hundreds of videos and video sets; hosted hundreds of thousands of educators at Professional Learning Communities at Work Institutes on four different continents; brought more than 150 PLC associates on board who have successfully led the PLC at Work process in schools that showed increased student achievement in at least three consecutive years; and has collectively worked in every state, Canadian province, and twenty-one different countries to help countless numbers of educators impact the lives of students for the better. As a company, we have launched new movements in response to intervention, priority schools, common formative assessment, leadership, and culture.

I have been so honored to travel side by side with Bob and Rick from the beginning of our journey and to have Solution Tree be the brawn behind their brains. Our partnership has truly been that—a partnership—and not a typical publisher-author partnership, but rather a team of individuals linked arm in arm to be become the leading pioneers in the national, and now international, PLC movement.

The true measure of leadership is when you are no longer the leader and your work continues and grows. With the passing of both Rick and Becky, there has been an overwhelming and unbelievable stepping up of PLC authors and associates to keep this PLC at Work family together to continue the important work. That is the result of true leadership by Bob, Rick, and Becky. Today Bob and I still work closely on protecting, maintaining, and building Professional Learning Communities at Work and our partnership, and, more importantly, our friendship continues to grow. As I reflected and wrote this piece, it became very clear to me that to have been a part of this incredible journey with three people whom I consider three of the closest friends I have ever had is a life fulfilled.

= *References and Resources* =

Ainsworth, L., & Viegut, D. (2006). *Common formative assessments: How to connect standards-based instruction and assessment.* Thousand Oaks, CA: Corwin Press.

Anderson, N. G. (Ed.). (2006). *Reading Faulkner: Introduction to the first thirteen novels.* Knoxville: University of Tennessee Press.

Bellon, J. J., Bellon, E. C., & Blank, M. A. (1992). *Teaching from a research knowledge base: A development and renewal process.* New York: Merrill.

Bellon, J., Eaker, R., Huffman, J., & Jones, R. (1976). *Classroom supervision and instructional improvement: A synergetic process.* Dubuque, IA: Kendall Hunt.

Bennis, W., & Nanus, B. (1985). *Leaders: Strategies for taking charge.* New York: Harper & Row.

Berliner, D. C. (1986). In pursuit of the expert pedagogue. *Educational Researcher, 15*(7), 5–13.

Blanchard, K. (2007). *Leading at a higher level: Blanchard on leadership and creating high performing organizations.* Upper Saddle River, NJ: Prentice Hall.

Bloom, B. S. (Ed.). (1956). *Taxonomy of educational objectives: The classification of educational goals; Handbook I: Cognitive domain.* New York: McKay.

Brookover, W., & Lezotte, L. (1979). *Changes in school characteristics coincident with changes in student achievement* [Occasional Paper No. 17]. East Lansing, MI: Institute for Research on Teaching.

Brown, A. (2014). *The myth of the strong leader: Political leadership in the modern age.* New York: Basic Books.

Brown v. Board of Education of Topeka, 347 U.S. 483 (1954).

Brualdi, A. C. (1998). *Classroom questions*. Washington, DC: ERIC Clearinghouse on Assessment and Evaluation. (ERIC Document Reproduction Service No. ED422407)

Buckley, W., Jr. (1983). *Overdrive: A personal documentary*. Boston: Little, Brown.

Burns, J. M. (1978). *Leadership*. New York: Harper & Row.

Champy, J. (1995). *Reengineering management: The mandate for new leadership*. New York: HarperBusiness.

Cogan, M. (1973). *Clinical supervision*. Boston: Houghton Mifflin.

Coleman, J. S., Campbell, E. Q., Hobson, C. J., McPartland, J., Mood, A. M., Weinfeld, F. D., et al. (1966). *Equality of educational opportunity* (Report No. OE-38001). Washington, DC: U.S. Department of Health, Education and Welfare.

Collins, J., & Porras, J. I. (1994). *Built to last: Successful habits of visionary companies*. New York: HarperBusiness.

Conroy, P. (1987). *The great Santini*. New York: Bantam.

Conroy, P. (2010). *My reading life*. New York: Doubleday.

Conroy, P. (2016). *A lowcountry heart: Reflections on a writing life*. New York: Doubleday.

Conzemius, A., & O'Neill, J. (2005). *The handbook for SMART school teams*. Bloomington, IN: Solution Tree Press.

Conzemius, A. E., & O'Neill, J. (2013). *The handbook for SMART school teams: Revitalizing best practices for collaboration*. Bloomington, IN: Solution Tree Press.

Cooper, H. M., & Good, T. L. (1983). *Pygmalion grows up: Studies in the expectation communication process*. New York: Longman.

Cotton, K. (1988). *Close-up #5: Classroom questioning* (School Improvement Research Series). Accessed at www.educationnorthwest.org/sites/default/files/ClassroomQuestioning.pdf on January 6, 2015.

Covey, S. (1996). Three roles of the leader in the new paradigm. In F. Hesselbein, M. Goldsmith, & R. Beckhard (Eds.), *The leader of the future: New visions, strategies and practices for the next era* (pp. 149–160). San Francisco: Jossey-Bass.

Darling-Hammond, L. (1996). What matters most: A competent teacher for every child. *Phi Delta Kappan, 78*(3), 193–200.

Deal, T. E., & Kennedy, A. A. (1982). *Corporate cultures: The rites and rituals of corporate life*. Reading, MA: Addison-Wesley.

Dewey, J. (1916). *Democracy and education: Introduction to the philosophy of education.* New York: Macmillan.

Dickinson, E. E. (2016). Coleman report set the standard for the study of public education. *Johns Hopkins Magazine.* Accessed at https://hub.jhu.edu /magazine/2016/winter/coleman-report-public-education on May 16, 2019.

Dilworth, R. (1995). The DNA of the learning organization. In C. Sarita & J. Renesch (Eds.), *Learning organizations: Developing cultures for tomorrow's workplace* (pp. 243–254). New York: Productivity Press.

Drucker, P. (1992). *Managing for the future: The 1990s and beyond.* New York: Truman Talley Books.

Duckett, W. (1986). An interview with Robert Eaker: Linking research and classroom practice. *Phi Delta Kappan, 68*(2), 161–164.

Duckworth, A. (2016). *Grit: The power of passion and perseverance.* New York: Scribner.

DuFour, R., DuFour, R., & Eaker, R. (2008). *Revisiting Professional Learning Communities at Work: New insights for improving schools.* Bloomington, IN: Solution Tree Press.

DuFour, R., DuFour, R., Eaker, R., & Karhanek, G. (2004). *Whatever it takes: How professional learning communities respond when kids don't learn.* Bloomington, IN: Solution Tree Press.

DuFour, R., DuFour, R., Eaker, R., & Karhanek, G. (2010). *Raising the bar and closing the gap: Whatever it takes.* Bloomington, IN: Solution Tree Press.

DuFour, R., DuFour, R., Eaker, R., & Many, T. (2006). *Learning by doing: A handbook for Professional Learning Communities at Work.* Bloomington, IN: Solution Tree Press.

DuFour, R., DuFour, R., Eaker, R., & Many, T. (2010). *Learning by doing: A handbook for Professional Learning Communities at Work* (2nd ed.). Bloomington, IN: Solution Tree Press.

DuFour, R., DuFour, R., Eaker, R., Many, T. W., & Mattos, M. (2016). *Learning by doing: A handbook for Professional Learning Communities at Work* (3rd ed.). Bloomington, IN: Solution Tree Press.

DuFour, R., & Eaker, R. (1987). *Fulfilling the promise of excellence: A practitioner's guide to school improvement.* Westbury, NY: Wilkerson.

DuFour, R., & Eaker, R. (1992). *Creating the new American school: A principal's guide to school improvement.* Bloomington, IN: Solution Tree Press.

DuFour, R., & Eaker, R. (1998). *Professional Learning Communities at Work: Best practices for enhancing student achievement.* Bloomington, IN: Solution Tree Press.

DuFour, R., Eaker, R., & DuFour, R. (Eds.). (2005). *On common ground: The power of professional learning communities.* Bloomington, IN: Solution Tree Press.

DuFour, R., Eaker, R., & DuFour, R. (2007). *The power of Professional Learning Communities at Work: Bringing the big ideas to life* [Video]. Bloomington, IN: Solution Tree Press.

Duke, A. (2018). *Thinking in bets: Make smarter decisions when you don't have all the facts.* New York: Portfolio.

Dweck, C. S. (2008). *Mindset: The new psychology of success.* New York: Ballantine Books.

Eaker, R., & Dillard, H. (2017, Winter). School culture and effective schools: The fifteen-thousand-hours study. *AllThingsPLC Magazine,* 40–41.

Eaker, R., DuFour, R., & DuFour, R. (2002). *Getting started: Reculturing schools to become professional learning communities.* Bloomington, IN: Solution Tree Press.

Eaker, R., & Friziellie, H. (2018, Fall). The Hawthorne effect. *AllThingsPLC Magazine,* 44–45.

Eaker, R., & Huffman, J. (1980). *Helping teachers use research findings: The consumer-validation process* [Occasional Paper No. 44]. East Lansing, MI: Institute for Research on Teaching.

Eaker, R., & Huffman, J. (1981). *Teacher perceptions of dissemination of research on teaching findings* [Occasional Paper No. 41]. East Lansing, MI: Institute for Research on Teaching.

Eaker, R., Huffman, J., & White, R. (1978). *A history of the Teacher Education Alliance for Metro, 1968–1977* [Monograph]. Murfreesboro: Middle Tennessee State University, Department of Educational Leadership.

Eaker, R., & Keating, J. (2012). *Every school, every team, every classroom: District leadership for growing Professional Learning Communities at Work.* Bloomington, IN: Solution Tree Press.

Eaker, R., & Keating, J. (2015). *Kid by kid, skill by skill: Teaching in a Professional Learning Community at Work.* Bloomington, IN: Solution Tree Press.

Eaker, R., & Sells, D. (2016). *A new way: Introducing higher education to Professional Learning Communities at Work.* Bloomington, IN: Solution Tree Press.

Edmonds, R. (1979). Effective schools for the urban poor. *Educational Leadership, 37*(1), 15–24.

Edmonds, R. R., & Frederiksen, J. R. (1978). *Search for effective schools: The identification and analysis of city schools that are instructionally effective for poor children.* Cambridge, MA: Harvard University Center for Urban Studies.

Eurich, T. (2017). *Insight: Why we're not as self-aware as we think, and how seeing ourselves clearly helps us succeed at work and in life.* New York: Crown Business.

Foreman, J. (Producer), & Hill, G. R. (Director). (1969). *Butch Cassidy and the sundance kid* [Motion picture]. United States: 20th Century Fox.

Fullan, M. (1993). *Change forces: Probing the depths of educational reform.* London: Falmer Press.

Fullan, M. (2005). *Leadership and sustainability: System thinkers in action.* Thousand Oaks, CA: Corwin Press.

Galbraith, J. K. (1981). *A life in our times: Memoirs.* Boston: Houghton Mifflin.

Good, T. L., & Brophy, J. E. (1980). *Educational psychology: A realistic approach* (2nd ed.). New York: Holt, Rinehart and Winston.

Grossman, N., Ostrowsky, I., & Schwarzman (Producers), & Tyldum, M. (Director). (2014). *The imitation game* [Motion picture]. United States: Weinstein.

Haley, A. (1965). *The autobiography of Malcom X.* New York: Grove Press.

Handy, C. (1995). Managing the dream. In S. Chawla & J. Renesch (Eds.), *Learning organizations: Developing cultures for tomorrow's workplace* (pp. 45–55). New York: Productivity Press.

Hattie, J. (2009). *Visible learning: A synthesis of over 800 meta-analyses relating to achievement.* New York: Routledge.

Hersey, P., Blanchard, K. H., & Johnson, D. E. (2001). *Management of organizational behavior: Leading human resources* (8th ed.). Upper Saddle, NJ: Prentice Hall.

Isaacson, W. (2017). *Leonardo da Vinci.* New York: Simon & Schuster.

Jencks, C. (1972). *Inequality: A reassessment of the effect of family and schooling in America.* New York: Basic Books.

Joyce, B., & Showers, B. (1995). Learning experiences in staff development. *The Developer, 3.*

Kanter, R. (1997, October). *Leading the change-adept organization with concepts, competence, and connections.* Keynote address presented at the Lessons in Leadership Conference, Boston.

Keating, J., Eaker, R., DuFour, R., & DuFour, R. (2008). *The journey to becoming a professional learning community.* Bloomington, IN: Solution Tree Press.

Kounin, J. S. (1970). *Discipline and group management in classrooms.* Huntington, NY: Krieger.

Kouzes, J. M., & Posner, B. Z. (1987). *The leadership challenge: How to get extraordinary things done in organizations.* San Francisco: Jossey-Bass.

Lepore, J. (2018). *These truths: A history of the United States.* New York: Norton.

Lezotte, L. W. (2005). More effective schools: Professional learning communities in action. In R. DuFour, R. DuFour, & R. Eaker (Eds.), *On common ground: The power of professional learning communities* (pp. 177–191). Bloomington, IN: Solution Tree Press.

Lezotte, L. W., & Snyder, K. M. (2011). *What effective schools do: Re-envisioning the correlates.* Bloomington, IN: Solution Tree Press.

Long, M., & Sato, C. (1983). Classroom foreign talk discourse: Forms and functions of teachers' questions. In H. W. Seliger & M. H. Long (Eds.), *Classroom oriented research in second language acquisition* (pp. 268–285). Rowley, MA: Newbury House.

Louis, K. S., Kruse, S., & Raywid, M. A. (1996). Putting teachers at the center of reform: Learning schools and professional communities. *NASSP Bulletin, 80*(580), 9–21.

Madden, J. V., Lawson, D. R., & Sweet. D. (1976). *California school effectiveness study: The first year, 1974–75—A report to the California legislature.* Unpublished manuscript.

Marzano, R. J. (2003). *What works in schools: Translating research into action.* Alexandria, VA: Association for Supervision and Curriculum Development.

Marzano, R. J. (2007). *The art and science of teaching: A comprehensive framework for effective instruction.* Alexandria, VA: Association for Supervision and Curriculum Development.

Marzano, R. J. (2017). *The new art and science of teaching.* Bloomington, IN: Solution Tree Press.

Marzano, R. J., Warrick, P. B., Rains, C. L., & DuFour, R. (2018). *Leading a high reliability school.* Bloomington, IN: Solution Tree Press.

Maslow, A. H. (1954). *Motivation and personality.* New York: Harper.

Maugham, W. S. (1919). *The moon and sixpence*. New York: Doran.

Maugham, W. S. (1938). *The summing up*. New York: Arno Press.

McCarthy, F. (Producer), & Schaffner, F. J. (Director). (1970). *Patton* [Motion picture]. United States: 20th Century Fox.

McGregor, D. (1960). *The human side of enterprise*. New York: McGraw-Hill.

Mohr, K. (1998). Teacher talk: A summary analysis of effective teachers' discourse during primary literacy lessons. *Journal of Classroom Interaction, 33*(2), 16–23.

Neville, M., Capotosto, C., & Ma, N. (Producers), & Neville, M. (Director). (2018). *Won't you be my neighbor?* [Motion picture]. United States: Tremolo Productions.

Newmann, F. M., & Associates (Eds.). (1996). *Authentic achievement: Restructuring schools for intellectual quality*. San Francisco: Jossey-Bass.

Newmann, F. M., & Wehlage, G. G. (1995). *Successful school restructuring: A report to the public and educators by the Center on Organization and Restructuring of Schools*. Madison: University of Wisconsin.

No Child Left Behind Act of 2001, Pub. L. No. 107–110, 20 U.S.C. § 6319 (2002).

Owens, R. G. (1970). *Organizational behavior in schools*. Englewood Cliffs, NJ: Prentice Hall.

Palimpsest. (n.d.). In *Oxford English Living Dictionaries online*. Accessed at https://en.oxforddictionaries.com/definition/palimpsest on May 17, 2019.

Peters, T. J., & Waterman, R. H., Jr. (1982). *In search of excellence: Lessons from America's best-run companies*. New York: Harper & Row.

Pfeffer, J., & Sutton, R. I. (2000). *The knowing-doing gap: How smart companies turn knowledge into action*. Boston: Harvard Business School Press.

Pinchot, G., & Pinchot, E. (1993). *The end of bureaucracy and the rise of the intelligent organization*. San Francisco: Berrett-Koehler.

Reeves, D. (2000). *Accountability in action: A blueprint for learning organizations*. Denver, CO: Advanced Learning Press.

Reeves, D., & Eaker, R. (2019). *100-day leaders: Turning short-term wins into long-term success in schools*. Bloomington, IN: Solution Tree Press.

Rogers, C. R. (1961). *On becoming a person: A therapist's view of psychotherapy*. Boston: Houghton Mifflin.

Rosenthal, R., & Jacobson, L. (1968). *Pygmalion in the classroom: Teacher expectation and pupils' intellectual development.* New York: Holt, Rinehart and Winston.

Rutter, M., Maughan, B., Mortimore, P., Ouston, J., & Smith, A. (1979). *Fifteen thousand hours: Secondary schools and their effects on children.* Cambridge, MA: Harvard University Press.

Saphier, J., Haley-Speca, M. A., & Gover, R. R. (2008). *The skillful teacher: Building your teaching skills* (6th ed.). Acton, MA: Research for Better Teaching.

Sarason, S. B. (1996). *Revisiting "the culture of the school and the problem of change."* New York: Teachers College Press.

Schmoker, M. (2004). Learning communities at the crossroads: Toward the best schools we've ever had. *Phi Delta Kappan, 86*(1), 84–88.

Senge, P. M. (1990). *The fifth discipline: The art and practice of the learning organization.* New York: Doubleday.

Senge, P. M. (1996). Leading learning organizations. In F. Hesselbein, M. Goldsmith, & R. Beckhard (Eds.), *The leader of the future* (pp. 41–58). San Francisco: Jossey-Bass.

Shaw, G. B. (2003). *Pygmalion.* London: Penguin Books. (Original work published 1916)

Sinek, S. (2009). *Start with why: How great leaders inspire everyone to take action.* New York: Portfolio.

Solomon, D. (2013). *American mirror: The life and art of Norman Rockwell.* New York: Farrar, Straus and Giroux.

State of New York Office of Education Performance Review, Albany. (1974). *School factors influencing reading achievement: A case study of two inner city schools.* New York: Author.

Steller, A. W. (1988). *Effective schools research: Promise and practice (fastback).* Arlington, VA: Phi Delta Kappa International.

Stiggins, R. (2005). Assessment FOR learning: Building a culture of confident learners. In R. DuFour, R. Eaker, & R. DuFour (Eds.), *On common ground: The power of professional learning communities* (pp. 65–83). Bloomington, IN: Solution Tree Press.

Taylor, F. W. (1911). *The principles of scientific management.* New York: Harper and Brothers.

Tomlinson, C. A., & Allan, S. D. (2000). *Leadership for differentiating schools and classrooms*. Alexandria, VA: Association for Supervision and Curriculum Development.

Thompson, J. W. (1995). The renaissance of learning in business. In C. Chawla & J. Renesch (Eds.), *Learning organizations: Developing cultures for tomorrow's workplace* (pp. 85–100). New York: Productivity Press.

Vidal, G. (1995). *Palimpsest: A memoir*. London: Penguin Books.

Ward, G. C., & Burns, K. (2014). *The Roosevelts: An intimate history*. New York: Knopf.

Warner, J. L. (Producer), & Cukor, G. (Director). (1964). *My fair lady* [Motion picture]. United States: Warner Bros. Pictures.

Weber, G. (1971). *Inner-city children can be taught to read: Four successful schools*. Washington, DC: Council for Basic Education.

Western Electric Company. (1924–1933). *Western Electric Company Hawthorne studies collection*. Cambridge, MA: Baker Library, Harvard Business School.

Wiliam, D. (2011). *Embedded formative assessment*. Bloomington, IN: Solution Tree Press.

Wiliam, D. (2018). *Embedded formative assessment* (2nd ed.). Bloomington, IN: Solution Tree Press.

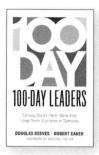

100-Day Leaders
Douglas Reeves and Robert Eaker
In only 100 days, schools can dramatically increase student achievement, transform faculty morale, reduce discipline issues, and much more.
BKF919

Learning by Doing, 3rd Edition
Richard DuFour, Rebecca DuFour, Robert Eaker, Thomas W. Many, and Mike Mattos
The third edition of this comprehensive action guide includes new strategies, tools, and tips for transforming your school or district into a high-performing PLC.
BKF746

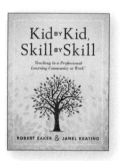

Kid by Kid, Skill by Skill
Robert Eaker and Janel Keating
This book explores PLCs from a teacher's perspective, focusing on best instructional practices, collaborative team actions, and lasting commitment to success.
BKF694

Every School, Every Team, Every Classroom
Robert Eaker and Janel Keating
With a focus on creating simultaneous top-down *and* bottom-up leadership, the authors show how to grow PLCs by encouraging innovation at every level.
BKF534

Solution Tree | Press

a division of
Solution Tree

Visit SolutionTree.com or call 800.733.6786 to order.

"Tremendous, tremendous, tremendous!

The speaker made me do some very deep internal reflection about the **PLC process** and the personal responsibility I have in making the school improvement process work **for ALL kids.**"

—Marc Rodriguez, teacher effectiveness coach,
Denver Public Schools, Colorado

PD Services

Our experts draw from decades of research and their own experiences to bring you practical strategies for building and sustaining a high-performing PLC. You can choose from a range of customizable services, from a one-day overview to a multiyear process.

Book your PLC PD today!
888.763.9045

Solution Tree